THE AUTHOR: Sawak̲o̲ ̲...
As a student she developed a deep interest in ...
modern drama and traditional Kabuki, and her own plays are wide-ly performed in Japan. Many of her novels have also been adapted for the stage, the cinema, and television.

Ariyoshi first rose to prominence in the 1950s as a writer of short stories, but has since built an impressive reputation as a novelist dealing with crucial social issues. Among her themes have been the problems faced by women in the traditional Japanese household (*Hanaoka seishū no tsuma*, 1967, translated as *The Doctor's Wife*), racial segregation in the United States (*Hishoku*, 1964), and environmental pollution (*Fukugō osen*, 1975). Her *Kōkotsu no hito* (*The Twilight Years*) was published in 1972 and sold over a million copies in less than a year.

Translations of her books have appeared throughout the world and include a French translation of *The Doctor's Wife*, which was a best-seller in France in 1981; *The River Ki*; *The Twilight Years*; and *Her Highness Princess Kazu*, awarded the prestigious Mainichi Cultural Prize in 1979.

Ariyoshi died in 1984.

THE TRANSLATOR: Mildred Tahara is Associate Professor of Japanese Literature at the University of Hawaii at Manoa. Her publications include *Tales of Yamato* (University of Hawaii Press, 1980) and translations of three Ariyoshi works: *The River Ki*, *The Twilight Years*, and *Her Highness Princess Kazu*.

The Twilight Years

SAWAKO ARIYOSHI

Translated by Mildred Tahara

KODANSHA INTERNATIONAL
Tokyo · New York · London

Publication of *The Twilight Years* was assisted by a grant from The
Japan Foundation. The original work was published in 1972 by
Shinchosha under the title *Kōkotsu no hito*. This English translation was first published in the United Kingdom by Peter Owen Pub-
lishers in 1984.

Distributed in the United States by Kodansha America, Inc., 114
Fifth Avenue, New York, N.Y. 10011, and in the United Kingdom
and continental Europe by Kodansha Europe Ltd., Gillingham
House, 38-44 Gillingham Street, London SW1V 1HU. Published by
Kodansha International Ltd., 17-14 Otowa 1-chome, Bunkyo-ku,
Tokyo 112, and Kodansha America, Inc. Copyright © Sawako
Ariyoshi, 1972. Translation copyright © Mildred Tahara, 1984. All
rights reserved. Printed in Japan.
First edition, 1984
First paperback edition, 1987

    93 94 95 7 6 5 4

LCC 84-47687
ISBN 0-87011-852-8
ISBN (Japan) 4-7700-1352-3

To Donald Keene, my mentor and friend

M.T.

TRANSLATOR'S ACKNOWLEDGEMENTS

I should like to acknowledge the financial assistance I received from the University of Hawaii Japan Studies Endowment, funded by a grant from the Japanese Government.

I must also thank Daniel Zoll and Robert Borgen, who read the translation in draft and offered many helpful suggestions.

M.T.

1

Akiko emerged from the subway station carrying a large shopping bag in each hand. A light snow was falling along Ōme Avenue. Akiko regularly bought her frozen foods on Saturday, and now, looking at the snow, she congratulated herself for having got her shopping done. It was an early snow, but judging from the cold, she felt that it would continue to fall.

Akiko stopped at the corner store on her way home. She bought a loaf of bread and, after a moment's pause, added a few sweet rolls, for recently her only son, soon to take his college entrance examination, had developed a voracious appetite. Though light, the bread was bulky and Akiko had difficulty balancing the two shopping bags. The bag containing the frozen food weighed heavily in her right hand, while with her left arm she hugged the other bag into which she had slipped the loaf of bread. Heavily laden with these groceries, she could barely walk.

As she struggled through the snow without an umbrella, Akiko wondered if she would run into her son, Satoshi, who ought to be coming home from his private tutoring around this time. The shopping bag in her right hand, which contained two frozen crabs, felt particularly heavy. But Akiko was happy as she trudged along, her eyes fixed on the falling snow. Her husband, who had been brought up in the north, was extremely fond of these crabs, and it pleased her to picture him in a good mood that night. Satoshi, on the other hand, found crab such a nuisance to eat that he refused to have any. Akiko herself had not cared for crab ever since she had been terribly sick after eating some about ten years before.

She turned into Umezato from Itsukaichi Avenue and stopped in her tracks. A tall old man was walking towards her up the street. He looked very pale. Although he was wearing a tie and leather shoes, he had neither an overcoat nor an umbrella. He did not seem appropriately dressed for taking a walk on a snowy day.

'Father, Father,' Akiko called out loudly to her father-in-law, who was approaching her at a rapid pace. Just as he was about to pass her, she cried out 'Grandpa!' in a different tone of voice, almost knocking him down as he brushed against the bag clasped to her chest. Only then did he notice her.

'Oh, it's you, Akiko,' said the old man, stopping abruptly. He had a strange expression on his face as he gazed at the wife of his only son.

'What's come over you, Grandpa? Don't you realize it's snowing?'

'Ah, yes. It's snowing.'

The old man's eyes, which had been momentarily fixed on Akiko, seemed lifeless as they gazed into the distance. Was she mistaken in thinking that he had looked menacing a moment ago? She could not be certain, for lately her eyes tired easily. But she could see that her father-in-law, though dressed properly in a suit and tie, had left the house without his overcoat. He was not at all his usual self. Akiko wondered why her mother-in-law, who was usually so fussy, had seen her husband off without making sure that he was properly dressed.

'Don't you feel cold, Grandpa? It's snowing.'

'No.'

'Where were you going?'

'Are you on your way home from work?'

'Yes. But what about you?'

'Oh, look! It's snowing.'

The old man looked up at the sky with a dreamy expression on his face. A moment later, accompanied by Akiko, he turned back in the direction from which he had come. Akiko was terribly worried that he might catch a cold, but after being married to his son for twenty years, she knew her father-in-law's character. If she were to lecture him about the way he was dressed, he would stubbornly contradict her and insist on going out lightly dressed. So she walked along with him in silence. Her mother-in-law handled Shigezō, her fastidious husband, with the utmost care. She had been so protective of him that he had continued to be wilful well into old age. Akiko could imagine how joyfully her mother-in-law would welcome him back into their warm cottage where the two of them lived a life of leisurely retirement. What urgent business could have made him leave the house on a day like this?

'I bought some crabs today, Grandpa. Crabs from Hokkaido. You know how much Nobutoshi likes them. You like them too, don't you?'

'Yes, I love them.'

'I won't be able to prepare them tonight because they're still frozen. I'll bring one over for your lunch tomorrow, though. Won't it be lovely to see some snow on the ground?'

Her father-in-law did not reply and gradually quickened his pace. As soon as their home came into view, he headed straight for the gate and disappeared inside without another glance at Akiko. She set down the two shopping bags on the side of the road, which was already covered with a thin layer of snow, and caught her breath. Gazing at the small gate of the Tachibana residence, she felt annoyed with Shigezō. So this is what a man of the Meiji era is like, she thought to herself. Shigezō, who was fully six feet tall, had watched his tiny daughter-in-law stagger under the weight of the two heavy shopping bags, but he had not offered to help her carry them. Although she had not expected the old man to carry the bags, she found his arrogance inexcusable. She regretted having promised to bring one of the crabs over the next day. With inflation so high, it was an extravagance for Akiko, whose husband was an ordinary office worker, to buy the crabs with no intention of sharing them with her in-laws, who lived in the detached cottage. Yet it was only because – against her father-in-law's wishes – she had a job, that she could afford to make such an expensive purchase. It pained her to recall how often Shigezō had sarcastically called her a 'working wife'. In Japan, much was made of the strained relationship between mother-in-law and daughter-in-law, but in this household it was her mother-in-law who had often interceded in her behalf when Shigezō treated her unkindly.

The snow began to form drifts along the deserted lane. Akiko smiled wryly. Wasn't it because she regretted having told her father-in-law that he could have one of the crabs that she was now remembering how he had tormented her in the past? She groaned as she lifted up the heavy shopping bags and passed through the gate.

Unlocking the front door and entering the house, Akiko was surprised to find it dark and deserted. Satoshi is probably late getting back from his private tutor, she thought. Akiko lit the kerosene stove and then, still wearing her overcoat, began to tidy up the house. As she worked full-time, she usually did all the household chores on Saturdays, starting in the afternoon and finishing late at night. Although she was not a Christian, she was deeply impressed by Christ's wisdom in setting aside Sunday as a day of rest. If she had to spend all day Sunday cleaning the house, she would not be able to work efficiently at the office during the week! She would therefore find it impossible to hold down a full-time job and look after the house as well. Akiko was convinced that in order to do both she had

9

to turn down all invitations to Saturday afternoon functions and spend the time doing her grocery shopping for the entire week.

The Japanese, who had enjoyed a leisure boom in recent years, considered it fashionable to spend the weekend up in the mountains or out hiking. Akiko, however, took no part in such frivolous activities. Fortunately, her husband, a busy employee of a trading company, who worked hard at the office six days out of seven, preferred to sleep on Sundays. This suited Akiko perfectly. Her son Satoshi was very independent because his parents had little time to spoil him. He used to go skiing or camping, but once he had entered high school and realized that the highly competitive college entrance examination was fast approaching, he had thrown himself into his studies.

Rain or shine, Akiko also did the laundry every Saturday; so the washing-machine churned away as usual that afternoon. Presently she switched on the automatic clothes dryer. Although its price had been exorbitant, she considered it a worthwhile investment for the inevitable rainy days. When the house began to warm up a bit, Akiko went up to the second floor, removed her coat and slipped into a sweater and a pair of trousers. As always, she began by cleaning the bedroom. The vacuum cleaner hummed. Troublesome though Japanese-style bedding was, Akiko still spread it out at night and folded it away in the morning, because her husband disliked sleeping in a bed. She had to admit, however, that a room without a bed was infinitely easier to keep tidy. A thick layer of dust had accumulated, for she cleaned the room only once a week. But today the air was still because of the snow outside, and she knew that the room would be immaculate in no time.

Akiko very rarely looked into her son's room, which Satoshi jealously regarded as his private territory. It was surprisingly neat and tidy, however, Satoshi being fastidious for a boy of his age, and she did not have to worry about that room.

As Akiko descended the stairs, Satoshi, who had been given his own key to the house when he was still quite young, walked in. It was unusual for him to find his mother at home.

'Hello Satoshi. Back already?'

'Yes.'

'You'll find some sweet rolls in the kitchen.'

'I'd rather have some noodles.'

'Would you like me to make a bowl for you?'

'Yes, please.'

Being very fond of noodles, Satoshi prepared himself a bowl of instant noodles most days when he returned home. Moreover, since

10

his parents often failed to get back in time for dinner, he sometimes had noodles again as an evening snack. This had become a routine after he started going to elementary school. Akiko did not feel sorry for her son, as it did not take much effort to prepare a bowl of instant noodles.

Akiko placed a pan of water over the gas flame. While waiting for it to boil, she removed the parcels from the shopping bags one by one, unwrapped them and stored the foodstuffs away in the refrigerator or freezer. She put the shelled clams and frozen fish into the freezer, along with the packages of frozen waffles and pizza. The clothes dryer and the freezer were two luxury appliances that might have seemed out of place in their modest home, but Akiko thought that they were indispensable when both the husband and wife worked. Some women frowned upon frozen foods and complained that they lacked taste. But for a working wife, speed and nutritional value came before taste. Furthermore, such remarkable progress had been made recently in the processing of frozen food that Akiko found it extremely difficult to distinguish fresh from frozen shrimp or other shellfish. Most of the fish on display in the fish markets was caught in American waters and frozen on the spot.

As she removed the two crabs from the package, Akiko hesitated for a moment. She put one of them into the freezer and the other in the refrigerator. It was not that she was reluctant to share the crab, but that she suddenly remembered how Shigezō had complained for years about his delicate stomach. During the first ten years of her marriage, he had told her endlessly how the bean-jam dumplings she had bought or the fish she had stewed had made him ill. When she had taken fish over to the cottage, he had even complained that that was indigestible. Akiko had therefore made up her mind never to serve her father-in-law anything she had cooked. Why, then, had she forgotten her resolution and mentioned the crab to Shigezō? If he were to eat crab on a snowy day like this, he was bound to come and say, 'Thanks to you, I've got the runs again, Akiko.'

'The water's boiling, Mum,' cried Satoshi. Akiko was brought abruptly back to the present.

'Can't you prepare the noodles yourself?'

'But Mum, you said you'd do them for me.'

This kind of easy banter came naturally to them. It took Akiko only a few minutes to prepare a delicious bowl of noodles, topped with two raw eggs and two slices of ham. All but thrusting his face into the bowl, Satoshi slurped up the tasty noodles.

'You know, Mum, your noodles taste special. "Mother's home cooking,"' he chuckled. 'Just like in the commercial!'

11

Akiko burst out laughing. She raised the lid of the dryer and removed the laundry.

She washed an extra amount of rice and placed it in the electric rice-cooker, for Nobutoshi had told her that he would be home for dinner, and it was only rarely that he ate with the family. Akiko pared potatoes and carrots and cut some string beans, working diligently to prepare a home-cooked meal. As both she and her husband worked all week, she had a longing for such dishes as miso soup and stewed vegetables. When she was younger, her body could tolerate a regular diet of fried food and cheap restaurant cooking, but in recent years both Akiko and Nobutoshi had developed a fondness for simple Japanese food. They now fully appreciated the stewed dishes which her mother-in-law sometimes brought over to them. Fearing the sarcastic comments her father-in-law might make about the crab, Akiko decided not to take him any but to share some of the stewed vegetables with the elderly couple instead. Despite the fact that the two families lived at the same address, they saw little of each other. More than ten years had passed since her mother-in-law and Nobutoshi had decided that the two households ought to live separately because of Shigezō's cruel treatment of Akiko. In Southern Europe it is considered ideal for an old couple to live close enough to their son's family for a hot bowl of soup to be carried from one household to the other. It was out of sheer necessity that Akiko's family conformed to this tradition. Since they had built a separate cottage for the old couple, on land that had formerly been the garden, the house that they themselves occupied no longer got much sunlight. Fortunately, this did not matter too much as both Akiko and her husband were out of the house during the day and returned home only to sleep at night. Their main concern was avoid any discord between the members of the two households.

Akiko parboiled the carrots, potatoes, string beans and dried mushrooms in separate pots and added the seasoning. The result was a mountain of stewed vegetables. Even if she shared some of it with her in-laws, there would still be enough left for ten helpings. In another pot, she stewed a generous amount of seaweed, far too much for a family of three. On Saturdays, Akiko usually prepared several dishes. She would keep back enough of each for one meal and store the rest in the freezer. She intended to defrost the stewed vegetables and seaweed during the week. That was her way of efficiently planning the meals for her family.

Akiko worked without a pause in the steam-filled room, which had all the appearance of a restaurant kitchen. It certainly wasn't because she disliked housework that she went out to work. She started to prepare the meals for the next week. Just when she realized that the clothes dryer had finished its cycle, she heard someone knocking on the kitchen window, which was clouded with steam.

'Who is it?' she asked in a loud voice.

'It's me. Akiko, it's me.'

The voice of her father-in-law, with whom she had parted at the gate a short while ago, came from the narrow space between the main house and the cottage.

'Please open the door for Grandpa, Satoshi.'

Shigezō, still dressed in the same clothes, slipped into the house. When he saw the stewed vegetables, his eyes lit up.

'Potatoes?' he asked.

'I was thinking of bringing you some,' said Akiko cheerfully. As she looked up, she was astonished to see her father-in-law grab a fistful of carrots and potatoes and cram them into his mouth.

'Goodness, Father. Let me serve you some in a dish. You must be hungry! You're not at all your usual self today!'

Flustered, Akiko took up a small dish. Shigezō looked enviously at the empty bowl in front of his grandson and said, 'Grandma refuses to get up and I'm starved!'

'Is Mother asleep?'

'If you mean Grandma, yes. I've asked her again and again to wake up, but she won't.'

'Perhaps she isn't feeling well.'

'I think she's ill. I don't know what's wrong, but she won't get up.'

Akiko quickly went through the kitchen door. Slipping into a pair of sandals, she walked to the cottage. Unlike Shigezō, her mother-in-law had always enjoyed perfect health. But she was now well over seventy, and it was quite possible that she had had a stroke.

2

The dentist's drill sounded shrill and harsh as it bore into his molar, sending vibrations up to Nobutoshi's ear-drums and brain. With his mouth wide open and his head thrown back, Nobutoshi groaned and sighed again and again while the dentist worked on his tooth. His saliva, which poured in an endless stream from under his tongue, was sucked up by a device that had been thrust into his mouth. Civilization had made remarkable advances, yet the dentist continued to drill in this old-fashioned manner, unchanged from the days before World War II. Nobutoshi was irritated at having to undergo this ordeal. He tried to remember how many times he had visited the dentist in the past three years. It did not take him long to get there because the surgery was located in the same building as his company office. Each time he came, he had his teeth cleaned, a tooth extracted or a cavity filled. But even after a gold filling had been put in, the tooth would begin to decay around the filling a few years later, causing him excruciating pain. For how many more years would this seemingly endless cycle be repeated?

When the dentist had finished, Nobutoshi, looking absolutely wretched, asked: 'Doctor, are bad teeth hereditary?'

'Heredity is a factor. Why do you ask?'

'I've just remembered how my father used to suffer on account of his teeth. He started to wear dentures at a relatively early age.'

The dentist's surgery was open for only half a day on Saturdays, and Nobutoshi was the last patient that day. Appearing eager to take off his white coat, the dentist said brusquely: 'It'd be easy enough for me to make you a set of dentures. All I'd have to do is pull out every one of your teeth. You would never have to pay me another visit. But I'm going to all this trouble so that you won't have to wear dentures.'

Sometimes, when the pain was unbearable, Nobutoshi had begged his dentist to extract all his teeth, but the dentist had adamantly

14

refused. Also, those of Nobutoshi's superiors who wore dentures had told him that they were exceedingly disagreeable. Caught in a helpless situation, Nobutoshi continued to let the dentist look after his teeth, but after each visit he would stalk out of the surgery looking very glum.

'I suppose it can't be helped. My father had terrible teeth.'

'But it's perfectly natural for teeth to deteriorate when one gets older,' the dentist said with a faint smile.

The point he was trying to make was that it was perfectly normal for a person of Nobutoshi's age to have trouble with his teeth. Nobutoshi's teeth had given him very little trouble when he was younger. It was only in the past ten years that his visits to the dentist had become frequent. He himself believed that his dental problems were due to the poor living conditions he had experienced during the war years and to his bad diet when he was in an internment camp. He was convinced, too, that he had inherited his father's bad teeth. For as long as he could remember, his father had complained constantly about his stomach and his teeth, and Nobutoshi remembered that, as a youngster, he had been disgusted with him. Since his mother had devoted herself completely to looking after her sickly husband, Nobutoshi, despite the fact that he was their only son, had avoided being spoiled. He had inherited his mother's strong physique and had been in excellent health all these years, until his teeth had begun to give him trouble.

Nobutoshi worked overtime that day, occasionally pressing one hand against his cheek and wondering whether he would end up like his father one day. Being such a difficult man to please, Shigezō had changed dentists again and again. He fought with every dentist he visited and had each one make him several sets of dentures. Then, when none of these were to his satisfaction, he would find himself a new dentist. In the end he bought his own tools and materials and made his own dentures, having learnt to make a set by observing the dentists produce one pair after another.

'Have you got toothache, sir?' asked a young man who had walked up to Nobutoshi and now stood directly in front of his desk.

'I'm afraid I have, and it's really quite depressing. You're probably too young to have experienced this kind of agony.'

'Oh, no. I had a terrible time with my teeth as a child, so now I brush my teeth after every meal.'

'Really? That's a good idea,' said Nobutoshi, looking up at the dazzling white teeth of the young man who had been employed in the office for several years now.

'Do you smoke?'

15

'No.'

'Ah, so you don't believe in such vile habits.'

'Not at all. I used to smoke when I was in college, but then my tonsils would get swollen.'

'Since you brush your teeth after every meal, you probably won't suffer like me when you get to my age. Was your mother very strict with you?'

'No, not really. Most of my classmates formed this habit. It's probably because we were made to brush our teeth after lunch when we were still at elementary school.'

'You were lucky to get such training!' said Nobutoshi in admiration. He wondered whether Satoshi also brushed his teeth after every meal.

'When you're young, it's difficult to imagine the trouble you'll have with your teeth in later years,' he told the young man. 'Dental problems aren't like headaches and stomach-aches. They don't go away leaving you feeling fully recovered. It's really unbearable when one tooth after another gives you trouble.'

The young man listened patiently, nodding from time to time. Suddenly his expression changed, as if he had made up his mind to take no more of Nobutoshi's idle chatter.

'Sir, would you put your seal on this for me, please.'

Nobutoshi collected his thoughts and dismissed the young man, angry at himself for having complained about his teeth. How could a young man possibly sympathize with him? But however hard he tried, he could not banish from his mind the memory of his father's attempts to make his own dentures. Did his father get the instructions from books? Day after day, Shigezō would produce several milk-white teeth which he then embedded in gums, also of his own making. Then he would whittle down the teeth he thought were too big or build up those that were too small. Nobutoshi recalled how exasperated he had been with his father when he worked away in this manner. In the end Shigezō had lost patience with the tedious process and declared that it was not necessary for dentures to be made up of thirty-two individual teeth. One of the sets he made consisted of two solid pieces, one for the top and another for the bottom, which produced a truly frightening effect. He had the annoying habit of showing off this unique set of dentures to everyone, no matter who they were. There was no space between the individual teeth and the solid curved surface of pure white, gleaming from between his parted lips, was a weird sight. Nowadays, Nobutoshi could understand the feelings of the old man, who had been constantly irritated by dental problems. In those days he had turned a deaf ear to his father's endless

16

complaining: now he was doing the same thing to his young colleague. How irritated the man must have been with him.

In recent years there had been talk at the company of having both Saturdays and Sundays off, but this had not yet become official policy. Having to work on Saturdays was extremely unpopular with the younger employees, whereas the older ones felt uncomfortable staying at home. Since the attitude of the managers had not been clearly expressed, an employee who had completed his share of work could leave for home without formally excusing himself. Young employees these days did not feel under an obligation to remain behind to keep their superiors company.

Nobutoshi, who had been left all alone in the office, suddenly realized that the heat had been turned off. He rose to his feet, rubbing his cheek to feel the tooth the dentist had worked on.

Although he had been sitting in the office for hours, he had made very little progress with his work. He had told his wife that he would be home for dinner rather than going out for a drink, for he knew that saké would taste bad after a visit to the dentist.

In the heart of the city, where the streets were lined with office buildings, a powdery snow had begun to fall. By the time Nobutoshi emerged from the subway station, the pavement was covered with a thin white layer.

'Snow,' he muttered, frowning.

Usually, Nobutoshi loved the snow. In his opinion there was nothing quite so beautiful as a snowscape. But today he walked along sullenly, thinking of the saké he would not now be able to enjoy. His teeth had ruined the one pleasure this world had to offer. The traffic grew heavy when he turned into Itsukaichi Avenue. Here, too, snow lay white along the roadside.

As he approached the house, Nobutoshi stopped momentarily in his tracks, sensing that something was not quite right. A small car he did not recognize was parked outside the gate. Then he found that the front door was unlocked and the heating was on. His wife and son were nowhere to be seen. Instead, a large man, his back turned to Nobutoshi, was squatting on the threshold between the ten-mat room and the wooden floor.

'What's happened, Father?'

Looking back over his shoulder, Shigezō stared at his son for a moment, then turned away without saying a word.

Nobutoshi removed his coat. When he peered over the old man's shoulders to see what he had in his hands, he was filled with disgust.

'What are you eating, Father?'

'Potatoes and carrots.'

17

Speechless, Nobutoshi watched his father eating with his hands like a child who did not know any better.

'Is Akiko back?'

'Yes.'

'Where is she?'

'In Grandma's room.'

'Oh? Anyway, Father, don't you think you'll get an upset stomach if you stuff yourself like that?'

'Well . . .'

Shigezō got down on all fours. Suddenly he raised his arms like a dancing spider and stood up. Nobutoshi was of medium height and build, but his father, despite his small bones, was a giant of six feet or more. As Shigezō stretched his long, thin limbs, he stepped down from the kitchen door and in slow motion groped about for some slippers.

At the same moment, Akiko pushed open the door from the outside and rushed into the kitchen.

'Oh, you're home!' she said, terribly agitated.

'Is anything wrong?'

'Grandma's had a stroke. I called the doctor right away, but . . .'

'Is that his car outside?'

'Yes. He's leaving now.'

'How's Mother?'

'Please go and see for yourself. Satoshi is with her,' said Akiko in a low voice as she looked up at her husband.

Then she turned to Shigezō and said sternly: 'Why didn't you tell me sooner, Father? You know our office numbers, don't you?'

Nobutoshi was startled to hear his wife sound so harsh.

'Is she all right?'

'She's dead. She's been dead for hours!'

Akiko flipped frantically through the pages of the telephone directory and dialled a number.

'Hello. Is that the Kokuriko Beauty Parlour? This is Mrs Tachibana. Did my mother-in-law have an appointment with you today? Oh? About what time? Was she behaving strangely at the time? She had a shampoo and set, didn't she? It appears that she had a stroke as soon as she got home, because she still had her shawl on,' said Akiko, speaking rapidly in a shrill voice.

Nobutoshi ran to the cottage, where he found his mother lying on bedding that had been spread out in the six-mat room. Satoshi sat cross-legged on the floor, leaning against a pillar. He seemed to be in a state of shock.

'When did it happen?'

18

'Just a while ago, Grandpa came to the main house complaining that Grandma wouldn't get up. When we came to have a look, we found her lying over there,' said Satoshi, pointing to the narrow entrance.

The lined face of Nobutoshi's mother looked incredibly peaceful, as if she were asleep. Her complexion, dotted here and there with old-age spots, appeared fairer than ever and had a youthful glow. Nobutoshi could not believe that she was really dead; he lifted one of her hands, which were folded on her breast, and felt her pulse.

'Doesn't her body feel cold? It's true what they say about a corpse being cold,' said Satoshi, sounding as casual as if he were merely reporting the results of some scientific experiment. But Nobutoshi was too stunned to say anything.

Was she really dead? For some strange reason, Nobutoshi felt let down. He had known all along that, because of her age, he had to prepare himself for her death. But it had been so unexpected! Since she had not been ill, he had not been at her side in her last moments. He had never imagined that his mother's death would be anything like this. He shed no tears, for the full impact of his loss had yet to hit him. He was too stunned to cling to his mother's corpse. After a while, Nobutoshi walked over to his son and sat down beside him. He heaved a sigh. Satoshi hugged his knees and rested his chin on his kneecaps. Although he stole a glance at his father's face, he did not say a word.

'Did the doctor give her an injection?' asked Nobutoshi after a long pause.

'Actually, he hardly did anything. He looked under her eyelids and felt her hands and said that she'd been dead for over four hours. Rigor mortis – or whatever you call it – had set in. He had a hard time folding her hands,' said Satoshi, rocking his knees with his arms still around them.

Akiko's hysterical voice could be heard coming from the main house as she made a series of phone calls.

'Has Mum been acting like that all this time?'

'Yes. She was really upset while she was spreading out the bedding, calling the doctor and changing Grandma's kimono. She should know by now that there's no point in telling me off.'

'Call her over.'

'She'll come soon enough and tick us off for sitting here doing nothing.'

But what was one supposed to do at a time like this? Nobutoshi was still too shocked to do anything but sit. Surely it would be all right for him to pause for a moment and think about what to do next?

19

Nobutoshi could not believe that his mother was dead. Although he thought long and carefully, he could not recall a time when she had been ill. She had always worked diligently, preparing complicated Chinese herbal medicines according to the directions given by her extremely fussy husband or wiping the corridors with a damp cloth. Nobutoshi could not remember ever seeing his mother – a woman of fair complexion and the picture of health – without a smile on her face. She was not vain about her looks, but because her husband was so particular, she was always immaculately groomed. Even now not a single hair was out of place. Her grey hair, which had a lovely sheen on it, was beautifully arranged and covered with a fine hairnet. Nobutoshi had an odd feeling that any moment now his mother would open her eyes, sit up and say, 'Oh dear! What's happened?'

'What are you two doing?'

Suddenly Akiko's shrill voice sounded above their heads. Satoshi gave an embarrassed smile and looked at his father. As for Nobutoshi, he replied with a question.

'Well, what do you expect us to do? The doctor said it was too late, didn't he? All we can do is to wait until she's resurrected.'

'The doctor said that she died four hours ago. When I phoned the undertaker just now, he asked if we would mind having the funeral on Monday morning, as tomorrow is Sunday! Of all the nerve! I told him that people also died at weekends. His answer to that was to say sarcastically that he might be an undertaker, but *he* was still alive.'

'What a callous thing to say!'

'Wasn't it! How insulting! Well, I just hung up on him. Then I phoned the doctor. His wife answered and I asked her whether her husband could perhaps recommend an undertaker. The woman became hysterical and slammed the receiver down.'

'You probably didn't introduce yourself.'

'Why, that's right! Satoshi, please go to Dr Sasayama's surgery for me. Tell him that you're from the Tachibana family, whom he's just visited.'

'Yes, Mum.'

'Don't forget to tell him that we've never had a death in the family before, so we don't know what to do.'

'It's all right, Mum. I know what to say.'

'When you've done that, be sure to come straight back.'

Where in the world would Satoshi wander off to at a time like this, Nobutoshi wondered, but he kept his thoughts to himself. The Tachibanas were indeed inexperienced. Death was not new to Nobutoshi, but he had never been responsible for arranging all the details. When he had been a prisoner of war in Siberia, his comrades had died in their hundreds. After each death had been reported to the Russian soldiers, two men would haul the corpse away and that would be that. Nobutoshi vividly recalled the horror he had lived through twenty years before, though he hardly ever gave it a thought these days. Then, he had been unmoved by death. But even now that he had lost his mother, death was not as profoundly moving for him as it was made out to be in books.

'Mother went to the beauty parlour today. When I laid her on her bed, I noticed how nice her hair smelled, so I phoned them. The hairdresser said that Mother got there a little after twelve. She had a shampoo and set and seemed to be her usual self. Grandpa's so fussy about her appearance. Fancy having her hair done on a cold day like this! After sitting under the hairdryer, she went out into the snow, and the sudden drop in her body temperature must have been too much for her. The doctor said she had a cerebral haemorrhage. Everyone at the beauty parlour was shocked to hear that she was dead. They finished with her at a little after two. When I got here, just after six, she was in a heap over there,' said Akiko, pointing to the spot Satoshi had indicated earlier. 'Her shawl was still wrapped around her shoulders when I found her.'

'Didn't Dad come to tell you about her?'

'No. All he did when he came to the main house was complain about being hungry. He begged us for a snack, saying Grandma wouldn't get up. I was afraid that she might not be feeling well, so I came over to have a look. I was so shocked to find her lying there! I called out to her, but she didn't move a muscle. Her body was stone cold. I got Dr Sasayama to come right away.'

'Satoshi mentioned that he didn't bother to give her an injection.'

'There was no point, dear. She died at once when she had the stroke. Don't you think it was an ideal way to go? She didn't suffer at all. To think that I was quite unaware she was dead, and was busily preparing stewed potatoes at the time.'

'Speaking of potatoes, I saw Dad eating some out of a pot.'

'That's right. All of a sudden he started helping himself to the potatoes – with his hands, too! Oh dear!'

Akiko and Nobutoshi looked at each other. Then Akiko dashed out of the cottage. A minute later she returned, pulling Shigezō by the hand.

'Father, we're going to have a wake for Grandma tonight. She's dead, you know. Please come in here.'

Shigezō slowly entered the cottage and peered at his wife's face, looking very strange. Then, with a quizzical expression, he glanced

21

at his son and sat down in formal Japanese fashion, his legs tucked under him.

'Father, where were you when Mother had her stroke?'

'If you mean Grandma, isn't that her?'

'Akiko put her to bed. Didn't you see Grandma fall at the entrance?'

'Grandma?' asked Shigezō, slowly shifting his gaze back to his daughter-in-law. 'What's the matter with her?'

'What do you mean "What's the matter?" Grandma's dead.'

'Oh?'

Nobutoshi and Akiko exchanged glances, their hearts beating.

'Listen, Akiko,' Nobutoshi started to say. At the same moment Akiko cried out hysterically, 'Father!'

She grabbed the lapel of her father-in-law's suit and shook him so hard that the top half of his body rocked back and forth. Then she bombarded him with questions.

'Why didn't you let us know right away? We've got neighbours, haven't we? If you'd spoken to Mrs Kihara or Mrs Kadotani, they'd have rushed over immediately. Why did you leave Grandma lying there like that? You practically ran into me in the street when I was coming back from work! Why didn't you tell me about Grandma then? Letting her lie there for hours in an unheated house – what kind of husband are you?'

Shigezō offered no resistance at all as Akiko went on abusing him. His head bobbed back and forth as she shook him with all her might. Nobutoshi, unable to look on in silence, forced his wife to stop.

'Don't, Akiko. Dad isn't himself.'

Gasping for breath, Akiko looked at her husband.

'Have you noticed that too?'

'Yes. He's probably acting strangely because of the shock of Grandma's death.'

'I think you're right. When I met him on my way home, he had an angry look in his eyes as he hurried towards me. He was wearing a suit and tie, but he didn't have his coat on and he wasn't carrying an umbrella even though it was snowing. I asked him in a loud voice where he was going, and all he did was to turn around and walk home with me.'

'Do you think he went out to summon a neighbour?'

'Yes. And he probably forgot what he'd set out for. We ran into one another just beyond the market.'

Akiko and Nobutoshi both scrutinized the old man out of the corners of their eyes. Akiko began to feel uneasy and rose to her feet.

'I'll go and tell the neighbours. After all, Grandma was very friendly with Mrs Kihara and Mrs Kadotani. I'll be back soon.' She hurriedly left the house.

Nobutoshi remained silent for some time, glancing from his father to his mother. Still in a daze, he thought about the blood-tie between himself and the old couple, even though his birth fifty years before now seemed an event belonging to the distant past.

Meanwhile, Shigezō continued to sit in formal fashion, maintaining a complete silence, his eyes fixed on his dead wife. Finally, he turned and asked Nobutoshi: 'How long will Grandma go on sleeping like this?'

Taken aback, Nobutoshi stared into his father's face. There was something very odd about the tone of his voice. He seemed to regard Nobutoshi as a complete stranger. Shigezō had never used the polite form of speech in addressing him before. 'Hey, Nobutoshi,' was his usual form of address. Could it be that his father had forgotten him? Trying not to believe what was only too obvious, Nobutoshi stared into Shigezō's unblinking eyes, which were a dull, lustreless yellow. Although they returned Nobutoshi's gaze, they were focused on some point in the distance. The old man seemed to be lost in a dream.

3

Akiko reported the death to her mother-in-law's friends in the neighbourhood. In the course of answering their many questions, she gradually recovered her composure, which had been badly shaken. She had been emotionally unprepared for her mother-in-law's sudden death. Yet, without anyone's help, she had summoned the doctor, laid her mother-in-law on her bedding and, after the doctor's departure, telephoned the undertaker. She had been angry with her father-in-law for failing to inform the neighbours, and then realized that this was the first thing she herself should have done. Having gone out into the world to work, she felt that she was as capable as anyone, but in an emergency like this she was still at a loss as to what to do. She finally realized that her husband was being far more honest by sitting in a daze at his mother's bedside. It seemed the most natural thing to do at a time like this.

But Akiko was not in a position to sit idly at her husband's side. As she entered her own house she was assailed by the smell of burnt soy sauce. A cloud of smoke was billowing from the pot of seaweed simmering on the gas burner. In a panic, Akiko turned off the flame, carried the pot to the sink and quickly turned on the tap. There was a loud sizzling noise, accompanied by clouds of steam. The stewed seaweed she had planned to serve with two meals that week was completely ruined. But Akiko had no time to cry over it.

She picked up the receiver and dialed her brother's number. Her sister-in-law answered the phone.

'Mitsuko, may I speak to my brother?'

'I'm sorry, he isn't in. He's late as usual.'

'Something terrible has happened here. Grandma has just died. She had a stroke about four hours ago, but Grandpa didn't tell us straight away. I called the doctor after I got home from work. When he got here, he said she had died of a cerebral haemorrhage. She hadn't even

24

taken off her shawl. She apparently had a stroke as soon as she got home from the beauty parlour.'

'Akiko, are you talking about Nobutoshi's mother?'

'Yes.'

'Then there must be an awful lot for you to do. I'll come over right away.'

'What about my brother?'

'I'll leave a note telling him where he can find me. It'll be all right. Please wait for me.'

Mitsuko was the first to hang up. Akiko sank to the ground, as though her knees had given away under her. She had not expected her sister-in-law's offer of help. Mitsuko was married to Akiko's older brother, but the two women were the same age and had been in the same class at school. Because of this, Akiko did not usually address Mitsuko as 'elder sister' except when she was teasing her. But here was Mitsuko rushing over to help her in response to a single telephone call. Of course, she was a member of the family and not just a friend. Akiko recalled that when her mother had been dying of liver cancer several years before, it was Mitsuko who had nursed her during her illness and who had been at her deathbed. Only later was Akiko to realize how experienced Mitsuko was with wakes, funerals, and the like.

The Kiharas and Kadotanis arrived. When they realized that Akiko was not doing anything about it, they began preparing for the wake. Both families had experienced the death of a close relative, so Akiko was given an opportunity to learn in detail the traditional Japanese way of caring for the dead.

Mrs Kihara came up to Akiko and said, 'We'll need a knife, Mrs Tachibana.'

'Yes, of course. What are you going to cut?'

'It isn't for cutting anything. We need something with a sharp edge to ward off evil spirits. We're going to put it on the breast of the Buddha.'

It took Akiko a moment to realize that by 'Buddha' Mrs Kihara was referring to her mother-in-law. She asked whether a kitchen knife would do, or a pair of scissors from her sewing-box, or Nobutoshi's safety razor. Mrs Kihara was not satisfied with any of these.

'We must have a small knife to ward off evil spirits.'

'Would a fruit knife do?'

'A fruit knife?' asked Mrs Kihara, pausing to think about it.

Just then Satoshi came into the house. 'What about my knife? It even has a case.' He ran upstairs to fetch it.

Next, Mrs Kihara asked for some bleached cotton.

25

'To wipe her body?'

'Oh no. We're going to cover her face with it.'

'Would a towel do?'

Now it was Akiko's turn to run upstairs to the master bedroom to look for a suitable towel. She had recently replaced all her plain Japanese-style towels with coloured Western-style ones. When at last she found a white towel, she descended the stairs only to find that Mrs Kihara and Satoshi had disappeared. Akiko suddenly recalled that Mrs Kihara's husband had passed away two years earlier.

When Akiko made her way to the cottage, Mrs Kadotani, who seemed to be waiting for her to arrive, asked her if she had contacted the temple.

'No, I haven't.'

'Which temple is your family affiliated with?'

Akiko had no idea. Shigezō, a second son, had formed a junior branch of the main family, which remained out in the provinces. He had had two children – Nobutoshi and Kyōko. But in all these years there had never been a death in the family. Shigezō was not religious, and Akiko did not recall ever hearing her mother-in-law mention her religious sect. As Akiko paused to think, Mrs Kadotani asked reproachfully: 'Doesn't your family have a Buddhist altar?'

The old woman peered into the altar in the cottage and immediately identified the Buddhist sect.

'Grandpa, does our family belong to the Sōtō Zen sect?'

'Yes, yes,' was Shigezō's vague answer.

This happened to be the same sect to which the Kadotanis belonged. It was decided that Akiko should phone the temple in Umahashi and summon the head priest. Akiko was visibly shaken when Mrs Kadotani came across a shroud in the drawer directly under the altar.

'Your mother-in-law was well prepared, wasn't she?' remarked Mrs Kadotani, wiping the tears from her eyes. She also discovered a piece of cloth of the right length and immediately covered the dead woman's face with it.

'How could we use that?' she asked in disgust when her eyes fell upon the towel Akiko had fetched. She would probably have gone on complaining if Mrs Kihara had not interceded on Akiko's behalf.

'We'll use the towel later when we bathe the corpse. Please give us a hand, Mrs Kadotani.'

The women moved the corpse, bedding and all, so that the head pointed north, in keeping with Buddhist custom. The low two-fold screen was set upside-down around the head of the corpse, and some

26

joss-sticks were placed in the container. Everything was now ready for the wake.

Having observed that Akiko was completely ignorant about how to prepare for the wake, Mrs Kadotani grew increasingly officious.

'Please come here for a moment, Akiko,' she said.

Then she ordered Akiko to fetch her mother-in-law's favourite kimono, which would be placed with the hem up and collar down over the corpse when it was laid in the coffin later.

'Now you must cook some rice, dear. It has to be offered to the deceased, you know. Be sure to insert a pair of chopsticks before making the offering.'

Akiko had no idea how the chopsticks should be inserted into the rice. Since neither her husband nor her son had yet had their dinner, she returned to the kitchen.

Mitsuko arrived in a taxi. After putting down a large bundle wrapped in a scarf, and a bouquet of white chrysanthemums, at the entrance, she bowed low.

'My deepest sympathy on your recent bereavement, Akiko. Let me pay my respects to the deceased,' she said solemnly, before hurrying off to the cottage.

Mitsuko returned a few minutes later. She removed an apron from the bundle and tied it around her waist. Next, she found a flower vase, filled it with water, and arranged the flowers. After taking the flowers to the cottage, she quickly returned to the entrance of the house. Akiko was utterly flabbergasted, for Mitsuko, whom she had known since her youth, seemed to be totally transformed.

'Is this the largest tea kettle you have?'

Mitsuko filled the kettle with water and placed it on the burner. She put some teacups on a tray and began to prepare tea for the mourners who had arrived for the wake.

'How practical you are, Mitsuko! I'm still too numb to think clearly. I'm afraid I'll be no help at all. A few minutes ago my next-door neighbour was complaining because I didn't bring her the Japanese-style towel she had asked for.'

'Funerals are very traditional. I learned a great deal when your mother died. Have they already washed the body for the burial? . . . No, I see that they haven't done so yet. It's supposed to be washed just before it's placed in the coffin. By the way, have you had your dinner?'

'Not yet,' Akiko replied. 'But I really don't feel hungry.'

'That won't do at all. You simply must eat. The wake is fixed for tonight. After that, things will become even more hectic. Here, these are for you.'

Mitsuko removed some seaweed, sweets and canned goods from the bundle – probably everything she could spare from her own house.

'There's no need to worry about the vegetables. I've stewed enough to serve ten,' said Akiko, then stopped abruptly.

She removed the cover of the large pot and found one potato and five small chunks of carrot – hardly enough for a single helping.

'This is terrible!'

'What's the matter?'

'They're gone. All the vegetables have disappeared! Oh dear!'

A chill ran down Akiko's spine. Had her father-in-law devoured them all?

But how could he have done? There had been enough for ten servings, and she had used the largest pot in the house to cook them. She suddenly recalled seeing Shigezō bent over the pot just outside the kitchen while she was scurrying back and forth between the main house and the cottage. Had he been eating out of the pot all that time? Yes, she remembered now. Her father-in-law had come into the kitchen, grabbed a potato, and crammed it into his mouth with his hands . . .

Mitsuko, who had not seen the pile of vegetables there had been to begin with, was not as surprised as Akiko, even after hearing what had happened.

'Miso soup will do, won't it? I brought some pork that I had in the house. I'll make some Satsuma pork stew for you, so don't worry about a thing.'

'I can't help worrying about Grandpa.'

'Whatever for?'

'He has a delicate stomach. No matter what I give him, he complains about my cooking. After eating all those vegetables, he's bound to end up with a stomach-ache, and he'll blame me for it.'

'He can complain as much as he likes, but he won't have time to until after the funeral.'

Mitsuko suggested that they immediately order some food from a restaurant, for dinner would have to be served to the mourners. As Umezato was near Ōme Avenue, there were a noodle shop and a sushi restaurant near by. Mitsuko thought that fried bean-curd sushi would be best and phoned the restaurant to place an order. She was told that, fortunately, there was enough sushi left to feed twelve. But as it was a Saturday, and a snowy one at that, the restaurant would not deliver to the house.

'I'll go myself.'

'Why not send Satoshi? Don't you go, Akiko.'

When the water had boiled, Mitsuko prepared some tea. The two women returned to the cottage just as the head priest arrived. No sooner had Satoshi rushed out of the house for the sushi than the priest began to intone the sutras. Akiko pressed her hands together in prayer and closed her eyes. Suddenly, her head felt terribly heavy, and she was overcome by deep remorse. Why had she not been told straight away that her mother-in-law had suffered a stroke? Why could she not have been with her in her last moments? After all, they lived in virtually the same house. She could hardly suppress her anger at Shigezō, who had wandered off while his wife lay on the floor. And when he finally did turn up at the main house, it was only to complain about being hungry. What sort of man was this father-in-law of hers?

Akiko slowly opened her eyes and looked at Shigezō. Sitting with his legs tucked under him and with a strange look on his face, he gazed at the profile of the priest as he raised his head to chant the sutras. He seemed at once fascinated and amused by the priest's droning voice. There was nothing about him to suggest a man grieving for the loss of a beloved wife after more than fifty years of marriage.

In the middle of the chanting, Akiko's brother entered the room carrying two tall bottles of saké. As he sat down, he nodded to Nobutoshi.

The young priest of the Sōtō Zen sect looked as though he had recently graduated from college. Instead of his head being shaved, his hair was as long as that of Nobutoshi and Akiko's brother, and he appeared to have used a generous amount of hair oil. Akiko had no idea what sutra chanting was supposed to be like at a wake, but it seemed to her that the priest finished very quickly. Then he turned to the family and said somewhat glibly, sounding rather like a television presenter, 'The family may now make their offering of incense.'

'Thank you for coming out in all this snow.'

'Not at all. It was no trouble. The snow won't last – it's still too early,' replied the priest with a very ordinary expression on his face.

Akiko was dumbfounded. A woman had died. Was this the proper attitude to adopt at a wake? But then she recalled that when she had lost her mother several years earlier, no one had clung to the corpse or collapsed in tears, probably because her mother had died in a hospital. If this was what it was like when a member of the family died at home, then all the lamentation one had come to expect was nothing but a romantic fiction. Also, while a death in the family deeply affected those who were close to the deceased, the formal details of the funeral had to be attended to.

'Did you summon the priest?' asked Mitsuko in a whisper.

'No, Mrs Kadotani did.'

'Have you asked her how much we ought to give him as a temple offering?'

'No.'

'Is that Mrs Kadotani?'

Akiko nodded. Mitsuko went over to Mrs Kadotani and whispered something in her ear. Nodding at the old woman's reply, she returned to consult her husband, then made her way to the main house. Akiko vaguely realized that money had to be offered when a priest's services were requested. How fortunate she was to have Mitsuko to help her! Akiko overheard her brother say to Nobutoshi, 'At our age it seems only natural for us to be attending the funeral of one of our parents.'

Akiko was appalled. She and her brother had lost their father when they were little, so their worries had ended when their mother died. But she and her husband still had Shigezō to worry about. What kind of sarcastic remarks would he make if he had happened to overhear those callous words? Flustered, Akiko cast anxious glance at her father-in-law, but she could not tell whether he had heard. He was still sitting in the same position as before; she had the impression that he was no longer looking at the priest. His eyes seemed to be fixed on some distant point, and even when urged by Nobutoshi to offer incense, he remained expressionless.

Mitsuko entered the cottage carrying a tray of drinking glasses. Her husband removed the cap from one of the saké bottles, poured some into a glass and offered it to the priest.

'Would you care for a drink? It's freezing outside!'

'I'd love some, but as you can see, I came by car,' said the young priest, refusing the glass. He looked very relaxed as he put away his rosary.

'Forgive me for asking, but are you really the head priest?'

'Yes. My father's still alive. He's retired, so I make the rounds. I look so young that everyone treats me like an acolyte. Actually, though, I have a wife and child. If I shaved my head, I would look even younger. I don't want to look like a hippie, but I'm seriously thinking of growing a beard.'

'You are a good son, to let your father retire when you're still so young.'

'Well, to be honest, he's completely paralysed and has been bedridden for the past three years. He's looked after by a nurse and lives on a special diet. Even though he was a priest, he must be guilty of some terrible sin to deserve such cruel punishment. I shouldn't say

30

this, but I think my father would envy someone like your mother-in-law. I imagine when one's bedridden, one isn't very happy about living to a ripe old age. The doctor says he'll probably last another ten years.'

'May I ask how old he is?'

'Seventy-nine.'

The garrulous young priest was obviously fond of saké, as he himself had admitted earlier. Looking longingly at the glass from time to time, he rambled on and on about the marvellous advances that had been made in medical science for those stricken with paralysis. Following her husband's instructions, Mitsuko handed the priest an envelope with an offering for the temple, along with a bottle of saké. The priest bowed smartly, slipped into his rubber boots and went out into the cold. Akiko and Mitsuko accompanied him to his small Japanese car. He got in and, before driving off into the snow, asked them to let him know as soon as they had decided when to have the funeral.

'I never dreamed that a priest could afford to buy a car of his own.'

'His temple must be flourishing. He probably has plans to build himself a condominium in the temple grounds.'

Just then three beauticians from the Kokuriko Beauty Parlour arrived with a bouquet of white chrysanthemums.

'I still can't believe she's dead. She was looking so well!'

'She was quite her usual self today.'

'Now I come to think of it, she did say something funny,' one of the young girls blurted out. When Akiko pressed her for further details, the girl explained: 'Mrs Tachibana said that the only time she could breathe easily was when she was at the hairdresser's. She never said "beauty parlour". It was always "the hairdresser's".'

'She always asked us to use really hot water when we shampooed her hair, but today all she said was, "This feels so good! I feel as if I'm in Heaven." She kept on repeating it.'

'Even while she was under the dryer, she kept babbling away.'

'When I teased her about having a little secret, she smiled and admitted that she had.'

The young girls did not use honorifics in their speech; the owner of the beauty parlour therefore chose her words very carefully.

'I thought that I might touch up her hair, so I've brought my combs. Oh, but every hair on her head is in place!'

'Yes. Thanks to you. And it has such a lovely sheen.'

'Your mother-in-law's hair was very fine and curled easily. She had very thick hair, so it was no trouble to set. She came to have it done regularly.'

31

Mitsuko suggested that Akiko and her family leave everything to her and have their dinner, so Nobutoshi, Satoshi and Akiko returned to the main house. Mitsuko had prepared some miso soup for them, to which she had added extra ingredients.

Nobutoshi and Satoshi were famished. They polished off their first bowl of rice and noisily slurped their soup without uttering a word. Then Satoshi looked up and asked: 'Isn't Grandpa having any dinner?'

'Speaking of Grandpa . . .'

Akiko turned to her husband and told him how Shigezō had gorged himself on the vegetables. Nobutoshi listened to her in silence.

'Yes, I know.'

'If he really ate them all, he's sure to have an upset stomach. That would be terrible!'

'Should we get him to take some medicine?'

'Yes, by all means. Grandpa must have his medicine.'

Shigezō regularly took different medications, for he had had trouble with his stomach all his life. In the morning and at night, he had Chinese herbal medicine prepared for him, which he sipped instead of tea. For some time now he had been obsessed by green vegetable juice. He was so concerned about the greens being fresh that he had planted some chrysanthemum greens along the southern edge of the garden. He would grind the fresh greens in the earthenware mortar, then strain the juice through a piece of cheesecloth. Akiko felt depressed at the thought that she would probably have to prepare his vegetable juice from now on.

Putting down his chopsticks, Nobutoshi said in a low voice: 'Actually, I thought Dad would be the first to go.'

'What a thing to say, dear!' cried Akiko, rebuking her husband in front of their son. But she felt relieved that her husband shared her own feelings.

Mitsuko put her head round the door.

'Excuse me, Akiko. Do you happen to know which rice bowl is Grandmother's?'

'Yes, of course.'

'I had to ask because that neighbour of yours is upset about the rice not being ready yet.'

'Wasn't it all right to serve sushi?'

'The rice isn't for the mourners. It's for your mother-in-law.'

Out in the kitchen, Akiko piled white rice into the bowl that her mother-in-law had used every day and thrust her chopsticks into the rice. She took the bowl over to the cottage and set it down near the pillow. Mrs Kadotani at last looked satisfied.

32

More neighbours had arrived. Saké seemed to go naturally with the wake, and Akiko noticed an additional bottle, which one of the mourners had brought as a gift. The traffic sounds were muffled by the snow.

'Mrs Tachibana had just told me that she would soon be joining the Association. We had planned to go and see a play once a month. What a shame that she died without having attended a single meeting!' exclaimed Mrs Kadotani, referring to the Widows' Association in their district.

'Don't they allow men to join the Association?' asked Mr Kihara in a loud voice.

'Of course not. Men are definitely not admitted. We're all virtuous, old-fashioned women, you know.'

Everyone burst out laughing.

'But it isn't fair to keep men out.'

'You must remember that women outlive men. That's why the group is called the Widows' Association.'

'I see. I know that women live longer. Isn't the average life-span something like seventy years?'

'Oh no. It's seventy-four years.'

'Then Mrs Tachibana lived one year longer than the average. And what about the average life-span for men?'

'That's sixty-nine. Which means that if two people of the same age marry, the woman could find herself a widow for the last five years of her life.'

Shigezō did not take part in this discussion. He had undoubtedly overheard some of it because everyone was speaking in a loud voice. How did it make him feel, having lived ten years longer than the average male? Akiko looked at him anxiously, as he sat in the opposite corner with his back to her. The striking thing about him was his unusual height. She went over to him, telling herself that she must get him to take his stomach medicine. Only then did she notice that he was holding a plate of sushi. Horrified, she said: 'You can't have that, Grandpa. Haven't you just eaten all those potatoes?'

Shigezō uttered no protest when Akiko removed the plate from him.

'How many of the sushi have you had, Grandpa?' she asked, shaking him by the shoulder.

'How many?' Shigezō really did not know, although he tried very hard to answer her. 'Come here a moment, dear!' cried Akiko to her husband. When she reported that his father had helped himself to at least five sushi, Nobutoshi looked worried and said: 'See that he takes his medicine.'

33

'Yes, dear. Please keep an eye on him while I look for it.'

Akiko could not even begin to guess where her mother-in-law had put the medicine, so she opened all the drawers and cupboards in the cottage at random. Everything was neat and tidy. Akiko searched the kitchen from one end to the other, and looked into every container, but she failed to find the medicine.

'Whatever are you looking for, Akiko?' asked Mitsuko.

'Father's stomach medicine. There's a large supply of it somewhere, but I can't find it. For some strange reason, he's developed a ravenous appetite, and I'm sure he'll get an upset stomach. It'll be awful if he gets sick at a time like this!'

Akiko's calm tone belied her emotional state. She got down on her knees and searched feverishly through the bottom drawer of a chest, although this was not likely to hold a large quantity of herbal medicine.

Mitsuko watched Akiko calmly but was finally unable to remain silent any longer. In order to get her sister-in-law's attention, she said: 'By the way, Akiko, your husband has a younger sister, hasn't he? Have you notified her?'

Akiko suddenly stopped rummaging in the drawer and looked up at Mitsuko. Why hadn't she thought about doing so before? Something was definitely wrong with her. How could she possibly have forgotten to contact her sister-in-law? She had phoned the doctor, the undertaker and the relatives on her side of the family, but she had not notified her mother-in-law's own flesh and blood.

Her first thought was that perhaps Nobutoshi had contacted his sister. This, however, was highly unlikely. Yet Shigezō ought to have remembered his own daughter before anyone else, and mentioned her, thought Akiko resentfully. But this was not the time for her to express such thoughts.

'Please come here a minute, dear,' she called as she hurried out of the kitchen to summon her husband.

4

Death induces tears of sorrow only in the world of poetry and fiction, thought Nobutoshi. His mother had suddenly died, but neither he nor Satoshi, whom she had doted on all those years, had shed a tear. In real life, the complicated details of arranging a funeral do not permit grief in those closest to the deceased. But Nobutoshi's younger sister, who lived in a little town in north-eastern Japan, experienced something altogether different. Having made her way by train from the provinces, which were not served by airplanes or the super express, she had had ample time to be plunged into grief at her mother's death. As she hastily made her way to the house from Ueno Station, her eyes were still swollen from weeping and her make-up badly needed retouching.

'Who'd have guessed Mother would die first? I thought at first that I had heard you wrong. She was old, so her death wasn't altogether a surprise, but isn't Father over eighty? I just can't believe that she is dead. She was ten years younger than Father. It makes me weep to think that she was the one to die first. Don't you feel the same way, Akiko? Mother was a slave to Father. He was so difficult to please. And yet she never once contradicted him. I remember Mother grinding food that looked like chicken feed! Father was such a hypochondriac! Remember how he complained endlessly about having a stomach-ache or diarrhoea? Mother devoted her entire life to looking after an invalid! And Father, with his temper, raged like the devil when anything displeased him, and always blamed Mother for his aches and pains. What a fuss he made, saying that one thing gave him a fever and another made him cough. I really admire her for her stoicism. She was a true Meiji woman. A woman today would divorce a man like that after three days of such treatment! Mother endured it all in silence and died without having known a moment's peace. I feel so sorry for her!'

It was clear that Kyōko had stored up all these thoughts during the long train journey, for no sooner did she step into the house than she began her seemingly endless soliloquy. The body had already been laid in the coffin. The funerary objects supplied by the undertaker had been set up according to custom and an odd assortment of plastic offerings, fruit and sweets had been placed on the white altar. Kyōko raised the coffin lid and brought her mother's hands together. Then, with tears streaming down her face, she dipped a cotton-tipped swab into a glass of water and moistened her mother's lips.

'I had just been saying to my husband that Mother should pay us a visit now that the children are grown-up. Father probably wouldn't have let her come by herself, though, and the thought of having him there as well was unbearable. Believe me, Akiko, I've really felt sorry for you all these years. Nothing we did ever pleased Father. He complained about everything my husband said or did, and I was caught in the middle. I felt so relieved when he began to talk about going to live with you in Tokyo after you and Nobutoshi got married. But I knew very well that, while it made things easier for me, you would have to suffer looking after him.'

Despite the fact that she was older, Kyōko, who would soon be turning fifty, addressed her sister-in-law with respect. Nobutoshi threw a look of disgust at his sister's dishevelled hair with its streaks of grey. How different she was from their mother!

'How about washing your face?' he said sharply. 'Mother must be appalled to see you looking so sloppy.'

'What an unkind thing to say, Nobutoshi! I didn't get much sleep last night. Besides, you must remember I'm growing old. Last year the joints in my arms were so swollen that I couldn't lift anything heavy. It's certainly true that you get trouble with your legs when you're forty and your back when you're fifty. I won't look any more presentable, even after I've washed my face.'

'Whatever are you saying?' said Akiko. So far she had not uttered a word because she had not known how to deal with her sister-in-law, who had burst into tears on her arrival and who now spoke with such intensity of feeling.

'Tell me, Akiko, did Mother have her stroke in this very room?'

'Yes, right after removing her slippers.'

'And what was Father doing at the time?'

'That's still a mystery,' said Akiko, speaking somewhat enigmatically.

Just then Kyōko became aware of her father's presence and said: 'You must be terribly sad, Father. After all, you're the one who'll miss Mother most.'

36

Sitting upright in a corner of the room, Shigezō glared suspiciously at Kyōko as she leant over him.

'And who are you?'

At first mere slits under her swollen eyelids, Kyōko's eyes grew round and dark with surprise. Her lips quivered, but she was too stunned to utter a word.

'You see, he doesn't recognize us any more,' said Nobutoshi.

Kyōko looked blankly, first at her brother, then at her father. 'Father, it's me, Kyōko.' Turning to Nobutoshi, she frowned and said: 'I don't believe you.'

'Kyōko?'

'Don't you recognize me, Father?'

'Let me see now. Who are you?'

'Your daughter Kyōko. Why, this is dreadful!'

Kyōko put her hand on her father's knee and gave him a good shake. There was a look of fear on her face as she turned round.

'I was right. He doesn't recognize me, either,' said Nobutoshi.

'Not even you? Surely you're joking?'

'See for yourself.'

'Father, do you know who this is? You don't? Then tell me who she is.'

Shigezō ignored Kyōko when she pointed to her brother, but when she pointed to Akiko, he squared his shoulders and said in a tone of exasperation: 'Of course I know her. That's Akiko.'

'Oh dear.'

'He recognizes me too, Auntie,' said Satoshi, who had been watching the scene from a corner of the room.

'Goodness, how you've grown, Satoshi! If you hadn't introduced yourself, I'd never have recognized you,' said Kyōko, then swallowed hard as she realized that her words sounded like a line from a play.

'How long has Father been like this, Nobutoshi?'

'I really don't know. We thought at first that his strange behaviour was only a temporary reaction to Mother's death, but that doesn't seem to be the case.'

'Has he become senile?'

'I'm afraid so.'

Kyōko remained silent for a long moment, her eyes fixed on her father. Then she suddenly clapped her hands. Shigezō turned around, glared at her, and remarked to Akiko with a touch of sarcasm: 'What a strange woman! Fancy clapping her hands at a funeral. Doesn't she realize that this isn't a Shintō service?'

37

'He does make sense, doesn't he?' said Kyōko in a subdued voice. 'He sounds quite like his old self!'

'But he doesn't know whose funeral it is,' Nobutoshi remarked.

'What? You must be joking.'

'I wouldn't make jokes at a time like this!'

Satoshi suddenly asked in a loud voice: 'Whose funeral is this, Grandpa?'

'It's Grandma's,' replied Shigezō, staring at his grandson.

'He knows all right.'

'Yes, there are times when he seems to know what's going on.'

Nobutoshi nodded, then explained how pandemonium had reigned that morning from the moment Shigezō had woken. When he had seen how different the house looked, he had tried to run away.

'He kept saying that he had to leave for home. When Akiko stopped him going outside, he asked her why she was here.'

'I explained to him that this was his home, but what I said made no sense to him,' Akiko said. 'He begged me again and and again to go home with him. He also asked me why Satoshi was here as well.'

'Do you mean to say that even though he doesn't recognize his own son and daughter, he knows you two?'

Kyōko sighed, having apparently run out of words. Nobutoshi knew how she was feeling. Although it is said that the Japanese place great emphasis on blood relationships and sincerely believe that blood is thicker than water, here before their very eyes was evidence to the contrary. Shigezō recognized neither his son nor his daughter. This was understandable in the case of Kyōko, whom he had not seen for ten years, but why was he unable to recognize his son? After all, they had been living next door to each other for the past fifteen years. But then, on his days off, Nobutoshi either stayed in bed or went out to play golf and so he actually saw very little of his father. While his mother often visited the main house to see how her son was, bringing with her a dish he was particularly fond of, Shigezō never came of his own accord to visit him. He was so preoccupied with his own health that he gradually neglected details of his daily life that were not important to him.

'Seeing Father like this is really shocking. I can't cry any more.'

'We've been stunned too.'

Akiko plunged into a full description of her father's odd behaviour from the time she ran into him in the snow.

'Did he really eat all that sushi as well?' asked Kyōko, listening in utter disbelief to Akiko's account. 'Didn't he get an upset stomach?'

'Two kinds of medicine were stuffed into the shutter-boxing next to the alcove: pills and herbal remedies. I made him take a few pills, then wrapped a body-warmer around his stomach.'

'Did he have loose bowels?'

'Well, I looked in on him while he was in the lavatory, and he seemed to be all right. To be doubly sure, I served him some rice gruel this morning for breakfast. It's odd that he hasn't complained about having a stomach-ache. Whenever I ask him how he feels, he replies that he's fine.'

'That isn't at all like him! In the past, if you asked him about his stomach, he'd spend a full hour describing its condition. Just after we were married, my husband was really shocked when Father described the size of his bowel movement. If he was in a particularly good mood, he'd describe its colour, shape and even its smell.'

'Now you mention it, he hasn't talked about it for the past couple of days.'

Nobutoshi and Akiko looked at each other.

'He must have become senile. How long has Father been like this?' asked Kyōko.

Nobutoshi and Akiko had also been wondering about this.

'Do you think that Mother was aware of Father's condition? I'm sure she was.'

No one answered Kyōko. Nobutoshi and Akiko had lived next door to the old couple all these years, but they were now painfully aware of the fact that they might just as well have lived miles away. What surprised them more than anything was the fact that Nobutoshi's mother had never complained about Shigezō. Everyone had kept a respectful distance from the crochety old man, who had no interest apart from his health and who spent each day grumbling at his wife.

'To think that Mother died first!' said Kyōko again and again.

The hearse did not come for the coffin that day, as the crematorium was closed on Sundays. On Monday morning, the body was at last cremated. Both Nobutoshi and Akiko took a day off from work, and Satoshi stayed home from school.

After his retirement from a loan company in his home town twenty years before, Shigezō had led a secluded life. Because he had very few friends of his own in Tokyo, only the members of his immediate family silently followed his wife's remains to the crematorium. The ladies in the neighbourhood who had been close to the deceased, were not Shigezō's friends.

When the coffin was placed in the furnace, Nobutoshi looked at his father's face. It showed no trace of emotion. When the door was

39

closed and the roar of fire or electricity became audible, Akiko closed her eyes and Kyōko covered her face with her hands.

As the family strolled over to the tea stall in front of the crematorium, Kyōko tried hard to gain some recognition from her father.

'You know me, don't you, Father? I'm your daughter!'

'Oh?'

'What do you mean? I'm telling you that I'm your daughter. Can't you get that into your head?'

'You're a strange woman,' said Shigezō, looking very annoyed. 'My daughter isn't an old hag like you.'

'Oh dear!'

Satoshi burst out laughing, but neither Nobutoshi nor Kyōko was amused. Akiko did not laugh either. 'Do you remember your daughter's name, Father?' Kyōko persisted. 'Can you tell me what it is?'

'You ask the funniest questions. How could I forget a thing like that?'

'Well then, say it.'

'All right.'

'You remember her name, don't you?'

'Of course.'

'What is it?'

'Akiko.'

'This is terrible! Isn't that Akiko over there?'

'That's right.'

'Do you mean to say that she's your daughter?'

'No.'

Nobutoshi interrupted at this point, saying, 'Stop tormenting Father, Kyōko.'

The snow in the garden of the crematorium had melted, leaving only a few muddy patches, but it was so cold Akiko felt that her legs were freezing. During the past few years she had taken to wearing trousers, which were the height of fashion. She had been wearing them every day since the early autumn. Now, dressed in a black dress and a pair of nylons for the funeral, she felt as if she were standing on her bare feet. She had been unable to find anything appropriate to wear during this period of mourning, as all the clothes she had made for herself over the last three years were in bright colours. Although she had often worn black when she was younger, she realized that the colour no longer suited her.

Kyōko was dressed in a mourning kimono, which she had brought with her from the country, and the toes of her white socks were

40

getting stained with mud as she walked along in the melting snow. Because of the cold, she was wearing a Japanese-style jacket of bright peony purple over her kimono. The powder on her dry skin made it look blotchy, probably because she had not had enough sleep the night before.

Nobutoshi could see why his father had forgotten his daughter. He himself had not seen Kyōko for many years, and he thought that she had aged considerably. At the same time he realized that his own wife had lost her youthful glow, and that he himself looked older than either of them. However much he tried, he could not put the thought out of his mind that in his old age he might turn into a dotard like his father. Was such wretchedness the inevitable consequence of the ageing process? If so, a person who realized that he was becoming senile must surely be filled with terrible despair.

'Mitsuko thought that Mother died in the best possible way,' said Akiko. 'She was healthy until the very end and she was no burden to anyone, so her death was mourned by all. On the other hand, look at the way my mother died after a long stay in hospital, summoning one member of the family after another and giving each one a different version of her will. She took so long to die that she upset the entire family. I still feel sorry for Mitsuko. I just hope that when my turn comes, I'll die like your mother. What perfect timing to die when you've just had your hair done!'

'Stop saying such morbid things, Akiko. Are you planning to die before me?' said Nobutoshi teasingly. Both Kyōko and Satoshi laughed. Startled to hear laughter in the vicinity of a crematorium, the old woman who ran the tea stall looked disapprovingly in their direction. But the laughter helped to ease the tension they were feeling.

'I wonder what it would be like if only Father and Nobutoshi were left?'

'I'd move out of the house!' joked Satoshi.

This time no one laughed and an awkward silence fell upon the group. Just then a man from the crematorium came to summon them. They were led up a long flight of stairs to a small room, where they found a white porcelain funerary urn and several pairs of bamboo chopsticks of different lengths.

While the machinery churned away, a pile of white bones slowly rose from a hole in the centre of the round table which stood in the middle of the room.

'Goodness! In Tokyo even the crematorium is mechanically operated!' cried Kyōko, deeply impressed. Earlier, she had wept and lamented over her mother's death, but at a solemn moment like this

41

she was capable of making lighthearted remarks. Her insensitivity offended Nobutoshi.

'You see, Satoshi, you use chopsticks of uneven length when you pick up the bones, and you pick up each one with a partner. I'm sure that's the way it's done, even in Tokyo.'

Kyōko became quite animated as she chattered away, sharing with the others the knowledge she had acquired from her past experience. No one realized that her garrulousness had been triggered by the shock of seeing her mother's remains.

Shigezō paired off with Akiko, and together they picked up the largest bone. Meanwhile, Nobutoshi and Satoshi tried to pick up a triangular bone which they promptly dropped. Finally they succeeded in picking up a bone that resembled a stick. Kyōko and one of the crematorium attendants chatted to each other as they dutifully picked up their share of the bones.

'What part of the body does this come from?'

'I think it's the skull.'

'Is this part of the spine?'

'No. It's an arm bone.'

Their conversation could just as easily have taken place in a biology class. Satoshi craned his neck to get a better look at the bones.

The machine, located somewhere in the building, began to churn noisily; it sifted out the remaining bones, which the official scooped up into the urn.

'Some of the bones have been burned to a cinder by the electricity. There really aren't many bones in a body, are there?' Kyōko remarked.

'Probably because she was old.'

'Do you mean to say that old people have fewer bones? That isn't the case where I come from. When my father-in-law died two years ago at the age of seventy, there were twice as many bones to pick up!'

Had his sister gone senile? Nobutoshi found her remarks truly callous.

The urn was wrapped in a piece of white cloth and handed over to Nobutoshi. At that moment, Shigezō bowed low and said in a clear voice: 'I'm sorry to have caused you so much trouble.' Everyone was startled by his remark. Thinking that Shigezō had been addressing him, the official responded by conveying his deepest condolences.

Nobutoshi and Akiko, however, were convinced that Shigezō had been speaking to the remains of his wife. Kyōko, who up until then had been talking non-stop, was stunned into silence.

The bereaved family moved silently along the muddy road.

Mitsuko had stayed behind to look after the house. During their

42

absence, the undertaker had cleared away all the objects he had set up for the funeral; he had even taken away the large floral wreaths wrapped in cellophane which had been presented by the Neighbourhood Association and the Widows' Association. The house was as silent and deserted as it had been before the funeral. It was rather strange that the Widows' Association had presented a floral wreath, as the husband of the deceased was still alive. The wreath had probably been sent at the urging of Mrs Kadotani. The cloth-wrapped urn was placed in the small Buddhist altar in the cottage.

'A funeral in Tokyo is so simple! In the country it's really quite an event. Day after day people come to offer their condolences, and the mistress of the house is expected to serve them dinner.'

As soon as Mitsuko had left, Kyōko began a detailed description of what had happened following her father-in-law's death. It did not bother her in the least that Nobutoshi read the evening paper, Akiko worked busily in the kitchen and Satoshi disappeared upstairs while she rambled on and on. She said that he had had a great number of relatives and friends in the provinces. Even after the funeral, mourners came in an endless stream to offer incense, each one saying that someone had told him about the death in the family.

'Every time anybody came to call, I'd go out to buy some saké and cook an extra quantity of rice. Things were absolutely hectic! My mother-in-law, though, was delighted to have all those visitors. My father-in-law was not as bad as Father, but he was old-fashioned and required a lot of attention. Isn't it strange that after a person dies you remember only the good things about them? My mother-in-law has been a saint ever since she lost her husband. She's the picture of contentment, always smiling and happy. I'm sure it's because she feels completely free. That's why I feel sorry for Mother. After all, a woman enjoys her greatest happiness as a widow.'

'Do you say things like that in front of your husband, Kyōko?'

'Why, of course!'

Akiko, who could no longer control herself, giggled.

'Women today are really monsters. Mother would never have said anything like that.'

'That's why I feel sorry for her.'

Akiko busied herself rearranging the food in the refrigerator. Right at the back, behind the various things Mitsuko had put in, she came across a crab, one of those she had bought the day her mother-in-law died.

'Here's a crab. Would you like some, dear?'

Nobutoshi said that he would like to have the crab with saké and became irritated when Akiko expressed concern about his drinking

43

night after night. How did she expect him to eat crab without saké?

'I remember thinking what a treat it would be for you to have some crab that snowy day, but until today I've had no chance to serve it.'

'Crabmeat doesn't really go very well with a funeral,' Nobutoshi remarked.

Thinking that a whole crab was a bit too much, Akiko cut it lengthwise down its back with a cleaver and placed half of it on a plate.

'May I have some too, Akiko?' asked Shigezō as they seated themselves at the table.

Without saying anything, Akiko put the other half on a plate and placed it in front of Shigezō. Worried about his delicate stomach, she secretly hoped that Nobutoshi or Kyōko would stop her.

'Don't you like crab, Satoshi?' asked Kyōko.

'It tastes all right, but it's so much trouble to eat.'

'Well then, I'll shell some for you.'

But when Kyōko took up a crab leg from Shigezō's plate, he said sharply: 'What do you think you're doing? Put that back.'

Kyōko was so startled that she did as she was told. She looked at Nobutoshi and Akiko and shrugged her shoulders.

They all watched silently while Shigezō ate the crab. Using his left hand and chopsticks, the old man carefully removed the shell, tossed the white crabmeat into his mouth and chewed it carefully. Occasionally they could hear his tongue swishing about in his mouth. A mound of empty shells soon began to pile up on his plate. Shigezō seemed to be performing some strange survival ritual.

'Did you like the crabmeat, Grandfather?' asked Akiko.

Shigezō looked up and replied simply, 'Yes.'

After a while, Nobutoshi, sounding very wretched indeed, announced that he had lost his appetite and pushed his plate away, even though he usually could not resist crab or shrimps. He made up his mind then and there never to eat at the same table with young people when he was old.

5

One of Kyōko's constant refrains was that she did not have to return home immediately, as her mother-in-law had been perfectly happy and content since her husband's death. Akiko found her sister-in-law's presence reassuring. After taking a day off for the funeral, Nobutoshi returned to work, and Satoshi went back to school. But before she could go back to work, Akiko had to put the cottage in order. She thought she ought to consult her sister-in-law on how to dispose of the old woman's possessions, so was glad that Kyōko would be staying a little longer. Kyōko, who was warm and generous by nature, disposed of her mother's few valuable possessions in a very businesslike manner. All she wanted for herself were several sash clips which she had found among her mother's things. Akiko and Kyōko looked for the old couple's bank deposit book, but all they could find was a post office savings book recording how they had deposited and withdrawn the money Nobutoshi and Akiko had given them periodically as spending money. It would have been surprising if they had owned anything of great value, as Shigezō had retired soon after the war. Because Shigezō had not got on well with Kyōko's in-laws, he and his wife had sold their house and moved to Tokyo. Even when Nobutoshi and Akiko were young and their combined income was very low, the old couple had lived with them and depended on them financially. It was out of their joint salaries that Nobutoshi and Akiko had built the cottage for them.

No one therefore expected Shigezō and his wife to own anything of great value. But it was a blow to Kyōko's pride that there was not a single kimono belonging to her mother that she could take back to her mother-in-law as a keepsake.

During their sorting-out, the women came across Shigezō's large supply of medicines. Bags containing what appeared to be Chinese herbal remedies were hanging from the kitchen ceiling. Shigezō had used the herbs regularly, some of which he substituted for tea.

'Chinese medicine is said to bring eternal youth and promote longevity. Father must have been drinking just the latter kind,' said Kyōko.

Akiko decided to send her mother-in-law's bedding to a local quilt-maker to have it remade. He arrived to collect it almost as soon as she put down the phone. There was hardly any other furniture to speak of in the cottage, so the two women were surprised to discover a cache of empty cans and bottles under the veranda.

'Don't you have refuse collectors in Tokyo?'

'But that can't be the reason for all this rubbish.'

Akiko was dumbfounded. Nearly all the empty containers were ones she had discarded. The old couple could not possibly have used so much cooking oil. Who could have amassed all these cans and bottles week after week, Shigezō or his wife? Wasn't this what a dog did when he took a wooden clog in his teeth and dragged it under the veranda?

Despite her untidy appearance, Kyōko sorted her parents' possessions with great efficiency. As she took things out of the closet, she separated them into two piles: one for items that were to be disposed of and the other for those that were to be kept. Most of the clothing and bric-à-brac had to be thrown away.

'I suppose Mother had a reason for holding on to these things. Could you find a use for them? I don't know who would want them,' said Kyōko, for even the annual charity drive preferred money to old clothes.

Kyōko got down on all fours, crawled into the closet and emerged dragging with her a square wooden box. She removed the cover and let out a piercing scream. Akiko, who was cleaning out another cupboard, rushed to Kyōko's side. When she saw what the box contained her knees went weak. Inside were several sets of dentures made up of rows of yellow teeth embedded in flesh-coloured bases, as well as broken combs and cracked hand mirrors. Some of the dentures were broken in half, others had teeth missing. Akiko recalled how angry Shigezō had been each time he had tried a new pair of dentures and found that they did not fit properly. Needless to say, the cost of having several sets of dentures made by different dentists had been exorbitant. Akiko described to Kyōko how in the end Shigezō had bought materials and tools to make his own.

'When was this?'

'About ten years ago.'

'Then these must be the ones he threw out at the time.'

'I suppose so.'

The women were horrified. The dentures were even more weird when scrutinized closely.

'It must have cost the earth.'

'Yes. Dentists charge a lot, you know. I don't remember how many sets he had made. Some of the dentists were not even in his insurance plan!'

Akiko could not bring herself to describe how Shigezō would nag endlessly for a new set of dentures until either she or Nobutoshi gave in and offered to pay for them.

'I wonder if he made the set he is wearing now.'

'I really wouldn't know.'

Shigezō sat sunning himself on the veranda, his arms around his knees, while his daughter and daughter-in-law put the cottage in order. The snow had been followed by fine weather, and the perennial smog was forgotten. Shigezō's eyes were fixed on the fresh green leaves of a camellia which was visible in the distance.

'Father, Father,' cried Kyōko in a loud voice.

The old man responded very slowly. Only when Kyōko had given up trying to attract his attention did he turn to ask Akiko: 'Isn't dinner ready yet, Akiko?'

'Really, Father! You've only just eaten! Why, it isn't even two yet, is it, Akiko?'

'But I'm hungry, Akiko.'

'You can't be, Father. I wouldn't want you to get a stomach-ache.'

'Isn't it time for dinner?'

Akiko did not pride herself on being particularly gentle, but now that Kyōko had appeared on the scene, she found that her approach to the old man was mild by comparison.

'I'll go and buy you a snack in a moment. Please be patient, Grandpa,' she said, exuding kindness.

'Hurry. I'm starved.'

'All right.'

How had she managed to sound so gentle? Strange that she seemed to grow calmer as Kyōko's voice rose in anger.

'I think we'd better have Grandpa examined by a doctor,' said Akiko.

'I agree. Something is definitely wrong with him. Would you take him? Come to think of it, though, I've never heard a doctor say that senility can be cured,' Kyōko remarked. Akiko found it difficult to believe that Kyōko was speaking about her own father.

Akiko left the house to do some shopping. On her way she called to see the doctor who had attended to her mother-in-law at the time

47

of her death, but the nurse told her that his hours were from six p.m. onwards and then quickly disappeared. Akiko announced in a loud voice that she would be back at six, feeling suddenly anxious as she did so. There had been so many expenses lately, all connected with her mother-in-law's funeral. Since she had never experienced a funeral at first hand before, Akiko was shocked when she went over the bills sent by the crematorium and the undertaker. At her request, the young priest had itemized each service rendered; he had added that any additional contribution she might make was entirely voluntary. Even without the voluntary contribution the total sum had been staggering. So Akiko consulted Mrs Kadotani, who in turn consulted her son. The Kadotanis agreed that the sum the priest had asked for was exorbitant. Mrs Kadotani added that she had been at the funeral and did not think that Akiko should have to pay so much for such a short reading of the sutras. But, she reminded Akiko, there was still Shigezō's funeral to consider. She therefore advised Akiko to think the matter over carefully. In the end, Akiko had no choice but to pay for the services as charged, although she omitted the voluntary contribution.

Akiko went carefully over the invoice she had received from the funeral parlour, drawing Kyōko's attention to the cost of the coffin. The expression on Kyōko's face indicated eloquently that here was a perfect example of the high cost of living in Tokyo. According to Kyōko, one simply could not afford to die unprepared. She joked about the high cost of coffins, especially as they could only be used once, but Akiko, who was responsible for the bills, was not at all amused.

Akiko wondered how a family with only one breadwinner could make ends meet in these times of rampant inflation. Since both she and her husband worked, they had somehow managed up till now, but their end-of-year bonuses had been used up on the funeral expenses, and the mid-year bonuses were still a long way off. Akiko felt disheartened when she thought about the cuts she would have to make in her household budget. Having lived next door to the elderly couple all these years, Akiko had known that she would one day have to go through a period of mourning. It was strange, therefore, that she had felt none of the intense emotions that she had come to expect after a death in the family. Rather, Akiko had been hit by the realization of how terribly expensive a funeral was. At last she understood why gifts of money were presented when someone died!

When Akiko and Shigezō arrived at the Sasayama Clinic at six, three other patients were already waiting to see the doctor. At the prescription window, Akiko filled out a form, entering Shigezō's

48

name, age, address and telephone number. She handed the form, with the money to cover the cost of the first visit, to the nurse, who, without a word, noisily closed the window. This made Akiko feel very uneasy.

When Shigezō's name was finally called, Akiko went with him into the examination room. Bowing low to the doctor, she thanked him for his assistance at the time of her mother-in-law's death.

'Oh, *that* Tachibana! My deepest condolences. You must be terribly exhausted,' said the doctor.

'Yes. My father-in-law has been acting a little strange lately, doctor, probably because of the shock of seeing his wife die,' said Akiko, flustered.

Looking over the chart which the nurse had filled in, the doctor asked: 'He's very old, isn't he? Has he been having his regular check-ups?'

'What check-ups?'

'The physical examination for senior citizens. Any person over sixty-five years of age is entitled to it.'

'No, not to my knowledge. I don't know for certain, though, because he and his wife lived in a separate cottage. I doubt that he's been to see a doctor recently,' said Akiko, remembering that it was because Shigezō harboured a deep distrust of all doctors that he had become so absorbed in Chinese medicine. However, this was neither the time nor the place for her to mention this. Fortunately, Shigezō remained docile during his physical examination.

'Now let me examine your chest.'

Shigezō began to remove his shirt. His movements were so slow and deliberate that Akiko felt compelled to assist him.

'What a splendid physique!' exclaimed the doctor. Neither Shigezō nor Akiko made any remark.

Akiko had not known her father-in-law as a young man, but she had heard that he had been handsome and strong. He certainly did have a fine physique for his age. It suddenly occurred to Akiko that his bones might not fit into an urn. An instant later, she reproached herself for having had such a thought.

'All right now, take a deep breath. That's fine. Once again,' said the doctor. Pressing his stethoscope against Shigezō's chest, he spoke in the cajoling tone of voice that he usually reserved for children. Shigezō meekly did as he was told.

The next few minutes were hectic. After giving the nurse some instructions, the doctor whisked Shigezō off to an adjacent room and took some X-rays. The machine made a loud clanking noise. Akiko, who had been very worried about money matters ever since her mother-in-law's funeral, nearly jumped up in panic. X-rays were by no means cheap, and neither the doctor nor the nurse had asked whether Shigezō was covered by health insurance. What was she to do if the X-rays had to be paid for in cash? She could hardly restrain herself from rushing into the next room and begging the doctor to stop the examination. She should not have brought Shigezō here in the first place, especially as he had not shown any symptoms of illness. Coming here was Kyōko's idea.

Akiko was furious that her sister-in-law could be so irresponsible about her own father's welfare. Kyōko responded cheerfully enough whenever Akiko consulted her about anything, but she offered no practical advice. Akiko was convinced that this was a defence against having to take on any financial responsibility. She felt so irritable at this point that, when Dr Sasayama emerged from the dark room, she walked up to him and asked bluntly: 'How much will the X-rays cost?'

Peering at her from behind his glasses, the doctor noted the grave expression on Akiko's face and replied very calmly: 'Every year during the one-month period following the Respect for the Elderly Day – that is to say, between 15 September and 15 October – anyone over sixty-five is entitled to a free health check-up.'

'Oh.'

Akiko had not known about this. She grew more despondent when she realized that, had they come a few weeks earlier, Shigezō could have been examined free of charge.

'I imagine you have a number of other expenses at this time. Since this is your first visit here, I'll think of something to ease the burden.'

'What do you mean?'

'You can pay for the examination at cost.'

Akiko felt so relieved that she nearly fainted. While she bowed again and again to express her heartfelt gratitude, the doctor went back into the dark room. Akiko sat down in a corner of the examination room while the doctor took an electrocardiogram test and collected a blood sample from Shigezō. As each stage of the examination was completed, Akiko felt truly grateful that she only had to pay for the doctor's services at cost. Meanwhile Shigezō, as docile as a child, did exactly as he was told.

After being told that the results would be ready in a week's time, Akiko again bowed low and, taking Shigezō by the hand, returned home. She was surprised to find that both Kyōko and Satoshi had helped themselves to some noodles and were sitting with their faces thrust into their bowls.

'I'm hungry, Akiko. Please may I have a snack?' begged Shigezō.

Looking up from her bowl, Kyōko asked: 'How did the examination go?'

Akiko gave her sister-in-law a detailed account. Then, as Shigezō was still complaining about being hungry, she went into the kitchen and began to prepare dinner. She felt famished herself. What has Kyōko been doing all this time? she wondered. She could at least have put the rice on. Instead, she had helped herself to a bowl of noodles. Her hunger pangs made Akiko feel even more upset.

'What do you think you're doing, Satoshi? How about bringing your bowl to the sink,' she snapped.

Kyōko was too dense to catch the hint.

'Oh? Free check-ups after September 15th? I'm glad to know about that. I'll have to take my mother-in-law for hers next year. I wonder if they are available only in Tokyo. By the way, did you find out what was wrong with Father?'

'The doctor will have the results ready a week from today.'

'He'll probably have the blood analysed at a university hospital that specializes in such things.'

'Just imagine. A whole week!'

After a pensive silence, Kyōko said: 'Akiko, I intend to return home after the seventh-day memorial services.'

Akiko stopped in her tracks and stared blankly at her sister-in-law.

'Well, I can't stay here indefinitely. After all, I have a mother-in-law and children to look after at home. As you know, I'm no longer a member of the Tachibana family.'

'Yes, of course.'

'But I'll be here for the seventh-day memorial services.'

Kyōko was right. It was high time she returned home.

Just then, Shigezō began to sob.

'What's the matter, Father?'

'I'm so hungry I feel quite weak.'

Akiko did not know what to do with her father-in-law, who was crying like a baby, his hands over his face. After sending Satoshi to the baker's for some pastries, she peered into the refrigerator and spotted the remains of the crab.

'Would you like some crab, Grandpa?'

Shigezō immediately stopped crying and happily seated himself at the dining-table. Taking up his chopsticks, he began to remove the crabmeat.

As a hush fell over the room, Akiko breathed a sigh of relief. She asked Kyōko to look after the house while she was away at work the next day. Kyōko cheerfully agreed.

6

Akiko could not remember exactly when part of Yūrakuchō had come to be called Nishi Ginza. The Fujieda Law Firm she worked for could, in one sense, be described as an office in the Ginza; however, it was actually located near the Yūrakuchō Underpass and the windows of the gloomy office rattled each time a train went past. The office building had been imposing enough when it was first constructed amidst the burnt-out ruins during the immediate post-war years, but the more important tenants had moved out one by one as the years went by. The Fujieda Law Firm was now the oldest office in the building. Previously, Akiko had worked for a trading company where she had met and married Nobutoshi; however, she had had to leave her job because the company did not approve of working wives. An acquaintance had introduced her to the law firm where she now worked as a Japanese-language typist. Having been with them for twenty years, Akiko was considered an old hand, second only to Mr Fujieda, the attorney. The office had a rather dismal air about it.

Whenever a court session was scheduled, Mr Fujieda and his partner would leave the office in the morning and return in the afternoon to write up their reports. One of Akiko's duties was to type these. While she had been away, her desk had become piled high with paperwork.

A Japanese-language typewriter has a greater number of characters than the alphabet. What's more, special characters have to be selected from a box containing spare keys. To operate such a machine was exceedingly laborious and time-consuming. Akiko had been brought up by her mother and had begun to work immediately after leaving the girls' high school, so she had not had a chance to acquire any special skills. When she realized that the Japanese-language typewriter, though extremely cumbersome, was indispensable, she

52

had painstakingly taught herself to become an expert typist. However, Akiko had many other responsibilities at the office besides typing. She not only answered the telephone, but also served tea to visitors and looked after the running of the office. It was therefore not surprising that so much work had accumulated during her absence.

'I'm truly sorry for the inconvenience I've caused you, but my mother-in-law's death was totally unexpected,' Akiko said to Mr Fujieda during the lunch break.

'I understand that she was seventy-five. It was fortunate that she didn't suffer from a protracted illness.'

'Yes, Sir. But we've discovered something else.'

'And what's that?'

'Her husband . . . that is to say, my husband's eighty-four-year-old father, has been acting very strangely.'

The lawyer looked at Akiko and pointed to his head. 'You mean up here?'

'Yes. How did you guess?'

'From what you have just told me about him.'

'He doesn't even recognize his own son and daughter. He seems to know me and my son, though.'

'Does he have trouble with his sense of direction?'

'What do you mean?'

'Well, does he lose his bearings and rush headlong in the wrong direction?'

'No. But why do you ask?'

'My father did that and he gave us all a terrible time. He'd suddenly get up and dart forward, and then bump into something. In the end he fell off the veranda.'

'Was he killed?'

'No. He broke his legs and was completely incapacitated. Things were infinitely easier for all of us after that.'

'That's not my father-in-law's trouble. He's constantly gorging himself, and then he cries like a baby when we refuse to give him more food.'

'In that case he won't last very long.'

'How many more years do you think he has?'

'I'd say no more than two or three. My father used to behave like that. Immediately after having his lunch, he'd ask us when lunch was going to be served. My wife was always worried that people would think she wasn't feeding him properly. He died two years later.'

Akiko heaved a sigh.

'My in-laws lived in a separate cottage. We rarely visited each other, so we didn't realize that anything was wrong with him. We haven't the faintest idea when he became senile. My mother-in-law was in perfect health, so she had complete charge of their household. As soon as she died, my husband and I realized how senile my father-in-law had become, and we've been terribly worried about him ever since,' confessed Akiko.

'Who's looking after him today?'

'My husband's younger sister. She'll be with us until the seventh-day memorial services. I don't know what I'll do after she returns home.'

'You've got a real problem on your hands.'

'Oh?'

'No doubt about it.'

Just then the telephone rang, interrupting their conversation. While typing, Akiko thought about the serious expression on the attorney's face.

No sooner had the two lawyers left the office than the young secretary said: 'Things must be terribly difficult for you, Mrs Tachibana.'

'Why do you say that?'

'When my grandmother became senile, she caused us all sorts of trouble. Even now all of us suffer on her account.'

'Really?'

'We couldn't let her out of our sight. She became as shrivelled as a pickled plum, but she was able to scurry about all over the house. Does your father-in-law play about with all the knobs and switches?'

'What do you mean?'

'Well, my grandmother used to turn on the water and the gas. She touched everything in sight. She would turn on radios and television sets, and as she was hard of hearing, the noise didn't bother her in the least. It worried the rest of us, though. The gas was especially dangerous! We had to turn it off at the mains when we weren't using any of the appliances. But then she'd go around turning the taps on when we weren't looking, so when the gas was turned on again, we'd smell it coming from the most unexpected corners of the house. That was really dangerous! One of us had to be with her all the time, but she was so agile that even we grandchildren found ourselves out of breath chasing after her. We used to take turns keeping an eye on her.'

'How old is she?'

'Ninety-six. She started acting strangely about eight years ago.'

'Oh dear!'

'At first she started telling one lie after the other. By the time we realized that she was no longer her old self, she had stopped talking

54

altogether. Then she started running around the house and garden, panting.'

'Is she still doing that?'

'Oh no. She had a stroke five years ago. We thought at first that she was dead, as she didn't move a muscle, but her heart kept beating. She's been in the hospital ever since, surviving on a liquid diet fed through a rubber tube in her nose. She's been a terrible financial burden on all of us because she isn't covered by any health insurance. She requires round-the-clock nursing care, and the monthly salary for the nurse is several times my own. Each of her six grandchildren pays a part of the cost. Whenever we get together, all we talk about is how we'll prepare red-rice and celebrate when she dies.'

'Oh dear!'

'Father comes from a family of three boys and there are six grandchildren in all. If I were the only grandchild, I'd probably never be able to get married.'

'Does your grandmother recognize you at all?'

'No. She can't even open her eyes.'

'What do you mean?'

'Well, she's suffering from an eye ailment. She even has to wear a nappy. I visit her in the hospital once a year, but she looks so awful that I can't bear to look at her. Father wonders why they don't just let her die.'

'What a thing to say!'

'But the hospital care she receives is terribly expensive, and the salary of the nurse who is looking after her keeps on going up. All they do is pour liquids down a tube. Ten years have gone by, and she still clings to life. Father says that he'll probably die before her. If he does, we've all decided to run away.'

Akiko made no further comment and banged away at the typewriter, rather more loudly than necessary. Although there were only four people employed here, three had either lived with a senile relative at some time in the past or were heavily burdened by one at present.

Akiko suddenly remembered her mother-in-law, painfully aware that for some time now she had not thought about her very much. She had had a delightful personality and despite the fact that the poor woman had been a slave to her crochety husband for over fifty years, she had always worn a smile on her unlined face. How grateful Akiko had been for the times her mother-in-law had interceded on her behalf! Though she had never said so, Akiko too had been convinced that her mother-in-law would outlive Shigezō. Had women in the past been forced to live as if they were their husbands' slaves? The life

55

of this poor woman, who had never given way to self-pity or complained about Shigezō's becoming senile, had suddenly ended one snowy day. Akiko heaved a sigh. How was one to describe such self-sacrifice? No woman today would put up with such a miserable life.

After debating whether or not to work overtime that day, Akiko decided to leave for home at the usual time, for she had not had a chance to go shopping. Her meal-planning had been considerably affected by the two additional mouths she now had to feed. She was no longer able to stock up on groceries and was often at a loss what to cook, as neither Kyōko nor Shigezō cared for easy-to-prepare foods, such as spaghetti and stir-fried dishes. Yet if Kyōko dislikes such dishes, she ought to make her own, thought Akiko. But Kyōko did not lift a finger around the house, either because she was reluctant to intrude in another woman's kitchen or because she was revelling in her temporary freedom from domestic duties. However, Kyōko would be leaving for home in a few days, so Akiko would not have to put up with her for much longer. Akiko had been offended when Kyōko, who felt uneasy about frozen foods, would not even agree to taste them. She was irritated by what she saw as a countrywoman's prejudice. She herself firmly believed that frozen herrings and clams were far fresher than the supposedly fresh variety.

As Akiko walked through the basement of the department store shopping for food, she found herself at a corner piled high with crabs. Remembering the crab she still had in her freezer, she hesitated for a moment and then bought two. She planned to divide the larger crab into several smaller portions for her husband and to serve her father-in-law the smaller one.

Akiko was famished, for all she had had for lunch was a cheap bowl of Chinese noodles near the office. Feeling that she had to fortify herself in order to face her sister-in-law at home, she had a hot dog at a stand near the subway entrance. Perhaps Kyōko was preparing dinner after all. But Akiko did not let herself expect too much, afraid that she might be disappointed. Middle-aged women in Tokyo did their best to avoid eating rice, but Kyōko insisted on having three bowls of rice three times a day. She had it with pickled vegetables if there was no side dish to her liking. Akiko tried not to serve her husband too many salty dishes because he had high blood pressure; it was therefore to please her sister-in-law that she had bought a variety of *tsukudani*.*

Holding a bag of groceries in each hand, Akiko emerged from the subway. There was no sign of rain, but a chill wind was blowing
*Preserved food boiled down in soy sauce.

along Ōme Avenue. She remembered that it had been snowing the day her mother-in-law had died. Akiko wanted to buy some bread, but today she simply could not carry anything more. As the cold wintry wind cut into her, Akiko congratulated herself on having worn a trouser suit. A cold day like this was sure to give her a stomach upset. She had never had trouble like that when she was young. Now, no longer vain about her appearance, she put on woollen trousers as soon as the December gales began to blow. She thought about the young secretary dressed in a miniskirt and dark blue stockings. She probably did not know yet what it was like to feel the cold.

Akiko paused at the entrance to her house and put down her shopping bags. Just as she was about to take out her key, she remembered that today there was no need to and turned the doorknob. How infinitely more comforting it is to have someone to come home to, thought Akiko. She called out cheerfully, 'I'm back!'

Akiko waited for a while but there was no response. When she finally stepped into the house, she found the place in a mess. What surprised her most was the pile of dirty dishes in the sink. Even when Nobutoshi and Satoshi were left at home by themselves, she had never found the house so untidy on her return. Akiko felt the blood rush to her head.

'Grandpa!' she called out in a loud voice. 'Kyōko!'

There was no reply.

Akiko slipped out of her overcoat and began to clean up the kitchen. Although she was a working wife, she was fastidious and could not tolerate dirty dishes in the sink. Nobutoshi and Satoshi, too, kept the house neat and tidy without being reminded. How could Kyōko be so slovenly?

Akiko let the hot water run while she noisily washed the dirty bowls. With a burst of energy fuelled by her anger, she proceeded to clean the kitchen from top to bottom. Just as she had finished vacuuming, Satoshi returned home. His face was flushed, as if he had raced all the way home on his bicycle.

'Have you been at school all this time, dear?'

'I got back a little while ago but Grandpa and Aunt Kyōko weren't here. I wondered where they'd gone, so I went out to look for them.'

'How long ago was that?'

'About an hour ago.'

'Really? How careless of her . . .'

Satoshi did not reply.

'Where could they have gone?'

'I checked at the doctor's and also went to the market and Myōhō-ji Temple.'

'That was clever of you.'

'I was afraid Grandpa might have died too. After all, he's eighty-four.'

Now that her anger had subsided, Akiko began to worry. Where on earth had the two of them gone? She walked over to the cottage. It saddened her to see the urn of ashes in the Buddhist altar, covered with a white cloth. Then she was struck by a problem she would soon have to face: Shigezō and Kyōko slept here in the cottage every night, but where would the old man sleep after Kyōko's departure? She remembered the young secretary's description of the old woman who turned on all the knobs in sight. The deserted cottage had hardly any furnishings to speak of, yet it looked untidy. Akiko attributed this to Kyōko's slovenly ways. Sitting down in front of the Buddhist altar, she offered a candle, lit some joss-sticks and pressed her hands together in prayer. The photograph of her mother-in-law, which had been enlarged by the undertaker and placed in a large frame, gazed at her serenely from beyond the urn. It had been taken by Satoshi several years before and had been in the family album.

'Mother . . . ,' murmured Akiko, 'where can Grandpa and Kyōko have gone?'

Akiko was pleased that she hadn't left Shigezō unattended up till now, but her heart felt heavy as she wondered what to do with him after Kyōko left. Ringing in her ears were Mr Fujieda's solemn words: she had quite a problem on her hands. Worried about the risk of fire, Akiko blew out the candle and went back to the main house.

How could Kyōko have gone off like this without locking up the house? In Tokyo one had to take every precaution before leaving one's house. How irresponsible she was!

As there was nothing she could do for the moment, Akiko decided to get dinner ready. Kyōko's voracious appetite matched that of Satoshi and Shigezō. If left alone, she was capable of consuming an unbelievable amount of food. Akiko found herself washing twice as much rice as she normally did. She turned on the electric rice-cooker, prepared some Japanese-style side dishes and marinated several fish fillets in soy sauce. When she had finished, there was still no sign of the missing pair, so Akiko carried on and heated the bath water.

'Are you hungry, Satoshi?' Akiko called in a loud voice. Satoshi came down the stairs and said: 'I'm so hungry, I could weep.'

'Stop being silly. If you're hungry, I'll get your dinner right away.'

'Great!'

Akiko was feeling ill-tempered again and wondered how far her son would go in teasing her. Satoshi sprawled out in the middle of the room and began to read the evening paper.

'Where could Grandpa and Aunt Kyōko have gone?'

'Well, the festival day in honour of the temple founder is long past,' said Akiko, adding, 'Please watch this fish for me, dear.'

'Where are you going, Mum? I meant to tell you that I've already checked with Mrs Kihara and Mrs Kadotani.'

'Weren't they there?'

Satoshi turned the page of the newspaper and said: 'It's possible, you know, that they went out separately.'

'Who are you talking about?'

'Grandpa and Aunt Kyōko, of course. Aunt Kyōko may have asked Grandpa to look after the house while she went out to do some sightseeing. Then Grandpa might have forgotten all about it and gone out himself.'

'Don't even suggest such a thing!'

'But don't you think we should consider every possibility?'

Akiko got Satoshi's dinner ready and set the table.

Satoshi began to eat heartily. Presently he looked up. 'Aren't you having any dinner, Mum?' he asked.

'I'm too upset to eat. Besides, it wouldn't be right to eat before Aunt Kyōko.'

'But aren't you hungry?'

'I'll be all right.'

It was a good thing she had had that hot dog, she thought, but of course she did not mention this to her son.

'Akiko! Akiko!'

'Grandpa! Wherever have you been?'

Akiko opened the kitchen door and Shigezō came in. His eyes fell on Satoshi and the dining-table. Without a moment's hesitation, he slipped off his shoes, stepped up into the kitchen and picked up his chopsticks.

'Grandpa, where's Kyōko?'

Shigezō was too busy gorging himself to reply. Akiko scrutinized her father-in-law, who was neatly dressed in a suit, and then looked at the shoes he had taken off. She tried to associate the way he was dressed with something at the back of her mind, but, much to her irritation, could not recall what it was.

'What's happened to Kyōko, Grandpa? Didn't you leave the house together?'

Akiko peered into the face of her father-in-law, who was sitting properly, with his legs tucked under him, and eating carefully so as not to spill any of his rice. She flung questions at him, but the old man was oblivious to everything except his food. He didn't stop chewing, sitting bolt upright with his rice bowl in his left hand and the chopsticks in his right.

'Where have you been all this time, Grandpa?' Akiko shouted hysterically.

'Don't, Mum!' Satoshi broke in, unable to look on in silence.

A little while later, Kyōko came in through the front door. Her hair was so dishevelled that both Akiko and Satoshi were startled. The collar of her kimono was twisted.

'Whatever happened, Kyōko?'

Kyōko was too exhausted to speak. Seeing that her father was having his dinner, she flopped down on the spot. When Akiko saw how breathless her sister-in-law was, she filled a glass with water and handed it to her. Kyōko drank the water in one gulp and sighed. Still unable to utter a word, she glared reproachfully at her father.

Just then Shigezō thrust out his empty bowl and asked Akiko for his third helping of rice.

'You've had quite enough, Grandpa. Three bowls would be too much for you. Have some tea instead. It'll be terrible if you get an upset stomach.'

Shigezō silently sipped the tea Akiko gave him.

At long last Kyōko said: 'I think Father's in love with you, Akiko.'

Stunned, Akiko looked at her sister-in-law. 'Really, Kyōko. You mustn't say such things.'

'He's got a crush on you. After all, he doesn't recognize Nobutoshi or me. Does he listen to anything we say to him? No. But he listens to you. I tell you, he really loves you.'

'That isn't funny. Since I married Nobutoshi he has never stopped tormenting me. I don't know how many times he's said spiteful things to my face and made me cry.'

Satoshi got up quietly and disappeared upstairs.

'I've heard about that from Mother. She often said in her letters that she felt sorry for you. When he was with us, Father was always making sarcastic remarks to my husband, and I was often on the verge of tears. He even picked quarrels with my in-laws, which meant that I had to get involved. I felt absolutely wretched. Believe me, my heart went out to you. But I think that all along Father felt differently towards you.'

'In what way?'

'You've heard of the saying "He who loves too much hates in like extreme," haven't you? Well, deep down, Father was in love with you.'

'Please stop saying that!'

Akiko spoke so sharply that Kyōko finally realized how much she had upset her sister-in-law by expressing her secret thoughts with such frankness. She changed the subject.

'I had such a terrible time today. Father really took me by surprise. He walked too fast for me to keep up with him. At one point I was so breathless I really thought I was going to die.'

Not wanting the relationship between herself and her sister-in-law to become even more strained and curious to know what had happened, Akiko leaned forward to listen to Kyōko's account of the day's events.

'Where did you go? We were so worried! Satoshi got on his bike and went to the clinic and the temple to look for you.'

'Well, Father dozed off in front of the TV and was quiet until after lunch. I was afraid of upsetting his stomach, so I prepared some rice porridge, and he finished it all in less than an hour. I cooked just under a cup of rice over a low flame, adding some chives and eggs. I don't think it will disagree with him. At one point I had to go to the bathroom. By the time I got back, he'd slipped out of the house. I found him in the back room of the cottage changing his clothes. When I asked him where he was going, he said that he was going to fetch Grandma.'

'Really?'

'Then I asked him where he thought Grandma had gone, and he said, "Tokyo". I explained to him again and again that this *was* Tokyo, but he didn't pay any attention. He tied his own tie and put on his shoes without my help. To watch him get dressed, you wouldn't think he was senile.

'At least he hasn't forgotten Mother altogether. It was admirable of Father to say that he was going to fetch her, after treating her so badly. When he started to leave the house without his overcoat, I grabbed my shawl and dashed out after him. He walked so fast he didn't seem a bit like an old man. I called out after him, but he kept marching straight ahead without once looking back. I had to run to keep up with him most of the time.'

'Where did he go?'

'He made his way to Itsukaichi Avenue, then turned right by the bicycle shop.'

'Oh, that's Ōme Avenue.'

'Yes, that's right. Then he started to walk straight ahead. I repeatedly grabbed him from behind, asking him where he was going and saying we should go home, but he completely ignored me. He actually used brute force to shake me off! He's terribly strong! Once I fell flat on my bottom.'

'Oh?'

'I must say that Tokyo people are terribly unfriendly. A few of them turned round to look at me, but no one tried to help. I finally managed to stop a taxi and explained the situation to the driver. I begged him to help me, then started grappling with Father. But by the time I got Father under control, the taxi had disappeared. People in Tokyo don't know how to be kind. Back home, someone would have lent a hand.

'I'm overweight, so I got a sharp pain in my chest from all that running. I felt dizzy too, and out of breath. How was I to know that Father would walk that far? He just kept walking straight along that wide avenue — what did you say it was called?'

'Ōme Avenue. You must have been going towards Shinjuku.'

'Yes, that's right. He kept walking straight ahead, ignoring the traffic lights. He didn't stop. I was terrified! Every time the lights turned red, I warned Father to look out, but he kept walking straight ahead. Then it suddenly occurred to me what he meant when he said he was going to fetch Mother. It made me feel quite faint. He probably intended to get himself run over and killed!'

'What a thought!'

'I chased after him like a madwoman, begging him to go home as you were probably worried about him. Suddenly he looked at me as though he'd come out of a trance, and stopped in his tracks. He stared at me and asked me what had happened to you.

'I told him once again that we ought to be going back, and that everyone at home must be worried sick. He nodded meekly, then he turned and made for home. I couldn't believe my eyes! But, afraid that he'd be hit by a car, I ran after him. It's a wonder he wasn't run over. Again and again, cars screeched to a stop and drivers swore at him. I was so terrified that I closed my eyes tight, but Father was oblivious of all the commotion. My feet ached and I was out of breath, so I suggested that we take a taxi home. He didn't even look round! I really don't know how long we walked. It was still light when we left the house, but it was starting to get dark by the time we finally turned back.'

'It's about two hours since Satoshi got back from school and went to look for you.'

'We must have walked longer than that. Even back home I've never walked as far as I have today. I thought that everything would be all right once I began to recognize where we were. But instead of

62

turning in the direction of Itsukaichi Avenue, Father kept walking straight ahead.'

'Oh dear!'

'I summoned up my last ounce of energy and grabbed him from behind, telling him that your house was in this direction. Only then did he begin heading this way. By that time I could hardly stand, so I slipped into the coffee shop on the corner and had some tea and cake. I was so desperate that I really didn't care whether or not Father got home safely. But after catching my breath, I started to worry about him, and I ran all the way home. I'm exhausted!'

'So that's what happened,' said Akiko. 'I had no idea where you had gone and was too upset to have any dinner.'

'Oh, I'm sorry to have kept you waiting.'

'You should have called us from a phone box. Satoshi or I would have got a taxi and rushed over to wherever you were.'

'Phoned you?'

Kyōko's mouth fell open, a dazed expression on her face. 'I didn't think of that! Of course! There's the public telephone. It didn't occur to me to phone you. Since neither of you were at home when we left the house, all I did was to run frantically after Father.'

When Kyōko took up her chopsticks, Akiko at last sat down to dinner. So this was what had happened that snowy day! If she hadn't met Shigezō, he would probably have walked for miles. According to Kyōko, he had walked along Ōme Avenue nearly as far as Shinjuku. What on earth was he thinking about as he rushed along like one possessed?

'I actually heard him say he was going to fetch Grandma. He must have a screw loose because he insisted that she had gone to Tokyo. He seems to think that he's out in the provinces where he was born and brought up.'

Kyōko looked as if she were trying to solve a difficult problem.

'But he was able to return home on his own once he found himself on Itsukaichi Avenue?'

'Yes, that's right. I've noticed that he returns to reality from time to time.'

'He does seem to be going back and forth between dream and reality, doesn't he?'

'Yes. I envy him. There are times when I'd like to forget harsh reality myself!'

Kyōko, who had inherited her mother's easy-going nature, had a special ability to laugh cheerfully in the middle of a serious discussion. How Akiko wished she was like her sister-in-law! Even in jest she couldn't bring herself to say that she envied her father-in-law. She realized that she would have to live with this man until the day he died. Kyōko, on the other hand, would be returning home in a few days, free of any responsibility for her father.

After her exertions, Kyōko ate heartily, despite the piece of cake at the coffee shop. She ate in silence, occasionally looking up to see how her father was. When she had consumed three bowls of rice, she sighed, then said: 'You're the only one he recognizes, Akiko.'

Akiko pretended not to hear.

Kyōko did not offer to help with the dishes after dinner. Standing at the kitchen sink with the water running, Akiko mentioned to her sister-in-law that the bath water was hot, but Kyōko said that she was too tired to have a bath.

'You know, Grandpa hasn't had a bath since the funeral.'

Akiko was certainly not going to bath Shigezō, especially after Kyōko had claimed that he was infatuated with her.

'I realize that,' Kyōko replied, 'but don't you think that Father's tired, too? He really did walk fast today. Though he may not be as exhausted as I am, he must be tired.'

'It wouldn't do to tire him out even more, would it?'

'No, it wouldn't. I'll just take him over to the cottage and put him to bed. I'd like to get some rest myself.'

Kyōko went over to the cottage to spread out the bedding, but returned to the main house a few minutes later. 'It's freezing over there. May I borrow a kerosene stove, Akiko?'

'Of course. I'll take it over for you, if you'll keep an eye on Grandpa.'

'Father, Father,' cried Kyōko, rousing him from his sleep. 'You're tired, Father. Let me tuck you up in bed. Come along.'

Shigezō eyed his daughter suspiciously, then looked at Akiko and rose slowly to his feet.

'Did you see that? You're the only one he trusts, Akiko.'

Akiko had expected her sister-in-law to make a remark like that.

As she walked through the garden with the kerosene stove in her arms, she wondered if the stove would prove to be a fire hazard.

While Kyōko helped her father into his night clothes, Akiko searched the tiny kitchen for some charcoal. She eventually found a supply under the floorboards. Propped up in the corner of the narrow entranceway were a charcoal fire-starter and a shovel. It had been years since Akiko had used this old-fashioned method of heating the house. Lighting the single gas burner, she placed the fire-starter with its charcoals over the flame. Profoundly moved by the old couple's lifestyle, so cosy and yet so wretched, Akiko found herself wanting to apologize to her mother-in-law. The nuclear

64

family! Following the general social trend, the two families had maintained separate households. Akiko asked herself whether this was an ideal way for human beings to live, but could not supply the answer. At first, Shigezō and his wife had moved in with them, but Akiko had found the constant friction between herself and her father-in-law impossible to tolerate. In desperation she had insisted on setting up separate households, regardless of how much money she and Nobutoshi had to borrow. Still young at the time, Akiko had not thought about the future consequences.

Nowadays, whenever she had a moment to herself, Akiko would try to imagine what she would be like when she herself was old. As she had a full-time job, the days flew by, but she knew that she would not be able to work at the law office until she was old and decrepit. Would she, when Satoshi was married and Nobutoshi had retired, find herself buried in a cheerless existence, lighting the only gas burner in the house and miserably waiting for death? Akiko was lost in thought until fiery red flames shot up from the black charcoals.

Kyōko used the fire shovel to transfer the blazing charcoals to the brazier in the corner of the room where Shigezō lay fast asleep.

'I feel quite wretched at seeing Father like this. I can't believe he's the man I once knew,' she remarked, sitting down at her father's bedside. 'Father has taken Mother's death harder than I imagined. Do you think he's really taken in what's happened?'

After adding more charcoals and sprinkling them with ashes, Akiko placed an iron kettle on the trivet. She shook her head and said quietly: 'I often chatted with Grandma, but she never complained, so we had no idea that Grandpa had become senile.'

'I wonder if he's run away like this before.'

'Probably,' said Akiko, thinking of how she had run into her father-in-law that snowy day.

'Then Mother must have died of sheer exhaustion,' said Kyōko with a sigh.

Akiko gazed silently at the white cloth covering the urn in the Buddhist altar and at the photograph behind it. Then she studied the face of the old man who was fast asleep.

Shigezō was breathing evenly. His finely-chiselled nose and mouth suggested that he had been strikingly handsome in his youth. Even today, everyone thought he was only seventy because he had retained most of his hair, which was still more black than grey. Gazing at Shigezō, she could almost feel the vitality radiating from him.

'Grandpa must have been good-looking when he was young.'

'He must have looked cross all the time. And he was probably all skin and bones because of his delicate stomach. It's hard to imagine that he was handsome. On the other hand, I've heard Mother say that she fell in love with him at first sight.'

'Then he must have been handsome.'

'But look at him now,' laughed Kyōko, pointing to the wretched old man.

Akiko was appalled that Kyōko could laugh at a time like this, but she managed to murmur something inoffensive and rose silently to her feet. She made a mental note not to forget to take her one and only kerosene stove back to the main house.

7

Akiko felt very grateful to those of her neighbours who remembered to attend the seventh-day memorial services and came to pay their respects. So this was what was meant by the saying 'A friend near by is better than a distant relative'! Akiko would have to turn to her neighbours for advice after Kyōko's departure.

'Why don't you ask Mrs Kadotani's help? She doesn't have enough to keep her busy and she's quite reliable. I'm sure she'd be delighted to look after your father-in-law,' suggested Mrs Kihara.

When Akiko asked Mrs Kadotani, the old woman leaned forward, her lined face radiant.

'Men aren't allowed to join the Widows' Association. But I'm also a member of the Umezato Senior Citizens' Centre, and I'll invite Mr Tachibana along. The centre is here in our district. Don't worry about a thing. It's really very near. But don't you think his wife will burn with jealousy if we go out together so soon after the seventh-day services?'

Mrs Kadotani let out a happy chuckle and coquettishly pressed the tips of her dry fingers to her lips. Akiko was startled. She had been timid about asking the old woman to look after Shigezō, but her neighbour had taken the request very casually and had immediately begun to make plans for a date with Shigezō. Surreptitiously, Akiko asked Mrs Kihara how old Mrs Kadotani was and was told that she was around seventy-two.

Akiko was quite convinced that her mother-in-law had planned her death to fall conveniently on a Saturday. By the following Sunday the memorial services had been held and Kyōko had left for home. Peace and tranquillity reigned once more in the Tachibana household, and Nobutoshi and Akiko were able to sit down and discuss plans for the immediate future.

First of all, they had to decide where Shigezō was to sleep. While

67

Kyōko had been staying, she had slept with him in the cottage. Kyōko had hoped that this would help her father to remember her, but she had been disappointed.

When they considered his advanced age and senile condition, they realized that they could not let Shigezō sleep alone in the cottage. But who was to sleep with him there? Nobutoshi, who usually returned home late from work, could not be relied upon. And Satoshi would soon be taking his college entrance examination, so his parents did not want to trouble him. They also knew that, even if they asked him, he would flatly refuse, because he was too young to face the reality of his grandfather's wretched condition. Akiko herself could not bear the thought of having to sleep next to her father-in-law. She might possibly have resigned herself to it if Kyōko had not said that Shigezō was in love with her. If that were really true, then she would never be able to sleep in the same room with him. But how could Shigezō possibly be in love with her? The whole idea was preposterous.

At a loss what to do, Nobutoshi was unable to state his personal opinions clearly and was of no help at all in making this important decision. He found it much easier to keep himself busy at the office than to have to solve the problems that currently troubled the Tachibana household.

'What do you think we ought to do, dear?'

'Well . . .'

'We can't very well let Father sleep by himself in the cottage, can we?'

'Absolutely not.'

The couple looked helplessly at Shigezō, who was sitting near by, gazing vacantly out at the garden. He was clearly not listening to their conversation. His eyes were fixed and expressionless, as if he was in a trance.

'Please be more definite. What do you suggest we do?'

'I'd tell you if I knew.'

'I suppose you would.'

'Why do you insist on his sleeping in the cottage? How about all of us living together under one roof? Wouldn't that be easier for you?'

'Where will he sleep?'

There were two rooms upstairs: Satoshi's bedroom and the master bedroom. The only way Shigezō could sleep under the same roof with them would be for Akiko to lay out his bedding in the big room downstairs.

'Would it be all right to let him sleep by himself?' Akiko asked.

'Kyōko didn't think it was a problem, did she?'

'No.'

'Then it should be all right.'

'Yes, but . . .,' mumbled Akiko.

Then she told her husband about the old woman who turned on every knob that she saw – water taps, gas jets, television and radio controls. Nobutoshi frowned as he listened to her.

'But Dad hasn't done anything like that, has he?'

'No. But it might be too risky to use a kerosene stove in the house. And, of course, I'll have to turn off the main gas valve before going to bed at night. Do you think it will be too cold for him to sleep in the room?'

'What are you talking about? What do you suggest we do if it gets too cold for him?' asked Nobutoshi, his voice rising in anger.

'Why are you so cross, dear? I can't seem to discuss anything with you.'

'How can you expect me to be in a good mood? Father is just showing me what I'll eventually be like. I break out in a cold sweat when I take a close look at him. I just can't stand it.'

'Don't let him hear you say that, dear.'

'He doesn't seem to be angry. That proves that he hasn't heard a word I've said. To become senile is terrifying, all right. This is the first time I've seen it with my own eyes. You can imagine what a shock it's been, considering he's my own father. I'm not like you. I just can't gallantly plan for the future.'

'I'm not being gallant, dear. I'm simply thinking about a problem that's disrupting our lives. We must decide what to do as from tomorrow. If you think Grandpa is capable of being on his own in the house while we're at work, I'll make him a box lunch before I go to work. Do you think that would work out?'

Nobutoshi didn't reply. His silence made Akiko feel terribly uneasy. Was her husband about to tell her that she could not go to work and leave his father unattended? Would he also say that it was high time she stayed at home where she belonged?

The younger generation probably had different views about the role of women, but the feudalistic attitude among men of Nobutoshi's age could not easily be brushed aside. Men of his generation did not acknowledge the fact that a family's financial situation was vastly improved when the wife worked. They gave the impression that they were simply letting their wives do as they pleased and put up with their neglect of their household duties with tolerance and patience. Most wives were very modest about their full-time jobs, and it was certainly not because of dissatisfaction with their husbands' incomes that they went out to work. There had been times when

Akiko had been terribly irritated with women who felt this way, but in the past twenty years she had been unable to persuade any of them to change their way of thinking. Because she herself had lost her father when she was young and had watched her mother struggle to support the family, she had been eager to find work as soon as possible. She had met Nobutoshi while working for a trading company. When they got married she had left and taken up her present job. Since the firm was a small one, there was no union to protect her rights. On the other hand, she enjoyed considerable freedom: she had worked right up to the time of her son's birth, and then stayed at home for two years. After that, she had left her son in her mother-in-law's care and gone back to work. Her husband had never acknowledged the fact that with his salary alone they could not have finished paying off the loan they had taken out in order to build their house and the cottage. Both properties were in his name. It had never occurred to Nobutoshi to register both their names as legal owners, and Akiko had found it curiously difficult to discuss the matter. Yet, if Nobutoshi were to die suddenly, Akiko and Satoshi would have to pay an inheritance tax in order to keep the property. That would be utterly absurd, thought Akiko. Although a legal code extolling Equal Rights had been forced upon the Japanese during the Allied Occupation, the idea that family property was built up by the joint efforts of husband and wife was still not widely accepted.

However, such issues seemed no longer relevant. Even if Nobutoshi accepted the fact that she wanted to work, he would probably say that they now had a house of their own, that their son would be entering university the year after next, and that he himself had reached a high position in his company which enabled him to bring home a decent salary. So he would ask her to leave her job.

Akiko found this idea totally unacceptable. Was it just for the money that she had worked all these years? Had her banging away at the typewriter been no different from the simple, repetitive tasks carried out by a factory worker day after day? Was it because they were incompetent that women were hired to perform menial tasks such as serving tea and typing – jobs that did not allow them to participate actively in society? Such thoughts filled Akiko with disgust. However small, her role at the office was by no means insignificant. Official business had been held up because she had stayed away from the office for three consecutive days at the time of her mother-in-law's death, and when she had taken her maternity leave the lawyers had been impatient for her to return. If Akiko were to announce her resignation after all these years, it would cause her employers great

70

inconvenience. Even if a Japanese-language typist could be found at short notice, it would take at least a year or two for the girl to perform smoothly such diverse duties as receiving visitors and tidying up the office. Akiko deeply resented the fact that her husband had no understanding of her position.

During Akiko's lengthy silence, Nobutoshi had been struck by a solemn thought.

'I don't think this kind of tragedy ever occurred when a man's average life-span was only fifty years. Now, thanks to an improved diet, we live much longer. But does the world realize what wretchedness awaits us in our old age?'

'There are so many elderly people around. As well as the grandmother of that girl at the office, there's Mr Fujieda and his old father. And remember what the priest said about his father at the wake? Suddenly there seems to be an old man or woman in every household.'

'What did the doctor have to say about Dad?'

'He'll have the results of the tests next week. I'll be seeing him again on Tuesday, but . . .'

'But what?'

'Well, Kyōko said that she had never heard of a doctor curing a person of senility.'

'What an irresponsible thing to say!'

Akiko decided to use the brazier to heat the room and went to fetch it from the cottage; she then buried some burning charcoals in the ashes. Her major problem now was what to do with Shigezō during the day. But first she had to make the customary round of visits to offer small presents to those who had given the family something at the time of the funeral. She had arranged for the department store to send gifts to those who had travelled some distance for the funeral, but she wanted to deliver them to her neighbours in person. After consulting Mitsuko, she had decided on attractively-boxed green tea. Her first visit would be to the Kiharas and Kadotanis to thank them for their help at the funeral and to ask them for their assistance in the future. It was essential that she find someone to look after Shigezō from the next day onwards.

Akiko could not forget what Mrs Kadotani had said about the Senior Citizens' Centre. She was eager to learn more about the place and, after lunch, set out for the Kadotani residence, taking with her a box of green tea.

'How kind of you to remember us when you must have so many other families to visit.'

The younger Mrs Kadotani, who was about Akiko's age, was

delighted when Akiko asked about the Centre and immediately went to summon her mother-in-law.

'Didn't you promise to take Mrs Tachibana's father-in-law to the Centre, Grandmother?'

'To the Centre? Oh, yes. The folk song group meets on Monday. The session begins in the afternoon, so I'll come round to collect him. They also meet on Thursdays. It's really great fun. There are also calligraphy and tea ceremony groups. The Matsunoki Senior Citizens' Centre has a bath, but my daughter-in-law is afraid that I'll catch a cold if I go there. That's why I go to the one in Umezato. Our club president fell ill a while ago, but he's better now.'

Akiko could hardly believe that the old woman had been so coquettish the other day. It was obvious that she had completely forgotten her promise to take Shigezō with her to the Centre. Akiko was grateful that her young neighbour had remembered it. But first she had to find out where the place was and how it was supervised. She therefore set out to take a look.

Akiko found it difficult to believe that the building stood right next to the children's playground, within ten minutes of her home. She did not know what the Western-style building had been used for originally. Peering in through the front door, which had been left slightly ajar, she saw an old man leaning on the shoe cupboard and slowly removing his clogs.

'Excuse me, but is this the Umezato Senior Citizens' Centre?'

In slow motion, the old man turned round to look at Akiko. His jaws quivered slightly. Akiko could see at a glance that he had recently suffered a stroke.

'What was that?'

'I was told that this is the Umezato Senior Citizens' Centre.'

'Yes, this is the Umezato Centre. We have all sorts of activities here. But the directors are having a meeting so there won't be any sessions today.'

Although he appeared frail, his voice was firm. How Akiko wished that Shigezō could be like this old man – able to think clearly and to answer questions, even if his limbs were impaired! Akiko learned a great deal from him. The Centres, which were supervised by the local Welfare Departments, had been established more than twenty years earlier. They could be found in every ward, and there were sixty in Suginami alone. The Umezato Centre had approximately 150 members. Any man or woman aged sixty or over, who lived in Matsunoki, Horinouchi or Umezato, could become a member and use the facilities without having to pay a fee. If they wanted to take part in any special group activities, however, they had to pay an annual subscription of 500 yen. Even on days when no activity was scheduled, a member could drop in to watch television or for a chat with another member who happened to be there.

'Some of the members bring their lunches with them.'

A social worker from the Ward Office was on duty in the office near the entrance between 8 a.m. and 5 p.m.

'Would you like to have a look inside? Please go on in.'

There was a large twenty-mat room at the north end of the building, and two adjoining Japanese-style ten-mat rooms at the south end. The communal area, where several old men and women were chatting, was furnished with desks and cushions. When Akiko asked the old man what the directors were meeting to discuss that day, he replied very enthusiastically that they were discussing the possibility of reunifying the Golden Age Club, which had split into two separate groups some time ago.

In the hall, Akiko saw a large sheet of paper pasted up on the wall. On it were written in sweeping, powerful strokes the words of 'The Song of the Elderly':

> Come and form a circle, friends.
> This Centre is our own.
> Our suntanned faces beaming,
> We've struggled through the years.
> Ever strong and hearty,
> Let's go on living longer.
> No moping in dark solitude!
> Let's get together for a chat
> And, working diligently,
> And ever full of cheer,
> Let's go on living longer still.

Lyrics by Nakano Kin'ichi

Later, Akiko reported her findings to her husband.

'Sixty Centres in Suginami Ward!' exclaimed Nobutoshi, deeply impressed.

'There are forty thousand throughout Japan.'

'Really?'

'So I don't have to worry about Grandpa any more. I'll make some lunch for him to take with him tomorrow. The folk song group will be meeting twice tomorrow, in the morning and again in the afternoon. I was told that he could sit in on both sessions.'

'Wonderful!'

'What a relief! The person on duty in the office is a young woman. She said that they can take Shigezō six days a week, including Saturday. And they even serve tea!'

'That's great!'

'On the days Mrs Kadotani doesn't go to the Centre, I'll take Grandpa over in the morning and leave him there. It'll be all right for me to ask Satoshi to bring him home, won't it? He should do that much at least.'

'Yes.'

'What's the matter, dear? I'm not talking about a complete stranger, you know. Remember, he's your father,' said Akiko, becoming agitated.

Nobutoshi raised his head morosely. 'I know you're discussing Dad. I was just wondering if I'll end up in a place like that when I'm old and grey.'

'What an unpleasant thought! Don't even think such a thing.'

But her husband's words had made her think. What would it be like when her hands no longer moved nimbly? It had taken a good five minutes for the old man at the Centre to remove his clogs and walk up the steps to the hall. What would it be like when she could no longer walk along briskly in her high heels? Ever since she had begun to wear trousers, she could no longer wear a miniskirt on a cold winter's day. Was this not proof enough that her legs were beginning to grow old? She might be troubled at this moment about Shigezō, but was there any guarantee that she herself would not suffer the same sad fate thirty or forty years hence?

'If there are over a hundred members at the Umezato Centre, there must be four or five million old people throughout Japan who've joined similar groups to keep busy,' said Nobutoshi.

'It's all right. Don't go on about it. I've seen old men who are mentally far more alert than Grandpa. Of course, the ones I saw probably belong to a special group, as the regular activities were cancelled today because of the directors' meeting.'

Shigezō, still sitting where Akiko had last seen him before she left the house, was nodding away. She had serious doubts about whether he would be capable of participating in group activities. For the present, however, she had to rely on the Centre if she wanted to go back to work.

As soon as Akiko began to set the table Shigezō sat down and took up his chopsticks. 'I'm starved, Akiko. Isn't dinner ready yet?'

He finally settled down when the family sat down to eat. Nobutoshi, a strange expression on his face, watched his father chewing his food. Then he asked: 'Don't you have trouble with your dentures any more, Dad?'

'You won't get his attention by calling him Dad, dear. He doesn't realize that you're talking to him.'

'Then how do I address him?'

'Grandpa!' cried Akiko. Shigezō slowly turned to look in her direction. 'How are your dentures?'

'Dentures? Whose dentures?'

'Why, yours, Grandpa!'

'These are my own teeth.'

'No, they aren't,' said Nobutoshi impatiently. 'You've worn dentures for years. Don't you remember? You made your own because you weren't happy with the ones the dentists made.'

Suddenly seeing in her mind's eye the box full of dentures, Akiko lost her appetite altogether. Why in the world had her husband brought up the subject of false teeth in the first place?

'No one can make his own teeth. I tell you they aren't dentures.'

'But you can take them out, can't you?'

'You say the oddest things! How could I do that?' said Shigezō, terribly offended. He used his hands to turn over the flounder he had been eating and began to pick at the other side of the fish, carefully removing its bones.

'That's enough, dear,' said Akiko. 'Whatever possessed you to ask about his teeth at the dinner table anyway?'

'Well, lately I've become very interested in signs of ageing in teeth,' replied Nobutoshi. 'I wonder when he began to think of his dentures as his own teeth?'

Before Akiko had a chance to protest, Satoshi cried out: 'Ugh! How disgusting! Please stop talking about teeth!'

Akiko and Satoshi thought that Nobutoshi would change the subject, but instead he turned to his son and said: 'You ought to listen carefully to what I have to say instead of objecting like that. Have you been brushing *your* teeth after every meal?'

'No, only in the morning.'

'Don't they teach you to brush your teeth after lunch at school? The young men at work always brush their teeth in the men's room after lunch. It's an excellent habit. You too should brush your teeth after every meal. You've got to take good care of them. By the time you're twelve, you've lost your milk teeth and have a permanent set. After that you have to rely on good dental care.'

All this talk about teeth ruined their dinner. As soon as the meal was over, Satoshi all but threw down his chopsticks and ran upstairs. Akiko sighed and looked across at her husband who was scowling fiercely. Shigezō, unperturbed, quietly concentrated on picking at the dorsal fin of the fish with the tips of his chopsticks and carrying the tiny morsels to his mouth. Akiko had learned from experience that Shigezō could consume a fish fillet in no time at all, but when he was served a whole fish or a crab he would spend a long time completely absorbed in devouring it. While crabs were expensive, a plastic bag containing three or four frozen flounder was very reasonable, and stewed fish was Shigezō's favourite food. He could eat three bowls of rice while helping himself to a whole flounder. After Akiko scolded him for requesting a fourth bowl, Shigezō quietly sipped his tea.

'By the way, dear. Grandma must be feeling lonely out there in the cottage by herself. Don't you think we ought to move the altar in here?'

'I suppose we weren't being very thoughtful. But where can we put it?'

'Where do you suggest? We'll also have to think about what to do with her remains. I once read that one can buy plots in the cemetery. I should have realized at the time that our family would need one eventually.'

'They must be terribly expensive.'

'But we can't afford not to buy one. After all, we'll all be laid to rest there one day.'

Akiko was surprised at herself for having brought up the subject so casually. Did a family have to own a plot of ground in order to bury someone in a cemetery? Flustered, she added: 'Or should we bury her remains in her old home town?'

'Oh no. It's too far away. Our family has no plot there any more, not since Father established a branch family. Also, it'll be awfully inconvenient if we're not buried in Tokyo. Do you suppose Satoshi will come to visit our graves?'

'What a macabre turn our conversation has taken!'

'I agree.'

Nobutoshi and Akiko rose and made their way through the garden to the cottage to move Shigezō's things over to the main house.

The altar, which contained a bell and an incense holder, had been left open. Akiko remembered that her mother-in-law's photograph had to be displayed until the forty-ninth day. Just as she was thinking to herself that she should have enlisted her son's help, Shigezō's figure suddenly appeared at the entrance. Ignoring Nobutoshi and Akiko, he entered the cottage and made straight for the toilet.

'Please take Grandma's remains to the main house before any of the other things, dear.'

'All right,' replied Nobutoshi and meekly did as he was told.

In the meantime, Akiko piled up Shigezō's bedding and night clothes in a corner of the room. Nobutoshi scurried back and forth, carrying things from the cottage to the main house.

Shigezō remained in the toilet for a long time.

'Do you have a stomach-ache, Grandpa?' asked Akiko, suddenly worried.

Akiko heard Shigezō moving about in the toilet before he finally emerged.

'What was the matter, Grandpa? Is your stomach all right?'

'Yes.'

'Was it a big one?' asked Akiko, as if she were talking to a child about his bowel movement.

Shigezō, turning to look at Akiko, answered: 'What do you mean? I was only peeing.'

Had it taken Shigezō all that time to urinate? Akiko had imagined him squatting in the narrow room behind the partition. A chill ran through her when she thought of how cold it must have been in there. She should not have hesitated to open the door and look in on him.

'You and I will be sleeping in the same house from now on, Grandpa. We've moved the altar to the main house, so Grandma won't feel lonely any more.'

Akiko did not know to what extent her father-in-law took in what she had said. Shigezō sat silently in the corner of the room, his buttocks flat against the *tatami* and his arms around his knees. Akiko closed the rain shutters of the cottage and locked the place up securely. Then she called to Shigezō, who obediently followed her back to the main house.

Shigezō sat at the *kotatsu** until his bedtime and, together with Nobutoshi, kept his eyes glued to the television screen. However, he showed no glimmer of interest in either the drama programmes or the news. He seemed to be in a trance. Nobutoshi tried the channels featuring slapstick comedy, but his father did not even chuckle.

Meanwhile, Akiko cleared away the dishes and planned the menu for the following week. She decided to take her own lunch to work from now on, since she would have to prepare one for Shigezō. Nobutoshi had his lunch in the company dining-room and Satoshi ate in the school cafeteria, thus Akiko had never had to bother with preparing lunches, a duty that in the past had been considered one of the more important responsibilities of a housewife. It was years since she had prepared a box lunch, but she found the prospect less annoying because she would be making her own as well as Shigezō's.

*A Japanese-style foot warmer (with a quilt-covered wooden frame).

'Look, Akiko. Dad's fallen asleep.'

After spreading out the bedding next to the *kotatsu*, Akiko removed Shigezō's sweater and trousers and got him into a flannel kimono. Shigezō was not yet sleeping deeply, for Akiko had no trouble moving his arms and legs while getting him ready for bed. This was the way she had dressed Satoshi when he was going to kindergarten, she remembered nostalgically.

Akiko tucked Shigezō into bed. While folding away his clothes, she complained to her husband: 'Please try to be a little more helpful, dear. It isn't very thoughtful of you to simply look on while I do everything.'

'But I don't know what to do. Dad's turned into a complete idiot!'

That night Akiko and Nobutoshi slept together as husband and wife for the first time in weeks. As her husband's body moved away from hers, Akiko was unable to suppress a deep feeling of sadness. 'Dear. If you die before me and Satoshi is married, I think I'll commit suicide.'

'I was just thinking the same thing. I'd like to be the first to go, even if it's only one day before you. They say widowers are always pathetic, but Dad is the most wretched example I've ever seen. If you die first, I'll kill myself and follow you to the other world.'

Akiko vaguely recalled how they had once exchanged a similar vow twenty years earlier, as two young people passionately in love. In those days the idea of dying had been completely removed from reality and their words had sounded so sweet! They had never dreamed then that one day, in a totally different context, they would be speaking to each other about dying. There was nothing romantic about their vows now.

Akiko had somehow managed to survive that hectic week. She had found it extremely difficult to get along with Kyōko during her stay. There was truth in the saying that a sister-in-law was like 4,000 demons! And that it takes time to get used to the ways of a stranger. Only now did Akiko feel that her family had at last returned to the life of privacy they had enjoyed previously. Kyōko was by no means a difficult person, but she had left Akiko feeling completely exhausted. For the first time in weeks Akiko was able to sleep soundly. As she listened to her husband's even breathing, she felt very tranquil and, before long, she too fell into a deep, luxurious slumber.

She was awakened in the middle of the night by a loud animal-like moan. At first she thought that she was dreaming, but then she heard the same eerie cry again, coming from downstairs. When she realized that it was Shigezō screaming and pounding on the door, she jumped out of bed and ran down the stairs.

In the dim light, which she had left on, Akiko was able to see Shigezō with his limbs spread out like a spider against the sliding glass doors facing the garden.

'What's the matter, Grandpa? Please calm down,' she cried, clinging to his back.

'Oh, Akiko. I have to pee.'

'The toilet's right over there.'

Akiko walked to the other end of the room, opened the toilet door and turned on the light. Shigezō entered, parting the front of his kimono.

'I can't pee here, Akiko.'

The Tachibanas had had a Western-style flush toilet installed in their home the previous summer, after a sewage system had finally been completed in the neighbourhood the year before. At the time they had seriously considered having one put into the cottage as well, but since the elderly couple preferred the old-fashioned toilet, the one in the cottage had been left as it was. In any case the cost of installing a flush toilet had been far greater than Akiko had anticipated, so she was glad that they had had only one Western-style toilet put in. Their efforts had been in vain as far as Shigezō was concerned. Akiko suddenly recalled that her father-in-law had always gone to the cottage when he wanted to use the toilet.

After a moment's hesitation, Akiko slid open the glass doors and rain shutters and made straight for the cottage with Shigezō in tow.

'I can't wait, Akiko. I've got to go right now.'

'Do it in the garden, then, Grandpa.'

'Right here?'

'Yes,' replied Akiko, nodding.

There was a sudden burst of sound accompanied by a white cloud rising from the ground. With her arms around Shigezō from behind to help him keep his balance, Akiko contemplated the gravity of the situation. Would this recur night after night? She had rushed out of the house dressed only in a single kimono, and she could feel the cold night air cutting into her body.

For a long time, Shigezō stood absolutely still.

'Grandpa!' cried Akiko. Only then did Shigezō finally notice her.

'Oh, Akiko. The moon is so lovely!'

Akiko looked up at the sky and saw the pale moon shining brightly. It was a cloudless night and the moon was nearly full. Akiko stood there at her father-in-law's side and gazed at it in silence.

8

The Tachibanas greeted the New Year quietly, for they were still in mourning. With a senile member of the family like Shigezō to look after, they were thankful for the old custom that exempted them from the usual New Year's formalities. Although everything had gone smoothly thus far, with the old man going to the Centre during the day, Akiko could not help worrying while she was away at work. January the second fell on a Sunday that year, and she was pleased that she could stay at home with Shigezō for five consecutive days.

Akiko had not ordered any special rice cakes from the rice dealer, but she had bought a plastic bag of the rice cakes that both Nobutoshi and Satoshi were fond of. She toasted some of them over the charcoal fire in the brazier.

'What a treat! This is the best way to have rice cakes,' exclaimed Nobutoshi.

Akiko dipped one of the cakes in soy sauce, wrapped some seaweed around it and handed it to Shigezō. At that moment, Mrs Kadotani, all smiles, looked over the garden fence.

'Is anyone at home?'

'Hello! Do come in. Thank you so much for looking after Grandpa.'

'Don't mention it. Happy New Year!'

Mrs Kadotani bowed low, making Akiko feel uneasy. Surely the old woman realized that the family was still in mourning? After all, she had been the one who had given explicit instructions about the white cloth to cover the face of the deceased and the knife to drive away evil spirits. But here she was calling on them.

'Grandpa, Mrs Kadotani is here,' cried Akiko.

Shigezō looked up from the other side of the *kotatsu*. 'Yes, yes,' he replied in a loud voice.

'There's a New Year's Party at the Centre, and I've come to invite Mr Tachibana along. I think he'll enjoy it.'

'You realize, of course, that we're still in mourning.'

'That doesn't matter. A family should celebrate when someone old dies. Would you care to join me, Mr Tachibana?'

It would be nice for Shigezō to go to what would probably be a lively gathering, thought Akiko. So she helped her father-in-law into a suit and an overcoat and asked Mrs Kadotani to keep an eye on him. Akiko walked with them to the gate and with concern watched Shigezō and the tiny old woman walking off hand in hand.

'The path of love never seems to grow dark, no matter how old one gets,' said Nobutoshi. 'So Father allowed himself to be led away without protesting? I wonder what old folks do at a New Year's Party?'

'Why don't you go and have a look, dear?'

'Not me!' He rose to his feet and, fetching his golf club, went out into the garden to practise his strokes. Akiko realized that this was the first time in years that her husband had spent the New Year holiday at home. On New Year's Day he usually visited the directors of his company and got thoroughly drunk on his way home. On the second or third of January he took part in a mah-jong tournament and played a round or two of golf. He must have turned down all these engagements this year because the family was still in mourning. Still, the rest would do him good. Though he had never noticed any ill effects when he was younger, Nobutoshi now felt completely exhausted the morning after drinking heavily. Akiko was suddenly reminded of what her husband had said about Shigezō representing what he himself would be like at the end of his own life. He is probably using his mother's death as an excuse to have a good rest, thought Akiko, who had every intention of doing the same.

Although the family was not formally celebrating the New Year, Akiko had hung up a salted salmon – an old Japanese custom – and had bought a variety of traditional New Year dishes. She had not, however, made any special plans for the holiday season. Shigezō's coming to live with them in the main house had marked the beginning of a new way of life. Every night the old man got up to empty his bladder, and since he still refused to use the Western-style toilet, Akiko now had to sleep downstairs with him. As soon as Shigezō woke up she automatically opened the rain shutters and led him out into the garden. By the New Year this had become a nightly ritual. But Shigezō could not control his bladder until he got to the cottage, so he urinated in the garden like a dog. So far this had not caused any problems as the weather had been fine, but what were they going

81

to do if it was raining or stormy? On 31 December, Akiko had bought a urine bottle which she made Shigezō try out after the bell of the Myōhō-ji Temple stopped tolling at midnight, but he loudly protested that he could not use such a receptacle. Nobutoshi was now practising his golf strokes on the very spot where his father relieved himself every night. Watching her husband, Akiko knew that if she mentioned this fact to him he would become sullen and stop practising.

It was five o'clock in the afternoon and Shigezō had not yet returned home. Nobutoshi realized that he could not burden his wife with everything, so he set out to see what was happening at the Centre. Akiko privately thought that there was nothing to worry about as long as Shigezō was with Mrs Kadotani. But if Nobutoshi were to find Mrs Kadotani there alone, the situation could be far more serious than the time when Kyōko had had to chase after her father. So it was with some anxiety that Akiko saw her husband off.

She turned to her son. 'Satoshi, dear. I know that next year will be difficult, with your college entrance exams and everything else, but please think about Grandpa's welfare, too. I'll try to get home from work as early as possible, but I'd like you to stay at home in the evenings.'

'All right, Mum.'

'Your father and I aren't used to taking care of Grandpa yet, but I think that everything will be fine once we get accustomed to his ways. Until then, please try to co-operate.'

'You should relax, Mum. Things would be much more difficult if he were as bad-tempered as he used to be.'

'Yes, I agree. Grandpa seems to have become a child again. It's certainly better than being snarled at and having him complain endlessly about his health.'

'He's not a child. He's an animal.'

'What a thing to say, Satoshi!'

'It's true. Dogs and cats have no difficulty in remembering their masters. Grandpa instinctively recognizes only the people who are absolutely necessary for his survival.'

Although Satoshi rarely discussed his grandfather with his parents, but it was clear that he had been observing him closely.

'Do you mean to say that he thinks of me as his owner?'

'Yes. After all, why should he bother to remember Dad when he doesn't do a thing for him? All this talk about Grandpa being Dad's and Aunt Kyōko's father is meaningless. They say that instinct is the innate wisdom necessary for survival.'

'But remember that Grandpa also recognizes you, dear.'

'Then he probably thinks that I'm of some use to him.'

'You might be right.'

'I agree that he's been a pain in the neck, though,' Satoshi remarked. 'Grandma was very nice, but Grandpa didn't do a thing for me when I was little. Once he was terribly cross with me for messing up the room. Another time he caught me peeing in the garden and really went for me – I think it was before I started going to kindergarten. I hated it when he got so angry. That's why I've always avoided Grandpa like the plague. But in spite of all that, he still recognizes me. I think it must be some kind of biological instinct.'

Akiko was surprised how sophisticated high school students were these days. They could talk quite casually about such things as 'biological instinct'. At the same time she was delighted to see how quickly her son was growing up. Nevertheless, the very idea that Shigezō regarded Akiko as his owner was shocking to say the least.

Some time later Nobutoshi returned home without Shigezō.

'I was really surprised by what goes on at the Centre. There are all kinds of old men and women there. They were singing folk songs and dancing to folk music. Although no saké had been served, they really were a rowdy bunch. Someone told me that one old woman who'd been dancing from the moment she arrived in the morning was about the same age as Father. She certainly wasn't senile! She talked and talked and even gave me a brief history of the Centre. The building was once an electricity substation. Then a group called the Senior Citizens Association took it over and converted it. The members personally laid out the *tatami* mats, so she refuses to go to any other centre. I never dreamed that a gathering of old people would be anything like that!'

'What was Grandpa doing all this time?'

'He was dozing away in a corner of the room with his arms round his knees.'

'Oh dear!'

'When I suggested that we went home, he looked scared and asked me who I was. Mrs Kadotani said that she would walk him home, so I left him there. She said that he'd eaten a lot of rice crackers and bean-jam cakes. That woman is behaving as though she were married to Dad.'

'You must be joking!'

'No, I'm not. She's really quite a flirt. Mother acted like Dad's nurse or housemaid, but Mrs Kadotani flirts with him outrageously.'

'And how does Grandpa react?'

'As far as I can tell, he ignores her completely.'

83

'He must have been quite a ladies' man to be popular with women even now that he's gone senile,' remarked Akiko, at the same time remembering her interview with the doctor when he had told her the results of Shigezō's medical examination. Apparently Shigezō's blood pressure was fine and his pulse normal. He was not anaemic and the X-rays showed no sign of cancer. The doctor had therefore given him a clean bill of health. When Akiko mentioned his voracious appetite, the doctor suggested that the family should make sure that he did not overeat. The fact that Shigezō did not recognize his own son was attributed to his advanced age. But, when Akiko asked if senility was an illness, the doctor became evasive and formal, announcing that the results of the examination showed Shigezō to be in perfect health. As he charged only for the actual cost of the examination, Akiko felt she could not press him any further. So she thanked him profusely and quickly excused herself.

Nobutoshi was silent for some time. He was thinking about what he had seen that afternoon. About forty old people had gathered at the Umezato Centre to celebrate the New Year. Some sang folk songs and others recited poems, each one performing spontaneously and giving himself as well as his audience great pleasure. Shigezō stood out conspicuously in that group. When Nobutoshi entered the hall, several old women were dancing to a record of 'The Flower-Decked Hat'. All the dancers seemed to be in perfect health. Women of seventy or eighty with their hats in their hands twirled and twisted their bodies from left to right. They did not make a single mistake, although one could not say that their hand-movements were particularly graceful. Mrs Kadotani danced as if she were the star performer.

Some of the old people sitting on the *tatami* moved their hands in time with the music while watching the dancing; others sat chatting, their backs turned to the dancers. Nobutoshi could not help noticing that it was the women who laughed most often. If Shigezō had begun going to the Centre regularly a few years earlier, he might not have become senile so quickly, thought Nobutoshi. But then he remembered what his father had been like before and realized that Shigezō would have felt uncomfortable in such company. Nobutoshi concluded that his father had only himself to blame for his wretched condition. Shigezō, with his arms around his knees, had dozed away in a corner of the room. When Nobutoshi tapped him on the shoulder and suggested that they go home, the old man had looked at him suspiciously with moist, rheumy eyes and asked him who he was. Nobutoshi had been shocked that his own father had not recognized him, especially in front of all these strangers.

'Well, back to work tomorrow,' he said in a valiant attempt to relieve the gloom.

Akiko laughed. 'You've been able to get quite a bit of rest over the holidays, haven't you, dear?'

'That's right. Perhaps I got a little too much rest and not enough exercise, but I really feel great! I'd hate to end up going senile like Dad, though.'

'What a thing to say!'

'Don't you think that ideally a man should die the minute he retires? I just can't see myself singing and dancing at a centre for senior citizens. All of a sudden I'm reminded of when I returned from the war.'

'Why is that?'

'Well, then I no longer had to worry about dying. I was glad to be alive. But when I look at Dad, I feel that I've just got to die before I go senile. Why do people live so much longer these days? It's frightening to think of a world where no one dies and everyone keeps growing older and older.'

Satoshi suddenly sprang to his feet and turned on the television. Akiko gestured to her husband, warning him to change the subject.

'What would you two like for dinner?'

Akiko was going back to work the next day, and meals would again be planned around simple dishes, so she wanted to prepare something special for dinner that night. but, much to her disappointment, Nobutoshi said that he was not hungry and Satoshi asked for some noodles.

Not long after, Shigezō arrived home, escorted by Mrs Kadotani. Akiko and Nobutoshi thanked the old woman who chuckled and said: 'He was really no trouble at all. I'll take him again tomorrow.'

'Welcome home, Grandpa.'

'Hello, Akiko.'

As he entered the house, Shigezō eyed Nobutoshi suspiciously. Nobutoshi looked at Akiko so helplessly that she found it difficult not to laugh.

'How was the New Year's party, Grandpa?' asked Akiko.

'Fine.'

'Did you have a lot of fun?'

'Yes.'

'I hear they served rice crackers and dumplings.'

Peering into the old man's face, Akiko continued to bombard him with questions, but Shigezō simply stared into space. Then he suddenly said with great urgency:

'Oh, Akiko. I'm starved. May I have my dinner?'

'What would you like, Grandpa? I'll get you whatever you like.'

Shigezō pursed his lips and began to concentrate, seizing this golden opportunity to communicate like a human being. Wondering what he would request for dinner, Akiko and Nobutoshi looked at each other. Even Satoshi turned round to look at his grandfather from his place in front of the television set.

The rock music blaring from the television filled the room and, for some strange reason, gave it an air of tranquillity. Shigezō, scrutinized by the other three members of the family, pursed his lips; he was a study in concentration. What special dish would he request, wondered Akiko, feeling rather worried. How could she say no if he asked for a dish for which she did not have the ingredients?

Presently Shigezō looked up.

'Grandma's dead, isn't she, Akiko?' he asked abruptly, startling the entire family.

'Oh? When did she die?'

'Don't you know? She was kicked by a horse and died after vomiting blood.'

'Is that how she died?'

'Yes.'

Akiko gave her husband a blank look. What on earth was Shigezō talking about? Nobutoshi racked his brains. Satoshi got up, removed his grandmother's photograph from the altar and showed it to his grandfather.

'Is this who you're talking about?'

Shigezō slowly looked up at Satoshi, then fixed his eyes on the photograph.

'Who is this woman?'

'Don't you recognize her? She's the one who died. But she wasn't kicked by a horse and she didn't vomit blood either,' Satoshi said.

'Whose horse are you talking about?'

'Didn't you just say something about a horse, Grandpa? You just said that Grandma was kicked by a horse. If you didn't mean this woman, who were you talking about?'

Shigezō appeared to be terribly confused. He looked at his grandson, then appealed to Akiko.

'Satoshi says the strangest things, Akiko. I don't recognize this woman.'

Akiko was too flabbergasted to say anything. She made her way to the kitchen, deciding that she really ought to get rid of all the New Year delicacies in one meal.

She had bought a large amount of rolled seaweed; she also had

86

some sweet potato and fish cake left over. All she had to do for dinner was to steam some hot rice and prepare a little miso soup.

Akiko carried the dishes of leftovers to the dining-table. As the family sat down at the table and took up their chopsticks, Nobutoshi suddenly blurted out:

'Of course! He's referring to that ancient story! Yes, I remember now. It happened forty years ago. No . . . forty-five, to be exact, before I'd started school. An old woman in our village died after being kicked by a horse. I never met her, but I remember going to see the horse that killed her. I can't recall whose it was. Yes, it's all coming back to me. It actually happened. The incident caused a big stir in the village.'

'I wonder why Grandpa suddenly remembered something that happened so long ago. Could he have been present when the old woman was kicked by the horse?'

'I really don't know what made him think of it.'

His son, daughter-in-law and grandson all looked at Shigezō as he held his rice bowl in his hand and chewed slowly. When Akiko served him a seaweed roll, he skilfully removed the gourd tie with the tips of his chopsticks. After unrolling the seaweed, he picked up the tiny fish at the centre of the roll and lifted it to his mouth. Satoshi placed another seaweed roll on his grandfather's plate and Shigezō repeated the delicate procedure. Mesmerized, Satoshi continued to put one roll after another on his grandfather's plate until the lacquered container was empty and the plate was piled high with seaweed. Shigezō paid no attention to Akiko when she told him that the seaweed was edible. She was appalled at how wasteful he was, but was not sorry to see the leftover food used up in this way. Observing how long it took Shigezō to get at the fish, Akiko realized that there was no danger of his overeating; she therefore let Satoshi serve him all the seaweed rolls.

'He seems to have forgotten Mother,' said Nobutoshi.

'How could a man possibly forget his wife after living with her for nearly sixty years?'

'Please, dear. He's the one who's forgotten her. There's no reason for you to glare at *me* like that.'

'How can he be so unfeeling? It makes me wonder what kept them together all these years.'

'But Dad remembers you well enough,' retorted Nobutoshi. Akiko felt terribly flustered. The last thing she wanted to hear was her husband making the same kind of remarks that Kyōko had made earlier. She changed the subject.

As usual, Shigezō got up in the middle of the night and, supported by Akiko, urinated in the garden. When she returned to the house, Akiko could not bear the thought of sleeping next to her father-in-law that night, and decided to spend the rest of the night with her husband. Taking up her pillow and blanket, she made her way upstairs.

When she caught sight of Nobutoshi snuggled comfortably in bed fast asleep, Akiko felt her anger rising. Nobutoshi expected her to take care of the old man's every need, even though Shigezō was *his* father. Men always tried their utmost to avoid the troublesome details of running a household. It was Akiko who got up every night when Shigezō had to relieve himself and who had to listen to him urinating in the garden. What's more, at the time of her mother-in-law's death, it had been Akiko who had taken care of all the details of the funeral, while her husband sat idly by, too dazed to lift a finger. Had he ever felt sorry for his wife when she had to accompany his father outside in the middle of the night? This man too would forget her completely if she died first. Suddenly unable to suppress her emotions, Akiko hit her sleeping husband with the pillow she had been hugging. Nobutoshi awoke with a start.

'What's happened?' he asked.

'Nothing, dear.'

Nobutoshi moaned and stretched, then turned over in bed and once more sank into a peaceful slumber. The silver in his hair glinted in the dim light, and Akiko remembered what her husband had said about how one day he would be like his father. She got no more sleep that night.

9

Akiko thought it a bit risky, but since there was nothing of great value in the cottage, she took Shigezō over there every morning after opening up the rain shutters. She would start a charcoal fire in the old brazier which she had taken out of storage, and cover it with ashes. Everything was arranged in such a way that Shigezō could leave the cottage just as it was when Mrs Kadotani came to fetch him. At the same time, she never failed to lock up the main house as securely as she had in the past. She also made sure that Satoshi called in at the Umezato Senior Citizens' Centre on his way back from school to escort Shigezō home on the days that Mrs Kadotani did not go. When Satoshi appeared at the Centre, Shigezō would call out his grandson's name, rise to his feet and return home with him. When they reached home, Satoshi would prepare two bowls of noodles for their afternoon snack.

As the days passed, Akiko grew accustomed to waking up in the middle of the night and helping her father-in-law out into the garden to relieve himself. After putting him back to bed, she made her way upstairs to the master bedroom and slept until morning. On working days, Nobutoshi usually returned home late, and on Sundays he slept until noon to catch up on his sleep. Seeing how well his senile father was being looked after, he felt that the family had worried unnecessarily.

The only problem was Mrs Kadotani, who gradually came to consider the cottage her own. Soon she went to the Centre only two or three times a week. On the other days, she turned up at the cottage in the morning and diligently looked after Shigezō all day. Satoshi, who had been the first to notice this new development, reported it to his mother; the next Saturday Akiko went over to the cottage in the morning and found the two old people sitting on opposite sides of the brazier. Shigezō sat facing the entrance with a blank expression on his face, while the old woman chatted away to her heart's content.

'Akiko, Akiko,' cried Shigezō when he noticed his daughter-in-law. He got up and came over to the door. 'I don't know what to do with this old woman. She says the strangest things and I don't know when she'll leave!'

Akiko grew alarmed, realizing that it would not do to have Mrs Kadotani hear him complaining about her.

'Oh, Akiko. Please don't worry about us. I thought that since Mr Tachibana had just lost his wife he must be feeling lonely. I'm trying to cheer him up, that's all.'

To Akiko's relief, the old woman, who was beaming happily, seemed not to have heard Shigezō's remarks. Akiko noticed the two lunches she had made early that morning near the brazier, together with several empty bowls. Going into the cottage, she saw a brisk fire burning in the brazier. Had Mrs Kadotani taken the liberty of getting charcoals and ashes from the kitchen?

'Thank you for looking after Grandpa. Aren't you two going to the Centre today?'

'No. There's nothing special scheduled for today. Anyway, Mr Tachibana said he preferred to sit here and talk,' said the old woman.

Akiko couldn't believe this: it was highly unlikely that Shigezō would make such a suggestion.

'I'm starved, Akiko. Can I have a little snack? Hasn't Satoshi come home yet?'

'Mr Tachibana suggested that we went out for a snack, but I refused. I told him that the key to a long life is never to feel completely full,' said the old woman, tittering.

Was this what her husband meant when he said that Mrs Kadotani was a flirt? Akiko now understood why Shigezō had complained that the old woman said the strangest things.

'I'm sorry to have troubled you. I'm going to prepare some noodles – please have some before you leave,' Akiko said.

'Did you hear that, Mr Tachibana? You're so lucky to have a kind and thoughtful daughter-in-law. Mine has never prepared noodles for me. I wonder whether I should have some. Aren't we lucky that Akiko came home early today? I love noodles and I'm sure you're fond of them too. We must have been predestined to meet like this.'

Mrs Kadotani beamed happily as she chattered away, while Akiko returned to the main house.

'What did I tell you?' asked Satoshi teasingly.

'How long has this been going on?'

'For about five days. I called at the Centre one afternoon and they told me that neither of them had shown up that day. Remembering how Aunt Kyōko once had to chase Grandpa, I ran all the way home. There they were in the cottage. I suppose you might call it love in December, though Grandpa obviously thinks she's a nuisance. When I turn up, he dashes up to me as if I had come to his rescue. She's so pushy! Still, the situation does have its funny side.'

'I wonder if her daughter-in-law knows about this?'

'I don't know. When Grandpa comes to the main house with me, she has no choice but to go home.'

Akiko firmly believed that a woman who worked full-time should always begin preparing the dinner as soon as she returned home. If she did not regard her duties at home as a continuation of her office duties and allowed herself a little breather, she would feel too tired to lift a finger. Akiko dropped the noodles she had bought on her way home into the boiling broth. Presently she scooped Satoshi's portion into a bowl, but let the noodles for the two elderly people simmer a little longer. While watching the noodles turn in the simmering broth, Akiko wondered how seriously she should regard the new relationship which Satoshi found so amusing. It was certainly no joking matter. If she were not careful, it could even result in a scandal. But how could any woman be attracted to a man as senile as Shigezō, she wondered.

Akiko placed two bowls of noodles on a tray and carried them to the cottage. When she entered the sitting-room, she found Mrs Kadotani warming her hands over the brazier, but there was no sign of Shigezō. Surprised, Akiko said: 'Oh dear. Where's Grandpa?'

'He's in the toilet,' replied the old woman, smiling. 'Please wait a minute.'

Akiko was even more startled when Mrs Kadotani strolled over to the toilet and called out, 'Are you done, Mr Tachibana? Akiko has brought us some noodles.'

Then she pushed open the toilet door. Akiko, who was still holding the tray, stood transfixed. It appeared that Shigezō had fallen flat on his seat in the toilet.

'Have your legs given out again, Mr Tachibana? The noodles are here. Do you think you can get up now? Please try to stand up.'

Akiko wondered whether to help them, but she lacked the courage to peer into the toilet. Instead, she sat down just where she was and waited until the two emerged, almost embracing each other. The old woman had even helped Shigezō to wipe himself with the toilet paper!

'Sorry to have kept you waiting, Akiko. Look, Mr Tachibana. Akiko has brought us some noodles.'

'Yes.'

'Now pick up your chopsticks,' said Mrs Kadotani, fussing over Shigezō.

The two elderly people helped themselves to the noodles, completely ignoring Akiko, who couldn't decide whether to stay or to return to the main house. In the end, she decided to see with her own eyes what her son had described as love in December, thinking that, as Shigezō's guardian, it was her responsibility to do so.

'Aren't the noodles delicious, Mr Tachibana? Akiko has seasoned them perfectly, don't you think? You know, I'm an expert at making home-made noodles. During the war I often kneaded together flour and water to make them. I'll make you some next time. I'm sure you'll find them tastier than Akiko's.'

The old woman was in high spirits. In recounting this incident to others, she will undoubtedly add that Shigezō expressed his desire to taste her home-made noodles, thought Akiko, without a trace of resentment. Just as Nobutoshi saw his father as the image of what he himself would be like one day, as she watched Mrs Kadotani Akiko saw her as her own future image. At this point she was reminded of an old anecdote: Ōoka, the provincial governor of Echizen, had once asked his mother at what age a woman ceased to be attracted to the opposite sex. Was it decent, she wondered, for a widow of over seventy to make advances to a widower of eighty-four and to conduct herself shamelessly as if she had been waiting for his wife to die? Akiko thought that she was open-minded about affairs of the heart, but she could not imagine herself ever becoming like this old woman, flirting outrageously and chattering vivaciously. Of course, since the old man seated before her was completely different from the man she had always thought her father-in-law would eventually become, she had no way of knowing what she herself would be like thirty or forty years hence. Everyone had to die one day, but when she was younger she had never dreamed that such a hellish fate awaited the elderly. Will I too find myself old and grey one day? What kind of old woman will I become? Akiko grew cold all over as she imagined herself and her husband moving about in slow motion as they helped each other to go to the toilet and ate overcooked noodles.

'Mrs Kadotani!' cried Akiko hoarsely. 'Aren't they expecting you at home? Your family must be terribly worried about you.'

The old woman looked at Akiko and replied calmly:

'Oh no. No one worries about me. They think I'm a terrible nuisance. They're all waiting for me to die. Yes, they are. I didn't choose to live this long, but if I kill myself, it'll make it difficult to arrange marriages for my grandchildren. Mr Tachibana and I talk about this all the time, don't we? We elderly folk must stick together and try to be independent. All we talk about at the Centre is how to keep from being a burden on our children. We remind each other that unless we take a lot of exercise, we'll grow weak, and unless we use our brains, we'll become senile. We all keep an eye on each other. I feel so happy whenever I talk about the past with Mr Tachibana. After all, we have a lot of memories to share. Young people can't stand it when we old folks talk about the past, and we can't follow them when they discuss what's happening today, so everything works out fine this way. All day today we talked about the Great Tokyo Earthquake of 1923. I saw the burnt-out ruins of the clothing warehouse in Honjo with my own eyes. I also saw a twelve-storey building beginning to burn from the top floor down, then breaking in two at the fourth floor. The fires raged for three days. My home was completely destroyed by fire during World War II, but the Earthquake was a far more terrifying experience. Don't you agree, Mr Tachibana?'

'Grandpa is from the Tōhoku district, so he doesn't know what it was like during the Earthquake.'

'Oh, really? No wonder he was fascinated! Now I know why he kept begging me to tell him about my experiences. Really, Mr Tachibana, that's what it was like. People were burnt to a cinder. The men who escaped with their lives found spears and formed vigilante groups. You must have taken up a bamboo spear yourself, Mr Tachibana. Besides being burnt out of our homes, we heard rumours of riots breaking out and hordes of people going on the rampage. That was around the time when Ōsugi Sakae and Itō Noe were killed. I remember thinking then that the world was coming to an end. We all had to line up in the hot sun to buy wheat cakes that sold for ten sen each, even though they had hardly any meat filling. We complained about the outrageous price, and yet we still queued up. After living through such hard times, people of our age are terrified of fires and food shortages. I'm appalled at the way my daughter-in-law wastes food, but if I speak to her about it, she glares at me. That's why I talk about it to Mr Tachibana. Isn't that right, Mr Tachibana?'

Shigezō had his eyes half-closed, too sleepy to pay any attention, but Mrs Kadotani took no notice and went on with her interminable chatter.

Akiko slipped out of the cottage, uncertain whether or not to report the situation to the Kadotanis. She finally decided to return to the main house first and seek her husband's advice when he returned.

Akiko finished her Saturday chores. When dinner was ready, she

93

went over to the cottage to inform Shigezō and Mrs Kadotani that it was time for them to part. At the mention of dinner, Shigezō slowly got to his feet and descended into the garden. Akiko noisily closed the shutters. Left alone, the old woman had no alternative but to return home.

Every Saturday Akiko did the laundry that had accumulated during the week and gave the house a thorough cleaning. After Shigezō had come to live with them, she had also taken to bathing him after dinner. He was still able to dress and undress himself, but when Akiko got him into the bathtub, he would soak himself for ages. Out of the tub, he would sit on the floor, and when Akiko handed him a bar of soap, he would rub his hands together until all the soap was gone. She therefore had to scrub him all over as if he was a child. When she asked him to lift his arms or stand up, he complied meekly. Although Akiko had bathed her son when he was little without feeling any revulsion, she found it most unpleasant to have to wash the lower half of Shigezō's body. She scrubbed his buttocks from behind with a towel using plenty of soap, then washed the suds off with hot water.

'Please wash yourself, Grandpa,' she pleaded, handing him a bar of soap.

'OK,' replied Shigezō, but all he did was to gaze blankly at the soap.

'Grandpa, you have to wash your penis,' shouted Akiko hysterically, losing her patience.

'OK, OK.'

But Shigezō merely looked down at his crotch and remained motionless. Akiko went on shouting at him, feeling absolutely wretched and wondering what might be going through her son's head as he sat listening to her not far from the bathroom. Akiko could not bring herself to wash her father-in-law's genitals for him. Finally, she poured some hot water over his crotch, thus completing the unpleasant chore. If only she could get Nobutoshi to bath his father! But he said it was out of the question and adamantly refused. The thought of the wrinkled mass of flesh dangling limply from between his father's legs filled him with revulsion.

By the time Nobutoshi returned home that night, his father was fast asleep and Akiko was in the room downstairs doing the ironing. Although she folded the underwear as it came out of the dryer, she still had to perform the laborious task of ironing things like cotton handkerchiefs and shirts.

'Welcome home, dear.'

'Um.'

94

In the Tachibana household, the wife did not serve her husband a cup of hot tea on his return home from work. It was not that Akiko did not believe in this traditional and elegant practice, but rather that in order to spend the kind of leisurely Sunday described in novels, she had to work like a madwoman on Saturdays. Thus Akiko went on with her ironing as she gave her husband a colourful report of the most recent development. Nobutoshi was surprised at her news, but did not make any comment. Presently he slipped away to take a bath, returning soon afterwards wearing a robe over his night kimono. Having seated himself at the *kotatsu* and lit a cigarette, he said, 'I'm amazed that Satoshi is familiar with an expression like "love in December".'

'Do you think he's teased Mrs Kadotani about it?'

'She's really been a great help. If she even helps Grandpa go to the toilet, we ought to pay her for her services.'

'Actually, I prepare three lunches every day, including one for Mrs Kadotani. But I am startled at the way she flirts with Grandpa. Imagine, at her age! It's disgusting. I keep wondering if I'll turn out to be like her in my old age.'

'Don't worry about it. I think it's wonderful to have sexual feelings until you die. It's infinitely better than becoming simple like Dad.'

'And she never stops talking. Today she kept telling me about the Great Tokyo Earthquake. According to her, she had to line up to buy wheat cakes at ten sen each.'

'Oh? I didn't know they had wheat cakes in the 'twenties. I thought they were only introduced after the war. How interesting!'

'You only say that because you don't know what Japan was like before that. Wheat cakes were sold throughout Japan during the war years.'

'That's what I thought, but didn't you just say that they were also sold at the time of the Earthquake?'

'According to Mrs Kadotani. But the cakes she described had a meat filling.'

Akiko finished the last handkerchief and put the ironing away. After seating herself at the *kotatsu*, she said: 'I wonder if when I get to her age I'll ramble on and on about the poverty of the post-war years. I'm always mentioning the food shortages right after the war whenever Satoshi complains about certain dishes. He can't bear to hear me talk about my wartime experiences.'

'Yes, I know. The young employees at work hate it whenever we reminisce about the war years.'

'Oh dear! Have we already begun behaving like old people?'

Akiko's question filled them with horror. Nobutoshi could not reply, and Akiko was taken aback at what she had said. They often repeated themselves these days. Was this a sign that they were growing old?

In the middle of the night Shigezō got up and told Akiko that he had to relieve himself. Akiko slipped into an overrobe. Earlier in the evening she had dressed Shigezō warmly in two night kimonos, but he was in such a hurry that she had not had the time to get him into a dressing-gown. His body temperature must have dropped after urinating, but he showed no sign of having caught a chill. Although Akiko was snugly dressed, the night air was so cold she continued to shiver long after she had crawled back into bed. It was generally believed that dogs and horses never catch colds. Akiko wondered if the same could be said of old men. Shigezō had once had a delicate stomach, but even though he had a voracious appetite he no longer suffered from diarrhoea. Had the nerves in his stomach grown dull?

With a heavy heart Akiko hugged her pillow to her breast, mounted the stairs and soon drifted back to sleep next to her husband. Some time later she was woken abruptly.

'Wake up, Akiko. Father's shouting his head off.'

'Why don't you do something for a change, dear? He's your father, isn't he? After all, tomorrow's Sunday,' said Akiko angrily.

Akiko turned her back to her husband. Had she made him angry or had she succeeded in making him realize how much truth there was to what she said? She had no way of knowing, but felt greatly relieved when she heard him go downstairs. He simply had to help out once in a while. It was unfair of him to expect her to do everything.

Shigezō's voice grew even louder. Presently, Nobutoshi came running up the stairs. 'I just won't do, honey. Please get up for my sake,' he said.

'What's the trouble now?'

'Dad doesn't recognize me. He keeps muttering that you've disappeared. He's crawling all over your bedding trying to find you.'

Akiko went downstairs and turned the light full on. Seeing her standing there, Shigezō said: 'Oh, there you are, Akiko!'

Shigezō had his long arms and legs spread out like a spider on the bedding that Akiko slept in during the early part of the night.

'What's the matter, Grandpa?'

'There's a burglar in the house. Call the police.'

'A burglar?'

'Yes. There he is!' cried Shigezō, pointing at Nobutoshi. Nobutoshi was dumbfounded.

96

'What are you saying, Dad? I'm your son!'

'Akiko, turn that man over to the police.'

'But, Grandpa, he isn't a burglar. He's a member of our family. Do you need to go out into the garden again?'

Akiko signalled to her husband with her eyes. Nobutoshi went back upstairs. Watching him disappear, Shigezō said in a low voice: 'Akiko, the burglar went upstairs. Please call the police.'

'All right. But first, would you like to go outside again?'

'No.'

'Well then, please go back to sleep.'

'All right.'

'It's still night-time, you know.'

'Yes.'

When she saw that Shigezō was fast asleep, Akiko tiptoed upstairs. Nobutoshi lay in bed wide awake.

'What a shock! I never thought Dad would ask to have me arrested.'

'He told me that the burglar went upstairs. Do you think he had a nightmare?'

'All I know is that by the time I got downstairs he was muttering to himself that you had disappeared. He turned over all the bedding frantically searching for you.'

'How awful!'

'But the minute you appeared, I became a burglar in his eyes. I wonder if rivalry between men lasts until their death.'

Akiko felt wretched the next day, having been up twice during the night. The family usually slept late on a Sunday morning, but by midday Akiko still felt that she had not enough sleep. There was a throbbing pain at the back of her head, but she knew she had to get up and prepare a proper meal for her family. As she made her way slowly downstairs, she found Shigezō with his eyes wide open.

'Oh, Akiko.'

Akiko silently opened the rain shutter. It was a lovely day, so she left the side facing the garden open and walked across to the washbasin. While she brushed her teeth, she wondered whether Shigezō had been brushing his dentures. In all the years he had worn them, she had never once seen him clean them. When she and Nobutoshi had questioned him about them, he had insisted that they were his own teeth. If he had not cleaned his dentures all these months, his mouth must be indescribably filthy. Such unpleasant thoughts so early in the morning distressed Akiko.

'I'm starved, Akiko. Can I have my breakfast?'

Akiko found it difficult not to show her irritation at moments like

97

these. She roughly folded away the bedding and said sharply: 'I can't get breakfast ready right away. Please be patient. Why don't you get dressed first?'

Shigezō followed Akiko with his eyes. Then he raised his long arms, covered his face with his upper arms and burst into tears.

'I'm starved and you won't let me have my breakfast!'

Akiko did not know how to placate her weeping father-in-law. Hurriedly, she handed him two slices of plain bread and, seething with anger, vacuumed the dusty room. Having to spread out two sets of bedding downstairs had added to the work she had to do every morning.

Akiko prepared a Western-style brunch of crisply toasted frozen waffles, various different types of bread, milk, scrambled eggs, sausages and coffee. Seated across the table from Nobutoshi and Satoshi, she drank cup after cup of coffee. Neither Nobutoshi nor Satoshi said anything, having overhead Shigezō's sobbing earlier. Nobutoshi spread out the newspaper and studied it carefully, while Satoshi watched television.

Shigezō slowly rose to his feet and went down into the garden.

'Please open up the cottage for Grandpa, Satoshi,' said Akiko, who knew that Shigezō wanted to use the toilet. Satoshi carried out her request without protesting. On his return, he helped himself to another waffle and, munching noisily, said: 'Mrs Kadotani was already there.'

'Oh? Where was she?'

'Sitting on the veranda. When she saw Grandpa, she looked very pleased.'

'What about Grandpa?'

'He disappeared into the toilet.'

If Mrs Kadotani was already there, Akiko would have to start a charcoal fire in the brazier right away, as the cottage would be freezing. As soon as the family had finished their breakfast, she went across to the cottage.

She was surprised to see that the old woman had already started a fire in the brazier and was preparing some tea. Shigezō, who had finished using the toilet, was sitting in front of the brazier. Akiko left the two in the cottage and hurried back to the main house. When she finished describing the scene she had just witnessed, her husband commented: 'They're behaving like a married couple. Won't this make things easier for you?'

'In what way? I'll still have to get up for him in the night. I couldn't stand it if that happened every night!'

'Then you should get Mrs Kadotani to sleep there at night. After all, the cottage has virtually become a home for the elderly,' said Nobutoshi.

What an insufferably selfish man her husband was! She wondered whether the Kadotanis were aware of the situation. Perhaps they knew and yet did nothing about it. What could they be thinking? Feeling that she ought to pay them a visit, Akiko set out with the box of cakes she had bought to present to the young woman at the Umezato Centre. Mr Kadotani was not at home, having gone fishing early that morning. His wife, who was about Akiko's age, accepted the gift and thanked Akiko profusely. Mrs Kadotani did not seem to know that her mother-in-law visited Shigezō in the cottage. She was a typical middle-aged housewife who, unlike Akiko, spent all her time at home. She was even unaware that Akiko prepared lunches for the two elderly people before leaving for work. Akiko could not help being appalled by her neighbour's lack of concern.

'Oh dear. I'm sorry that she's been so much trouble to you. She's such a nuisance at home that we don't know what to do with her.'

'Actually, she's been no trouble at all! On the contrary, it's a great help to have her around, so I'd like to thank *you* for everything. Is it really all right to have her help me so much?'

'Are you sure she isn't a nuisance? She's so talkative she must be a pain in the neck. I really do apologize.'

'Not at all. The cottage seems to have become a home for the elderly. We could leave things as they are, if it's all right with your family. After all, we are neighbours.'

'Yes, that's true. If we leave things as they are, it'll be easier for me as well. As you can see for yourself, my mother-in-law is still in perfect health. When she's at home she keeps ordering me about, and by the end of the day I'm utterly exhausted. I hear that she says cruel things about me at the Centre, but I'd rather have her there than at home. She never stops talking, and it's always about the Great Tokyo Earthquake.'

'I heard all about it yesterday. I found her account fascinating. It's remarkable that she can remember all those details.'

'It may be interesting to hear about it once in a while, but if you had to hear the same old story day after day as I have to, you'd be sick of it too. I never want to hear another word about people burned to a cinder and buying wheat cakes. The other day when she was watching the news about student activists on television, she got terribly excited, thinking it was a rice riot. I was born in the 'twenties, but I never want to hear another word about those difficult days. It was bad enough trying to survive during the war years.'

'But you're fortunate that your mother-in-law is able to think so clearly. It's wonderful that she can go to the Centre all by herself. My father-in-law can't do a thing on his own.'

'But Grandma finds him attractive.'

'Oh?'

'Well, ever since his wife passed away, not a day goes by without Grandma mentioning Mr Tachibana. She says that he's very handsome and that he carries himself like a lord. According to her, it's your father-in-law who insists that she comes to visit him. My husband says he feels uncomfortable when he sees his mother behaving so brazenly.'

'Oh?'

'I'm sure it's just an infatuation. But I must admit that I too find her behaviour rather disturbing, especially when I remember how old she is. But then I tell myself that she'd be no match for some of those women at the Centre who are even more active. Lately I've noticed that she is rather agitated when she leaves the house in the morning, and that she returns home late. Still, it's so much easier for me to have her out of the house. I never dreamed that she was going to your home! I'm terribly sorry! We've been talking about putting Grandma into a home, but I never imagined that there was one right in our neighbourhood!'

Akiko remained silent.

'I know I shouldn't interfere in such a private matter as their relationship, but isn't Mr Tachibana eighty-seven years old?'

'No, he's eighty-four. But he'll be eighty-five soon.'

'Then he must be impotent. Those two are just enjoying each other's company, so don't worry about what the neighbours will say. Wouldn't it be all right as long as we have an understanding?'

'I should think so. As you know, I work full-time, so I can't keep an eye on them during the day. I'll continue to make lunches for them, but I'd appreciate it if you looked in on them from time to time.'

'Everything will be fine. Grandma will be around for some time. Didn't she tell you that they do exercises at the Centre to make them live longer? I was so disappointed when I heard that!'

Akiko bowed and, asking Mrs Kadotani for her co-operation, excused herself. On her way home, she began to suspect that the woman had known about the situation all along. She also remembered what the old woman had said about everyone at home waiting for her to die. Didn't the younger woman realize that she herself would one day grow old?

Storming into the house in a rage, Akiko prepared a special afternoon snack for the old couple and took it over to the cottage.

Mrs Kadotani thanked Akiko profusely, tears streaming down her cheeks.

'Your daughter-in-law is such a lovely person! You don't know how lucky you are, Mr Tachibana. My daughter-in-law has never treated me to a snack like this. I have to prepare my own tea and at mealtimes she always has something sarcastic to say to me. That's why I get so depressed when I stay at home.'

Then, as though a dam had broken, she abused her daughter-in-law viciously. By this time Akiko was thoroughly disgusted with both women. Painfully reminded of how Shigezō had once treated her, she could not bear to listen to her neighbour a moment longer. Shigezō had become so childlike that Akiko had all but forgotten her old grudge, but now that she was reminded of the bitter past, all her resentment returned. Shigezō's sarcastic remarks used to be malicious and unpleasant, but all he did now was to stuff himself, perform his bodily functions or stare vacantly into space.

Ten years from now this old woman would probably be as helpless as Shigezō was today, and no longer have the energy to abuse her daughter-in-law. Akiko felt terribly annoyed. The intense cold made her shiver as she hurried off towards the main house.

'Akiko's gone. Akiko! Akiko!' cried Shigezō.

Akiko went downstairs, turned up the neon light which had been left burning low and found her father-in-law searching through her bedding. She was not a flea, so how could she be buried under the covers? Far from being amused, Akiko began to lose her temper.

'Oh, there you are, Akiko. I thought you'd disappeared.'

'I won't disappear, so try to get some sleep.'

'All right.'

Patting him gently on the back, Akiko recalled an incident that had taken place ten years earlier. Satoshi had woken up in the middle of the night and, half asleep, had begun groping for her. Akiko had taken him into her bedding and spent the rest of the night with her arms around him. Now it was her father-in-law who had been searching for her. Resigning herself to the inevitable, Akiko decided to begin sleeping in the same bedding with him. This would be easier for her than to go upstairs every time she put him back to sleep, she thought. As she drifted off to sleep, she recalled what Mrs Kadotani had said about Shigezō being impotent, and she knew that she would not be able to sleep soundly that night.

101

10

Once past Shinjuku Station on the subway coming home from work, Akiko could move about a little on the crowded train, although the carriage she was in was still unbearably stuffy. When she reached the top of the stairs at Shinkōenji Station, the cold air was exhilarating. Akiko had stayed behind at the office until she had finished her share of the work. It was long past dusk and the streets were dark. A light snow had begun to fall. Akiko stopped when she saw the snow but was roughly pushed aside by the crowd of young people who were surging up the stairs behind her. For a moment she lost her balance, then steadied herself. As she began to walk home, the snow made her reflect that more than two months had slipped by since her mother-in-law's death. She realized that from now on she would always be reminded of that day whenever it snowed.

As she approached the house she saw a light in the window. How comforting it was to have someone to come home to!

'I'm home, Satoshi. Sorry I'm late,' she called out as she entered the house.

A fire was burning briskly in the kerosene stove, and the room was warm and cosy. Shigezō was seated at the *kotatsu* watching television.

'Hello, Grandpa.'

'Welcome home, Akiko.'

Akiko noticed two empty bowls in the kitchen sink. So Satoshi had prepared some instant noodles. But something was amiss today, for she usually found Shigezō in the cottage with Mrs Kadotani when she returned. Akiko threw open the window and peered out at the cottage. It was completely dark. Worried, she walked across to have a look. The doors of the cottage were open and the rim of the porcelain brazier was as cold as ice. The fire must have gone out some time before.

Akiko shook her sleepy father-in-law by the shoulders. 'What happened to Mrs Kadotani, Grandpa?'

'Do you mean the old woman?'

'Yes. What happened to her?'

'She died.'

'What do you mean? Did she really die?'

'Yes.'

Akiko was still in a state of shock when Satoshi came downstairs.

'Well, Mum, it looks as if Grandpa's been jilted.'

Akiko did not know whom to believe.

'What do you mean, Satoshi? Tell me what happened.'

According to Satoshi, he had received a telephone call from the caretaker at the Umezato Centre. It was closing time and Shigezō was still there. Since Shigezō did not know how to get home, she wanted someone to come and fetch him. So Satoshi had rushed over to the Centre and brought Shigezō home. It had not occurred to him to ask why his grandfather had been abandoned, and Akiko feared that he had probably not even thanked the caretaker properly.

'Grandpa has just told me that Mrs Kadotani has died.'

'That isn't true. No one that healthy could die.'

'You can never tell. After all, it happened to Grandma.'

Akiko thought it quite possible for Mrs Kadotani to have suddenly died like her mother-in-law. Feeling very distressed, she went round to the Kadotanis'.

Mrs Kadotani's daughter-in-law greeted her at the entrance. Smiling broadly, she said in a low voice: 'It appears that Grandma has fallen out of love.' She chuckled after making this announcement.

'Whatever could have happened?'

'I really don't know, but do come in. We've already heard Grandma's version of the story. It may cheer her up to have someone else to listen to her,' said the daughter-in-law, obviously very much amused.

Almost against her will, Akiko found herself entering the house. When the old woman caught sight of her, she launched into an interminable monologue.

'Really, Akiko. It's the end when a man becomes that senile. It really is. I've put up with it long enough. Everyone makes fun of Mr Tachibana at the Centre. They say they'd rather die than be like him. All he says is "Uh-huh" or "All right". He never laughs or talks. Have you noticed that funny look on his face, as if he were in a trance? When he does say anything, it's always to complain about being hungry. I can't look after him any more. All my friends have begun to make fun of me. They say I must be a fool to look after such a

103

dotard. I've been terribly upset. Will my dead husband ever forgive me? I'm quite sure that Mrs Tachibana died of sheer disgust. How could any woman stand being married to a man like that? It was a good thing she died when she did. No woman could be a dutiful wife to such a wreck of a man. Not possibly! Why, I'd have died of shame if my husband had become that senile! I could never have covered up for him!'

Akiko was dumbfounded. Still, there were a few things that she wished to say as Shigezō's daughter-in-law. It was strange that her neighbour should say such things now. True, she had been the one to ask Mrs Kadotani to take Shigezō with her to the Centre, but it was the old woman who had flirted with him so shamelessly. Was it not possible that Shigezō had been annoyed with her? Had she forgotten how she had forced her way into the cottage and had delighted in pretending that they were a married couple?

'I'm sorry we caused you so much trouble. But you must remember, Mrs Kadotani, that a man of his age is likely to become senile.'

'Not necessarily! Mr Tachibana is eighty-four, isn't he? At the Centre you'll find people who are still alert at ninety-two. Senility is a state of mind. They all say that Mr Tachibana became senile because he didn't exercise his mind or his body. They also say that he was probably lazy. A man can slow down the ageing process by keeping mentally and physically active. Mr Tachibana must have made his wife work like a slave while he did absolutely nothing. People used to think that men deteriorated physically while women became senile. It's not true! Women rarely become senile, because they have to use their brains – whether they're sewing or doing the laundry. That's why I tell my daughter-in-law that the automatic washing-machine may be convenient and wonderful to have in the house, but in the future women will become senile at a younger age because they no longer have to be as active as women in the past. My daughter-in-law thinks I'm saying this out of spite, but I'm only giving her the facts. People won't become senile as long as they keep themselves fit, mentally and physically.'

Rendered speechless by the old woman's views on ageing, Akiko felt that she had much to learn from her. Here, before her very eyes, was a woman who had accumulated a wealth of knowledge through the years. A person had to keep physically fit. Akiko, who had begun to show signs of age, had to admit that this was the best advice anyone could give her at this time.

But Akiko's immediate problem was what to do with Shigezō, who had no doubt deteriorated to this extent as a result of his laziness.

If Mrs Kadotani had really given up on him, Akiko had a serious problem on her hands. Who would look after her father-in-law now, while she was at work? With a heavy heart, Akiko trudged home through the snow.

In the meantime, Nobutoshi was in the amusement centre under Shimbashi Station, going from one small bar to another. When he was young, the drunker he became, the louder he sang. Now, although he still went drinking with the same old gang, they took up very different topics of conversation.

Less than three per cent of the Japanese population was born in the Meiji era, one of the men pointed out, and yet Nobutoshi's company was still controlled by men belonging to this small and exclusive group. Another member of the group agreed wholeheartedly. How well their company demonstrated the fact that the Japanese population was growing older, he added. Nobutoshi's companions, who were all approaching fifty, believed that these older men were preventing them from being promoted. Their frustration was understandable, because they were so close to attaining their goal in life. Then the conversation took a new turn as they began to gossip about the executives of the company. They also discussed various personnel problems that had arisen during the previous ten years.

'Do you know what's become of Sakakibara, the Executive Director?' asked one of the men.

Sakakibara had clashed with the company president about three years before and had been forced to resign. As a young man, he had done exceptionally well in the company and had been posted to various foreign branch offices. Being extremely competent, he had achieved rapid promotion.

'What about him?'

'I'll bet you think he's been keeping a low profile, waiting for the right opportunity to make a comeback.'

'After all, why should a brilliant man like that remain buried in obscurity? How can the company afford to go on ignoring him? Now that international trade is becoming so complex, don't you think Sakakibara is about the only man who can help the company plan for the future?'

'I would think the politicians have their eyes on him. Hasn't he become someone's adviser?'

'Absolutely not. I paid him a New Year's visit, as he served as go-between at my wedding, and it was pitiful to see him.'

'Has he had a stroke?'

'No, he's become senile. He struggled just to remember my name, and then he got it wrong. So I told him I was Sasaki. He repeated the name correctly, as if he realized his mistake, but the next minute he was calling me Kato. He must have been thinking of Kato of the Personnel Department, though I don't look like him at all. And it wasn't only names that troubled him. He kept rambling on and on about America and China, but nothing he said made any sense. Later I realized that he'd been describing the situation way back in the 'thirties.'

'I don't believe it!'

'He's only sixty, so I too could hardly believe my eyes. He'd waited at home doing nothing, confident that the company would ask him to come back. Even my wife was amazed at how senile he'd become.'

'Whatever happened to him?'

'Did he drink too much?'

The men, who had themselves had too much alcohol, were sobered by this story. Recalling what Sakakibara had been like when he was a company director, they felt as though they had been struck by lightning. One of the men stated emphatically that his condition could not possibly be the result of a drinking problem, and everyone nodded in agreement. They wondered if Sakakibara had become prematurely senile because he had led a life of idleness at home. At this point, Nobutoshi and his friends began to gossip about other employees of the company who had recently retired. Some of the men had used their retirement money to become directors of subsidiary companies; others had built apartment buildings. One of these men, who was interested only in earning a high salary so that he could support his many children, had become a night watchman. Nobutoshi and his friends concluded that it was men who were financially secure who tended to become senile.

'Could it be that our bodies function like treadmills? While a man's employed he's completely absorbed in treading away, but once he begins to relax, he becomes senile. What a dreadful fate!'

At this point the bar hostess said angrily from where she stood behind the counter:

'Must you speak about such unlucky things? There isn't a single old man or woman in this place! Rumi, pour them some cold saké. It's water from the fountain of youth. I'll join them in a drink. Here I am, brimming with youth, and what's more, I've been a virgin for some time.'

'Come to think of it, so have I for about a month.'

'Whatever are you saying, you drunken fool!'

106

Their spirits lifted temporarily, they had another drink. But they all felt as if they had been touched by a chill wind. One member of the group announced that he preferred mah-jong to saké or women, and Nobutoshi shouted back that he agreed. When four people sit round a table playing mah-jong, they might quarrel amongst themselves, but they are too preoccupied with the game to gossip about other people. A player who is doing badly might feel depressed, but there is no danger that all four will enter into a gloomy discussion.

'The Chinese, who invented mah-jong, are a great people! I learned the game from an overseas Chinese, who firmly believed that a person who plays mah-jong will never become senile. I was very young when I started playing, so I didn't realize it then, but the game is good exercise for your brain.'

'The same thing could well be said of *go* and *shōgi*.'

'True. My grandfather was a landlord and led a life of leisure, but he loved to play *go*. Even at the age of ninety, he was still mentally alert.'

'Here we are, still on the same subject.'

Everyone laughed weakly and decided that it was high time they were going home. When they emerged from the subway station, it was snowing hard. They were shocked to realize how late it was. The problem of the elderly was forgotten as they concentrated on finding a taxi. The trains had already stopped running, and they had to persuade a sour-faced taxi driver to take them home. They closed their eyes to the extortionate rates he quoted them, and got into the taxi. The driver told them bluntly that, because of the snow, he would not turn into any narrow streets. Nobutoshi shared the taxi with two colleagues whose homes lay in the same direction. Glancing at his wristwatch, he saw that it was nearly two o'clock. One of the men remarked that he had never dreamed Sakakibara would become senile. He had been so certain that the former director would embark on a successful new venture. One never knew about the future, he sadly concluded. At this point, Nobutoshi mentioned that his father was eighty-four. The third passenger began to complain about his problems, as though he had been waiting all along for this opportunity.

'I have my mother at home, she's bedridden and very weak. She deteriorated when my father died and now she thinks she's living in the Taishō era. She says strange things like "the noon hour has struck" or "it's lamp-lighting time" and gives our children paper-wrapped 100-yen coins, which she calls *giza*. It was all rather quaint until she became disabled. The doctor says that she has an incurable hernia. We've put the television set near her bed, but she can no

107

longer distinguish between what she sees on TV and reality. When she sees a man on TV, she imagines he's a burglar or a murderer and lets out a blood-curdling scream! Over the past few months, my wife's become terribly irritable. In fact, our marriage is on the rocks and our arguments are becoming more violent. I sometimes wonder if we'll be divorced before Mother dies, because no nursing home will take in anyone who's bedridden.'

'Really?'

'In order to get a place, a elderly person has to be healthy in mind and body, which my mother is not. My wife firmly believes that she has to develop a strong back so that she won't end up like Mother, so she goes bowling on Sundays when I'm at home. I'm afraid that if she isn't given a chance to let off some steam, she'll break under the strain.'

The men were so engrossed in their conversation that, before they were aware of it, the taxi had come to a stop at the corner of Itsukaichi Avenue. The driver told Nobutoshi that he could not take him any closer to his home, so Nobutoshi got out and paid his share of the fare.

The snow was still falling in flurries, and was settling heavily on the ground. Nobutoshi could see the path in front of him, but the snow clung tenaciously to the soles of his shoes. Slipping each time he took a step, he found it extremely difficult to make his way. Arriving home at last, he pressed the buzzer, but no one came to the door to let him in. Akiko is probably in bed, he thought, angry with me for being so late. Nobutoshi took the key dangling from the wallet containing his season ticket and unlocked the door.

All he could see in the dim light were two sets of empty bedding laid out on the floor. One of the rain shutters facing the garden was open. Rubbing his hands together for warmth, Nobutoshi walked on to the veranda and peered out into the garden. When his eyes fell on his father and his wife embracing there, he stood rooted to the spot. A moment later, however, he realized that they were not locked in a lovers' embrace. His wife, supporting Shigezō from behind, was looking the other way. Petite though she was, Akiko somehow managed to keep her father-in-law from falling over. Neither uttered a word. While listening to his father urinating, Nobutoshi watched the snow melt away, revealing a round dark patch of earth about a foot away from where his father was standing. The scene reminded him of a poem by Bashō. As the snow continued to fall, the small hole resembled a dark abyss.

As soon as Shigezō finished urinating Nobutoshi turned and fled up the stairs. How could he face his wife when she had to perform this unpleasant duty every night? How could he bear to look at his decrepit father, or hear him demand yet again that he be turned over to the police? While slipping into his nightclothes, Nobutoshi tried hard to recall the lines of the poem by Bashō, but was unable to do so. He thought that it must be one of the poems in *The Narrow Road of Oku*. Instead, he remembered two other poems: 'How pitiful! A grasshopper under the helmet' and 'How wonderful it is here in Minamidani where the snow is made fragrant'. It was natural for him to think of the first, which was composed in memory of Sanemori who, after dyeing his grey hair, had fought valiantly and died in battle. But the second had absolutely no association with the scene he had just witnessed. The snow in the poem referred to the snow covering the peak of a distant mountain, and the phrase 'to be fragrant' had been used because it was early summer. If he now associated the urine and snow which he had just seen with the poem, all his youthful efforts to master the art of haiku composition had been in vain. When he was young, he had no difficulty at all in quoting Bashō's poems. Why, then, was he no longer able to remember the lines of that famous verse?

Nobutoshi felt that, before going to bed, he ought to thank Akiko for her efforts. Instead, he called out brusquely, 'Hey, honey. I'm home!'

'My, how delicate you are!' she replied from the foot of the stairs.

'I'm sorry you have to go through that every night.'

'Oh, did you see us out there?'

Instead of answering, Nobutoshi buried himself in the quilts. It was then that the lines of the poem came back to him: 'Fleas and lice; the horse urinating near my bed.' Bashō had composed it to describe his wretched lodgings in the mountains of Dewa in *The Narrow Road of Oku*. The instant he recalled the verse, Nobutoshi felt at once relieved and frightened. He had become very forgetful in recent years. It took him much longer now to remember things. Suddenly to remember the lines of a poem like that – wasn't it just like his aged father suddenly remembering the old woman who had been killed by a horse? Indeed, was it not *actual proof* of the fact that he himself had already begun to grow old?

The words of apology that her husband had all but shouted from upstairs echoed in Akiko's ears and completely dispelled the irritation that had built up in her during the day. For the past two months she had waited eagerly to hear him say these words. So Nobutoshi realized what she was going through! He must have seen her out in the garden with his father. Despite the brusqueness of his words, her husband, although both embarrassed and upset, was

109

clearly grateful for her efforts. Akiko lay down next to Shigezō and buried her face in her pillow. With her husband's words echoing softly in her ears like a lullaby, she soon fell into a peaceful slumber.

As dawn approached, Akiko was woken by a crushing weight on her breast and was startled to find Shigezō sitting on her on top of the covers. He was moaning softly. Akiko frantically pushed her father-in-law aside and jumped to her feet.

'What is it, Grandpa?'

'Oh, oh. Akiko's gone. She's disappeared.'

Shigezō got down on his knees, lifted the bottom of Akiko's quilt and peered under it. Fascinated, Akiko stepped back and watched her father-in-law pick up the pillow and shake it hard. Then he peered cautiously under the quilt again as if he were looking for a cockroach he had spotted crawling under the covers.

Akiko turned up the neon lights.

'Grandpa!' she cried.

Only then did Shigezō realize that Akiko was standing in front of him. All at once his limbs went limp and, like a puppet with its strings snapped, he flopped down on the quilt.

'I've been here all along, Grandpa.'

'Oh.'

'What's the matter?'

'Uh . . .'

'Do you have to go outside?'

'Yes.'

'Again?'

'No.'

'Then why don't you go back to sleep?' she asked sharply.

Akiko dragged Shigezō back into bed. The old man, very docile now, lay still. Akiko sighed. During the day she had felt indignation at her young neighbour's remarks, but now she found herself plunged into despair. How long could she go on living like this? Things would be infinitely easier for her if Shigezō died! She no longer felt guilty about her secret thoughts. Her anger mounted as she remembered her husband's words of apology. If he really felt sorry for her, he would do his share in looking after his father. As the head of the household, he foisted all the unpleasant duties on her. Suppressing her anger, Akiko gazed at the wretched old man. Shigezō seemed to have drifted off to sleep and was breathing evenly. Akiko heaved a sigh of relief. Hestitating for a moment, she decided to leave the light on. She pressed the pillow against her ear and stretched out in the bedding. She desperately needed some sleeping pills. She was afraid to think of what the future would be like for her if she were to be woken up regularly twice a night from now on.

Just as she was about to drop off to sleep, she heard Shigezō screaming: 'Akiko! Akiko!'

She sat up and looked around, but Shigezō was nowhere in sight. 'Where are you, Grandpa?' she called, getting to her feet.

'Here I am! Here I am!'

The room was brightly lit. Following the sound of his voice, Akiko finally found Shigezō crouching by the shoe cupboard near the entrance.

'What's the matter, Grandpa?'

'Akiko! Call the police. There's a burglar in the house.'

'You must have been dreaming, Grandpa. I've locked up the house securely so no one could have broken in.' Then Akiko realized that her father-in-law might have seen Satoshi or Nobutoshi come down to use the toilet.

'Where did the burglar break into the house, Grandpa?'

Shigezō pointed to the kitchen window, but Akiko reassured him that it was securely fastened. Shigezō was trembling with fear. She took him by the hand and drew him back into the room.

'And where did the burglar go?'

Akiko thought that Shigezō would point upstairs, but he did not. Instead, he pointed fearfully at the closet. Akiko opened the door loudly and made him look inside. She also opened the toilet door and said: 'See. There no burglar in here, either. Now please go back to sleep. Everything's all right.'

Though she spoke gently, Akiko shoved Shigezō into his bed. After switching off the light, she saw that, because of the snow, it was already growing light outside. Realizing that her father-in-law was rapidly deteriorating, she had a premonition of worse to come.

Indeed, from that night on, each time Shigezō awoke – which he did frequently – he would shout that a burglar had broken into the house. There was little Akiko could do about not getting enough sleep.

11

Akiko had always prided herself on her strength and courage, but the next morning she felt too weak to get out of bed. It had stopped snowing. The city of Tokyo, now buried under a heavy snowfall, seemed covered with silver. Akiko's view, from where she lay, was limited, and to her the dazzling white snow seemed harsh and cold. The garden in which the Tachibanas had built the cottage had never been more than a narrow strip of land. Only a tiny space between the house and the fence separated their property from that of their neighbours. The snow during the night had so completely covered the black hole made by Shigezō that not even a slight depression could be discerned.

Nobutoshi, who had slept as late as possible, caught only a glimpse of his wife's face, which showed clearly that she had not had enough sleep. However, before rushing off to work, he was told that his father had been abandoned by Mrs Kadotani and that he had got up three times in the night. Satoshi too was in a hurry. Akiko wondered if he would come home from school as soon as his classes were finished, as she had requested.

'Please get up, Akiko. I'm starved. May I have my breakfast?'

Akiko handed her father-in-law a loaf of bread and a small bottle of milk to keep him from bursting into tears. Then, heedless of the consequences, she made her way upstairs, threw herself on her husband's bed and fell into a deep sleep.

When she awoke, sunlight was streaming in through the window and her head felt refreshingly clear. She realized that she hadn't told the office she wouldn't be coming to work, and went downstairs to the phone. Only then did she notice that Shigezō was nowhere to be seen. The two sets of bedding lay just as she had left them earlier that morning. It annoyed her to see such slovenliness, and she quickly folded away the quilts. Before doing anything else, however, she had

112

to look for Shigezō. The garden gate had been left open. Looking outside, Akiko saw footprints in the snow leading to the cottage. Ah, yes. She had gone back to sleep without opening up the rain shutters in the cottage. Had Shigezō managed to get inside to use the toilet? She remembered that she had not helped him to get dressed that morning. The thought of Shigezō walking through the snow dressed in only one layer of clothing, perhaps standing outside the cottage unable to get inside, made her feel very worried. Not bothering to look for her sandals, which were buried under the snow, she jumped down into the garden in her bare feet.

One of the shutters at the far end of the cottage had been knocked down. Akiko wondered if Shigezō had flung his body against it in sheer desperation.

'Grandpa!'

There was no sign of anyone inside the dimly-lit cottage.

'Where are you, Grandpa?' cried Akiko, her voice rising.

Akiko opened the door to the toilet, peered inside and found Shigezō sitting in front of the urinal with his arms around his knees.

'Grandpa!'

'Hello, Akiko.'

'How long have you been sitting there, Grandpa? You must be freezing. Come on back to the main house.'

'All right.'

Shigezō's thin bare feet were visible below the hem of his kimono. Since there was nothing for him to wear, Akiko carried him piggy-back through the snow in her bare feet, which by now were too numb to feel the cold. The soles of her feet ached, but she was feeling too guilty to think about the pain. While waiting for the water to boil, she grated some garlic and mixed it with a soup base; then she poured the boiling water over the mixture and got Shigezō to drink the steaming broth. He made a gurgling sound as he swallowed, quickly draining the bowl. Now that she had warmed the inside of his body, Akiko bundled him up warmly. Next, she prepared two servings of instant noodles, cooking Shigezo's portion a little longer than her own. She grated some garlic, which her family believed in as a restorative, into her bowl of noodles.

'Do you feel cold, Grandpa?'

'Yes, a little.'

'I'm sorry I left you alone. I went upstairs to rest because I didn't get much sleep last night. Have you got a headache?'

'No.'

Akiko went to fetch a thermometer and slipped it under Shigezo's arm. She wondered what she would do if he developed a fever. His temperature was 96.1, but Akiko had no way of knowing whether this was normal for him.

It was already past noon when Akiko finally got round to phoning her office. No one answered. It was possible that the office was closed for the day because of the heavy snowfall.

After lunch Akiko cleared a narrow path between the main house and the cottage. She opened the remaining rain shutters in the cottage and noticed that the frame of the one Shigezō had knocked down was cracked. Although she managed to fix it, she wondered how Shigezō had mustered the strength to break it down.

She returned to the main house and lit the kerosene stove. After cleaning up the room, she set up the electric *kotatsu* for Shigezō. She usually helped him to change his clothes and, after escorting him to the cottage, returned to the house alone. But after what had happened today, she felt that he had to stay in the warm. Now that she had caught up on her sleep, Akiko busied herself with the housework and worked as she did on Saturdays. She even gave the cottage a thorough cleaning. As she scrubbed the filthy toilet, she was assailed by the foul smell that pervaded the tiny cubicle. When she had finished her chores, she examined his clothes, positive that they smelled badly, and was startled to find them absolutely filthy. Every night Akiko had got Shigezō to change into clean underwear and had thrown the dirty items into the washer. Had she known that his clothes were as filthy as this, she would not have washed them with the rest of the laundry. Examining the cardigan which he wore every day, she discovered that the front was sticky with spilt food. His trousers were as threadbare as a tramp's. Akiko felt terribly embarrassed that she had let her father-in-law go to the Centre dressed in such wretched clothes. After helping Shigezō into some clean clothes, she thought about making him wear a smock. Then she took his temperature again and found that it was still 96.1. She concluded that this was probably his normal temperature and that, because of his advanced age, very likely his blood had cooled. Before she realized it, she was taking her own temperature and found it to be 97.7. At this point, she knew that she had to pull herself together.

Satoshi returned home shortly after three. Akiko pounced on him as if she had been lying in wait for him and gave him a detailed account of the events of the previous night.

'Satoshi, I can't take any more of this. This morning I was so tired I went upstairs and fell asleep. By the time I came downstairs, Grandpa had forced his way into the cottage. I found him sitting in the toilet. I have to keep my eye on him all the time. Now that he's been abandoned by Mrs Kadotani, what am I to do?'

114

Satoshi looked very glum as he listened to his mother, neither nodding nor making any comment. When she asked him for his opinion, he replied nonchalantly: 'Why don't you put him in an old people's home?'

Hearing a terrible ringing in her ears, Akiko quickly replied: 'Yes, that's the only solution. Why don't you mention it to your father. I'm not in a position to do so.'

'Why not?'

'Because Grandpa's my father-in-law. I can't bring myself to make such a suggestion. Surely you realize that Grandpa and I are not blood relations. So please speak to your father about it.'

'All right, Mum.'

'Will you really?'

'All I have to do is to bring it up, right? Of course I'll talk to Dad.'

Akiko's heart felt empty. She quickly picked up her shopping basket and, after asking Satoshi to keep an eye on his grandfather, stepped outside. She usually did her grocery shopping on Saturdays. This particular afternoon she planned to do some shopping at the local market, since she had not had a chance to go downtown. But although several stores in the area had a frozen foods department, the variety was not as great as in the basement of the department store. When she asked Satoshi to watch Shigezō, she thought that she must first visit the Umezato Senior Citizens' Centre and try to find out what had upset Mrs Kadotani the previous day. There was the additional incentive that the caretaker would undoubtedly be well-informed about problems concerning the elderly; she would be able to give the best advice regarding nursing homes. Akiko hoped to learn as much as she could about the subject. Her son's words had upset her terribly, though his suggestion was not an original one. It was because his thoughts mirrored the very depths of her own that Akiko felt so distressed.

Akiko bought a box of cakes at a local bakery and made her way to the Centre. When she entered the building, directly in front of her she noticed an office resembling a police box. Sitting inside was a young woman, who followed Akiko with her eyes. She looked puzzled as she rose to her feet.

'I'm Mrs Tachibana. Thank you for looking after my father-in-law. I'm sorry that he was so much trouble yesterday.'

'Not at all. I would gladly have walked him home, but since he didn't know the way, I had to phone.'

'Please accept these cakes as a token of my appreciation.'

The young woman seemed embarrassed. Was it wrong to present a gift to an employee of a public institution? Or were the cakes inappropriate as a token of appreciation?

'I've come for some advice on a serious matter,' said Akiko solemnly.

The young woman invited Akiko in and offered her a cushion to sit on in the corner of the Japanese-style room. A group of about twenty old men and women were practising folk songs and folk dances. Some of them danced well, others were exceedingly clumsy, but they were all enjoying themselves. Several old men had joined the group, and one had an exceptionally fine singing voice.

'Did Mrs Kadotani come here today?'

'No, she didn't. I had a telephone call from her a while ago, though. She said that she very much wanted to come, but she had been asked to look after the house. The old people have so much fun here that they really look forward to coming. Those who are free to come whenever they wish are the lucky ones. A few long to come, but aren't allowed to because their families think of the Centre as a kind of nursing home and feel that it would be a disgrace to have a member of the family take part in the activities here. In other cases, the daughter-in-law is afraid that her mother-in-law might say unkind things about her behind her back, so she doesn't allow her to come. Many of the elderly are forced to stay home and look after the children. They can't join in the fun, because bringing children along is strictly against the regulations.'

'Oh? I didn't know that.'

'I realize that some families need someone to look after the children, so I'm not too strict about enforcing the rule. Others are, however, and turn away anyone who brings small children.'

'You do have a difficult job!'

'Yes, but I'm on very friendly terms with the regular members. Being the only young one here, they all make a fuss over me. Once when I had a cold and stayed at home, several of them visited me. One old woman brought me some burdock.'

'Burdock?'

'She urged me to drink a broth made by pouring boiling water onto a mixture of soya-bean paste and grated raw burdock. It worked wonders! The old woman who gave me this cold remedy was nearly eighty-five.'

'Grated burdock?'

'Yes. And when I came back to work everyone was so kind! They asked me why I had been away and told me how worried they'd been. They are so concerned about me that I don't have the heart to stay at home because of a simple cold.'

116

'What a wonderful job you have!'

'I agree. When I first came here I thought I'd simply be a nursemaid to the elderly. The one thing I've come to realize is that, though they may be stubborn, they're all very sweet!'

The young woman went on chattering gaily, smiling all the while. Being surrounded by old men and women day after day, it was rare for her to find herself with a woman of Akiko's age. She was therefore longing to talk and bubbling over with enthusiasm, so that Akiko found it increasingly difficult to bring up the subject of nursing homes.

'Mrs Kadotani and Mr Tachibana were such close friends. She took very good care of your father-in-law and seemed to enjoy being teased by the others about their relationship. It was obvious that she was very much attached to him. Yesterday, though, Mrs Kadotani left the Centre in a huff. When I called her home, her daughter-in-law answered the phone and said her mother-in-law had finally had more than she could take of Mr Tachibana. I was so surprised to hear that! I'm afraid I still don't know what actually happened between them.'

'Did you notice if my father-in-law was particularly troublesome yesterday?'

'Not really. He's always so quiet. Actually, the Matsunoki Centre might be a better place for him. The building itself is more modern and it even has a communal bath. And there are more men there. After all, he's had a fight with Mrs Kadotani, and a feud between two elderly people is frightening. It usually results in one of them not coming at all for a time, and when that one does show up, it's only to abuse the other. As you probably know, Mrs Kadotani has been coming here since the Centre opened.'

Was the woman suggesting that Shigezō should not come any more? Perhaps this was why she had hesitated to accept the cakes. In any case, Akiko made up her mind to be philosophical about the situation. She asked the woman a number of questions and received businesslike replies. When she asked where she could find a doctor specializing in geriatrics, she was told that this was the responsibility of the Health Centre. According to the caretaker, any resident of Suginami Ward over sixty-five years of age could join the senior citizens' centre of his choice. However, he could belong to only one centre because government funds were allocated on a per capita basis. Each centre came under the jurisdiction of the Welfare Department of the Bureau of Public Welfare and was staffed by civil servants of the Welfare Department.

'Tell me, do nursing homes come under the jurisdiction of the Ward Office?'

'No. They're under Welfare.'

'Welfare?'

'The Welfare Offices in each district are run by the Bureau of Social Services of the Ministry of Public Welfare. In this neighbourhood, the Eastern District Welfare Office in Wadahommachi supervises the nursing homes. But how can anyone even think about sending his parents to such a place? The elderly are happiest living together with their children and grandchildren. Those who are able to come to the Centre too are very fortunate! Here, they can enjoy each other's company and at home they're surrounded by their children and grandchildren.

'I can't understand how anyone can send their parents to a nursing home,' the caretaker repeated, shaking her head. 'Young people should realize that one day they'll find themselves old and grey. Don't you think it's cruel to commit old people to nursing homes?'

'Are there many people like that?'

'I'm afraid so. In fact there are so many of them that the government can't cope with the problem. All this stems from the fact that the young are no longer taught to respect the elderly. Do you know that Mr Tachibana is the only one here whose grandson comes to fetch him? I've been at this job for nearly five years, and today's the first time anyone has thanked me for my efforts. I was really flabbergasted! Mr Tachibana is very lucky to have such a kind daughter-in-law and such a fine grandson.'

Akiko made no comment.

'Once an old man slipped in the corridor and fractured his kneecap. I carried him piggy-back all the way to his home, but his daughter-in-law ignored me completely. All she did was yell at him, saying that this was why she had told him so often not to go to the Centre. Don't you think she ought to have first summoned the doctor and put the poor man to bed? Well, I got angrier and angrier because she was scolding a man who'd hurt himself accidentally. I felt she was being unreasonable and cruel and I reminded her that one day she would be an old woman. The next day, she stormed into the Ward Office and filed a complaint against me; she even went so far as to say that I was to blame for the accident. Some daughters-in-law are really incredible! Since that incident, I've made a point of associating with the members only here at the Centre. But there are certainly as many different kinds of daughters-in-law as there are old men and women. You're the first one I know who's taken the trouble to look at the place. It was good of you to come.'

The woman was dressed conservatively, and yet she was full of life and obviously single. She radiated cheerfulness. Her youth and

118

candour surprised Akiko. In the young woman's eyes, Akiko was a kind-hearted daughter-in-law, unusual in this day and age, to whom, out of the kindness of her heart, she had recommended the Matsunoki Centre. She was not rejecting Shigezō, but genuinely believed that the facilities at the other centre were better. Her desire to avoid any trouble between Shigezō and Mrs Kadotani was quite understandable, and her advice was based on previous experience. Akiko blushed with embarrassment to hear the young woman criticize in hushed tones the general trend among the younger generation to send elderly members of the family to nursing homes, never dreaming that Akiko was thinking of sending Shigezō away.

Akiko hesitated to go directly to the Welfare Office. Instead, she set off in the direction of the Matsunoki Centre. According to the young woman, a branch of the Suginami Ward Office was located in Matsunoki and the Centre occupied the entire second floor of the building. Akiko wondered why a centre for senior citizens should be located on the second floor: she was finding it difficult enough to help Shigezō out into the garden in the middle of the night. Although he was able to get in and out of the house on his own, his movements were so slow that she felt compelled to assist him. How was a man like that ever going to get up a flight of stairs on his own?

Akiko's fears were allayed when she arrived at the Matsunoki branch of the Ward Office. The ultra-modern, ferro-concrete building had been constructed several years previously. There was a signboard displaying the characters 'Matsunoki Senior Citizens' Centre' and, right next to it, a gently sloping ramp which reminded her of a slide in a playground. The ramp was ingeniously designed with only one bend in it. A person making his way up its gentle incline would find himself at the entrance to the Centre without having had to climb a single step. Now Akiko understood why the young woman had said that the facilities at this centre were far superior. Deeply impressed by the fact that the architect had had the elderly in mind in every detail of his design, Akiko paused for a moment to look about her. Matsunoki was adjacent to Umezato, and so it was not far from her home. No sound of traffic could be heard in this quiet residential area, lush with greenery, situated some distance from Ōme Avenue. Before the war, a number of professional military men had lived in this neighbourhood and, even now, she had heard that Horinouchi was inhabited by a better class of people than Umezato. The mere fact that such a magnificent building could be found here confirmed this.

The front door opened when Akiko pushed it. To the right was a tidy office, and the sonorous chanting of a Nō text could be heard

119

down the hall, where several old women were practising a Nō dance. She was amazed that the residents of two adjoining districts could be so different! A young woman dressed in a dark green smock saw Akiko enter and made her way towards her from the Japanese-style room at the far end of the hall. Akiko could tell at a glance that she was a member of the staff. She was young-looking, with a lovely complexion. Akiko bowed and introduced herself.

'I live in this neighbourhood. My husband's father is eighty-four and I've heard that this centre is especially good, so I've come to look around.'

'Please come in. I'll be happy to show you round.'

'It's certainly lively here, isn't it?'

'Yes. Three interest groups are meeting at the same time today. There are five groups altogether. This centre has a reputation for being very cultured, and most of the old people who come here are exceptionally intelligent and well-educated. In fact, some of the women are college graduates.'

'Which group do you think my father-in-law should join? He has no particular interest or hobby.'

'I imagine he'll select his own friends as he wanders about the Centre. Ask him to come whenever it's convenient for you. There's a communal bath over there that you might like to look at. The women are in there at the moment. They're allowed to bathe between two and four, but I can never get everyone out before five. It's very spacious. Please go on in.'

Akiko opened the door, peered inside and saw that the room was full of old women who were still physically attractive. The women took turns washing each other's backs as they chattered away, pretending that they were at a hot spring resort.

The Japanese-style rooms were far more magnificent and spacious than any at the Umezato Centre. There were two adjoining fifteen-mat rooms. Two teams of old men were playing *go* in one of the rooms which had a decorative alcove, and Akiko listened for a while to the clicking of *go* stones. One of the old men folded his arms and sank into a pensive silence.

'Can you believe that he's ninety years old? He comes here every day and looks for a partner to play with. His mind is still extraordinarily keen, and his speech is clear and lucid.'

Bald, with a head like an octopus's, the old man had a benign expression on his face. There was a loud clicking sound as he placed a white stone on the board. His opponent, who appeared to be much younger, suddenly groaned, for he had lost the match.

Akiko gave the caretaker her name and address. She also

120

mentioned that she had a job and that, though she would accompany her father-in-law to the Centre in the mornings, she would get her son to collect him on his way home from school. Then, very humbly, she asked the woman to look after Shigezō from Monday. The woman looked somewhat taken aback. After inviting Akiko to come again, she echoed the words of the woman at the Umezato Centre.

'It's really unusual to have a person like you come here. This is the first time since I began working with old people that a daughter-in-law has come to introduce herself and to look over the Centre. We get in touch with the family when anything goes wrong, but only a few of the daughters-in-law have thanked us.'

'Well, I would be happy to think of my father-in-law spending the day at a place like this. I don't want to leave him at home by himself.'

'You should certainly avail yourself of the facilities here. They are available even on Sundays. But many of our members are asked to stay at home and look after the house on Sundays, so no one turns up. Families clearly take advantage of the elderly.'

'You're very young to have a responsible job like this,' said Akiko, meaning what she said.

The young woman smiled and said: 'Working with the elderly has been a real education. There are many wise old men and women here who've taught me a lot. When I first came, I had pimples all over my face. One of the old women urged me to eat barley gruel. She even gave me some barley and taught me how to cook the gruel. It cleared up my complexion.'

'The barley is responsible for that? I couldn't help noticing your beautiful complexion.'

'Many people have told me so. At home we all have barley gruel for breakfast every morning. I've learned a great deal just by being here. Once when I came down with a cold . . .'

Suddenly, the ninety-year-old man seated in front of the *go* board went rigid; a moment later, he fell forward, his face crashing onto the black and white stones. The young woman dashed into the room, leaving Akiko in the corridor.

'Mr Suzuki!'

She lifted up the old man and laid him out on the *tatami*. The man remained limp and motionless. Akiko was too stunned to move. The elderly people around her, however, all stood up. The young woman ran into the office, dialled a number on the telephone and summoned an ambulance. Akiko was forgotten as the woman phoned the old man's family and told them what had happened. She requested that someone should come to the Centre immediately. There wasn't a hint of panic in her voice.

121

The group who had been chanting the Nō texts stopped abruptly. They slipped into the room to see what had happened, then gathered out in the corridor and began to whisper to each other.

The man's partner seemed to be in a state of shock. He watched the caretaker feel for the man's pulse. Then he stammered:

'How terrible! Mr Suzuki always launched into a long lecture at the end of a match. He was unusually quiet today and I wondered if anything was the matter. He should've told me he wasn't feeling well. We could've taken a little break. He really startled me when he fell over like that. Are you in pain, Mr Suzuki? How is his pulse?' he asked, peering into the young woman's face.

An ambulance arrived, its siren wailing. A young doctor in a white uniform rushed into the room. He pressed a stethoscope against the old man's chest and looked into his pupils, then sat down in formal Japanese fashion and bowed low.

'He's dead.'

Taking this pronouncement as a signal, the old people seated themselves on the floor and pressed their hands together in prayer. Completely overwhelmed, Akiko sat down in the corridor and also brought her hands together. The old man had been a complete stranger, and yet, by some quirk of fate, she had been present when he breathed his last. Led by the members of his family who had come for him, the dead man was carried out of the Centre on a stretcher. No one shed a single tear.

'He was lucky never to have known a day's illness all these years and to have died without suffering any pain.'

'Imagine, he dropped dead after playing his favourite game!'

'And he won the match, didn't he? He couldn't have had any regrets at all.'

'How I envy him.'

'I wouldn't mind dying like that.'

'You shouldn't be talking about dying. After all, you're twenty years younger than him.'

'But life is so uncertain. For all I know, it may be my turn tomorrow. I wouldn't mind dying after winning a game of *go*.'

There was no hint of sadness or grief in the snatches of conversation that Akiko overheard. Every elderly person present viewed the death dispassionately – they even envied the dead man. An old woman who had just emerged from the bathroom was bewildered by all the commotion.

'What's happened?' she asked.

'Mr Suzuki has just died.'

'But I thought he was playing *go* in the other room.'

122

'He was, but he had a stroke just as the game ended. By the time the ambulance arrived, he was already dead.'

'How old was he?'

'Ninety.'

'A man who's lived that long should have no regrets. He was lucky never to have known a day of illness.'

Akiko realized that it was time for her to go. She and the caretaker were the only young people at the Centre, and Akiko felt embarrassed about not having been of any assistance in the emergency. Up till now she believed that the centres for senior citizens were not governed by any set of regulations, but as she was putting on her shoes, she glanced up and saw posted on the wall a handwritten contract for all members. As Akiko read through it line by line, her eye was caught by one particular item.

'Membership in this Senior Citizens' Centre is open to all old people who are healthy in mind and body. Each member should do his best not to trouble other members.'

The words lingered in Akiko's mind as she walked out of the building and descended the concrete ramp. The man who had just died had been a perfect specimen of an old person sound in mind and body. But what about Shigezō? The doctor had given him a clean bill of health, but Akiko knew that his mental state did not meet the standards of the Centre. This realization plunged her into utter despair. With her own eyes, she had seen a ninety-year-old man play *go*. He had had many friends, had enjoyed various pleasures in life, and had not gone senile. All Shigezō had ever done was to complain and to indulge himself excessively. Never once had he become enthusiastic about a hobby. In other words, he had lived too long without finding any pleasure in life. What had he lived for all these years? He had cared for no one, not even his son or his wife. He had persecuted his daughter-in-law and had never shown his grandson any affection. Hadn't he become senile because he had worried endlessly about his delicate stomach? Now, every night, he cried out that a burglar had broken into the house and insisted that she call the police. Did this strange behaviour have any special significance? Why should Shigezō think that a burglar was breaking into the house when there was nothing of great value in it?

The snow that had fallen the previous night was thawing more quickly than Akiko had expected, and the centre of the road had turned to dirty slush. Though it had been warm during the day, the wind had grown cold while Akiko was visiting the Matsunoki Centre. Although she had left the house intending to stock up on groceries, all she had bought at the market was enough food for

123

dinner that night and for the next day's meals. What would Satoshi say when she reported how she had seen an old man die right before her eyes? Akiko was not sure whether she could describe what she had seen. Shigezō was five years short of turning ninety, and five years in his case would seem like an eternity. If the events of the previous night were to recur night after night, she would die of sheer exhaustion within a year or two. Akiko remembered hearing about an experiment with rats: one was fed well but not allowed to sleep, the other was allowed to sleep but given no food. The rat that did not get any sleep died immediately. Akiko was convinced that if the situation remained unchanged, she would die before Shigezō did.

The front gate had been left open. Akiko, who could not tolerate such carelessness, quickly walked up to the front door.

'Satoshi! You ought to be more careful, dear! Don't ever leave the gate open again,' she said in a loud voice.

There was no sign of Satoshi or Shigezō in the room. Feeling suddenly afraid, Akiko called out their names in turn. She looked upstairs, then checked the toilet downstairs. Next she ran across to the cottage, but the two were nowhere in sight.

Akiko set the shopping bag down on the floor. Not knowing what to do, she went outside, walked around the main house and the cottage and even peered under the two buildings. She checked the toilet in the cottage, then made her way back to the house and looked in the bathroom. Nothing seemed to be amiss. The gate had been left open, so they might have rushed out of the house. Perhaps Shigezō had had a stroke and Satoshi had summoned an ambulance.

In her mind's eye Akiko vividly saw the scene she had just witnessed at the Centre. The same thing could have happened here. If Shigezō had had a stroke, where could he have been taken? The body of that ninety-year-old man had been taken home, but Shigezō was not here. So he must have survived his attack. Had he been whisked away to a hospital? Surely the neighbours would have heard the siren of the ambulance. Just as Akiko was about to go over to the Kiharas, the telephone rang.

'Hello.'

'Mum, it's me. I've been trying to get in touch with you.'

'Where are you calling from? How is Grandpa?'

'We've been walking non-stop for over an hour. At this moment we're on Ōme Avenue. A few minutes ago we crossed the overpass at Ogikubo. You'll find us on your left as you head this way. *Please* come after us in a taxi.'

'Could you repeat the directions, dear?'

'Grandpa's walking straight ahead as fast as he can. He refuses to

124

turn back. Hurry, Mum. Be sure to bring some money with you. We're a little way beyond the Ogikubo overpass. You'll find us on your left.'

'Hold on a minute, Satoshi.'

'I can't, Mum. Grandpa's still walking. I've got to keep him in sight, so I'm going to hang up now. As I told you, we're on Ōme Avenue. Please come after us in a taxi. We'll be on your left.'

Satoshi hung up, leaving Akiko dumbfounded. But this was no time for her to stand there wondering. She grabbed her purse, ran out of the house and, moments later, found herself on Ōme Avenue. The main thoroughfare was heavy with rush-hour traffic. She realized that it would take her a while to hail a taxi. Getting increasingly agitated, she hurried in the direction of Ogikubo, turning back repeatedly in the hope that a taxi be cruising by. What would happen if Shigezō turned into a side street before she got there? Whenever she caught sight of a taxi, Akiko stopped, calling out loudly and waving frantically. But all the taxis were occupied and sped past her. She silently prayed that a patrol car would come along. A number of empty taxis were heading in the opposite direction, but she could not hail them from her side of the street. She seriously considered crossing over to the other side, but hesitated in case a taxi came along just as she had done so.

Eventually Akiko succeeded in hailing a taxi near the Suginami Ward Office.

'Where to?' asked the driver.

'Please keep driving in this direction. I'm looking for an old man walking along the left-hand side of the street. He ran away from home and he's somewhere beyond the overpass.'

The taxi driver said nothing as he noisily closed the automatic door and stepped on the accelerator. Akiko wondered whether he had understood her directions. How could he just remain silent after having been told that an old man had run away from home?

When the taxi crossed the overpass and headed for the crowded streets of Ogikubo, Akiko said: 'Would you please slow down a little?'

The driver either failed to hear her or pretended not to, for he maintained a sullen silence. Akiko glared resentfully at his thick shoulders. She realized that this was not the time to give him a piece of her mind, as it was imperative that she find Shigezō and Satoshi without delay. Looking out of the window on her left and scanning the people teeming on the streets, she grew alarmed. How would she ever be able to find Shigezō in this crowd?

125

'Please drive closer to the curb. My father-in-law should be somewhere around here. Please slow down.'

The driver remained silent and showed no sign of complying with her request. Akiko was seething with indignation, but she could not afford to look away from the window for even a second.

After they had left the bustling shopping district behind, Akiko noticed that there were fewer pedestrians and her uneasiness intensified. She was cruising along Ōme Avenue just as Satoshi had asked her to, but having never been in this part of Tokyo before, everything looked unfamiliar. She felt exceedingly uncomfortable whenever she asked the driver where they were and he failed to reply; moreover, her anger seemed to mount with each passing minute. She noted that the meter registered 420 yen and realized that the taxi had covered a greater distance than that between Umezato and Shinjuku.

'There he is! Please stop at the next corner. That's the man I've been looking for!'

Akiko was so excited at recognizing Shigezō, who was walking straight ahead, and Satoshi, who was running behind him, that she bounced up and down in the taxi and almost screamed at the driver. The taxi overtook Shigezō and screeched to a halt. Hardly able to wait for the door to open, Akiko tumbled out of the vehicle.

'Grandpa!' Akiko planted herself directly in front of Shigezō, assuming that he would stop as soon as she addressed him. Instead, he shoved her aside with such force that she fell to the ground. She realized that it would be no easy task to stop the old man.

'Grandpa! It's me,' she shouted, roughly grabbing hold of him. Shigezō struggled, then suddenly recognized his daughter-in-law and grew quiet. With an odd expression on his face, he stopped in his tracks and, apparently in a daze, gazed at Akiko. Then he looked across at his grandson.

'Grandpa, let's all go home together.'

They climbed into the taxi which was standing at the curb. Without saying a word, the driver turned round and headed back to Umezato. Akiko was amused by the man's determination not to speak to his passengers. Driving a taxi might be his job, but he ought at least to express a word of sympathy at a time like this, she thought. Shigezō had walked all the way from Kōenji. Was this not an astonishing feat? Akiko and Satoshi seated themselves in the back seat with Shigezō sandwiched between them and did not speak for some time. Satoshi was panting harder than Shigezō.

'What a distance you covered, Satoshi. On the phone, you said you were somewhere beyond the overpass, so I kept a lookout for you

126

after reaching Ogikubo. I was beginning to think that we'd driven right past you.'

'Boy, did we walk! I didn't know exactly where we were when I called you, but I really thought we were outside the city limits. You picked us up in Nerima Ward. I think I saw a sign saying Sekimachi. Is that right?'

The taxi driver did not reply, so Akiko quickly said: 'So that was Nerima Ward! I thought we were already in Tama. What a monstrous city Tokyo is! Oh, but I'm glad I found you. Whatever possessed Grandpa to run away from home?'

'He suddenly started yelling that there was a burglar in the house. He was near the entrance, shaking with fear. I tried to calm him down, but he was so terrified that I just left him there. A few moments later I heard a sound, and when I looked, he was putting on his shoes. The next thing I knew, he was running out of the house. I remembered what happened to Aunt Kyōko, so I made sure I had thirty yen in my pocket before I ran after him. I must have called you at least fifteen times. I was just about to dial emergency.'

'I'm terribly sorry, dear. An old man died while I was at the Centre, so I was late getting home.'

When the taxi turned right into a side road, Akiko leaned forward to give the driver more explicit directions on how to get to their home. The three of them got out of the taxi after Akiko paid the fare of over a thousand yen, and the taxi sped away, emitting a cloud of smoke.

'What a grouch!' said Satoshi angrily.

Akiko shared his disgust with the taxi driver. When that surly driver grows too old to drive a taxi, she said to herself, he'll become senile. These days, whenever Akiko wanted to spite someone who had offended her, she would predict for him a future as wretched as Shigezō's. The taxi driver was not 'healthy in mind and body': he would never qualify for membership of a senior citizens' group!

As they entered the house, she said, 'You must be hungry, Satoshi,' wanting to reward her son for his trouble. It was Shigezō who answered.

'Yes, I am. I'd like a snack.'

Satoshi keeled over, imitating the antics of a comedian he had seen on television. If a boy like Satoshi felt exhausted, Akiko could imagine how tired Shigezō must be after having covered such a distance. But he sat there unperturbed, as though nothing unusual had occurred. Surely he will sleep soundly tonight, thought Akiko as she lowered some frozen fish into a pot and lit the burner underneath it. She too felt utterly drained. She decided to prepare a

127

meat dish for herself and her son, without waiting for her husband's return. At the same time she wondered what the future had in store for the family. The floorboards seemed to shake under her feet as she reached out, took three vitamin pills from a bottle on the shelf and swallowed them with a glass of tap water.

12

It was a glorious Sunday, one the entire family should have enjoyed. Instead, from early morning onwards, everyone was glum and a stifling atmosphere pervaded the house. Nobutoshi had already finished reading the morning paper, but he could not settle down to either watching television or stretching out in some sunny spot. Although he had grown tired of listening to his wife repeat the same story over and over again, he knew that all hell would break loose if he dared to tell her so. This made him feel helplessly trapped. It was obvious that Satoshi shared his feelings. Maintaining a stony silence, he sat on the floor with his legs outstretched and his back against the chest of drawers. Satoshi was taller than his father and long-legged like other youths of his generation, who did not resemble in the least the typical Japanese of the past. He had a nervous habit of rocking his body to and fro, which made the altar on the chest above him shake almost imperceptibly. A square, box-like cover was fitted over the urn, to which a piece of damask cloth with an embossed pattern of gold thread on a white ground was glued. The cover was so large that it protruded precariously from the altar. Nobutoshi wondered how his mother could possibly rest in peace while his father, a pathetic wreck of his former self, remained alive.

As for Shigezō, he sat quietly on the veranda, his arms around his knees. He did not seem at all affected by the great distance he had walked along Ōme Avenue. Akiko had before her an old map of Tokyo, and her finger moved along a green line which marked the path Shigezō and Satoshi had taken. The map was on a scale of 1:24,000, so the line was only about twenty-three centimetres long, but it was clear that they had covered an extraordinary distance. Akiko pinpointed the exact spot where Shigezō had finally been stopped, at the junction of Ōme Avenue and Mejiro Highway, at Yanagizawa in Tanashi. Beyond Tanashi lay Higashikurume City and Higashimurayama City. It was really quite incredible.

129

'I agree with Kyōko that people in Tokyo are unfeeling! I must have looked desperate, but no one asked me what was the matter. And the taxi driver didn't even say a word, although he was well aware of the agony I was going through! As for Mrs Kadotani, all she did was laugh and say that the love affair was over. Since then, she hasn't asked once about Grandpa. I'm completely exhausted and even Satoshi was too tired to speak when we got home. I put Grandpa to bed without giving him a bath, but last night he woke up *four* times, each time screaming that a burglar had broken into the house. There was no way I could ignore him and go back to sleep. You didn't help me once, dear. Each time Grandpa got up, I had to get out of bed, show him that the doors were properly locked and check the closet and toilet with him. Then I made him go back to sleep and practically smothered him with the quilt. If this goes on night after night, I'll just die. Are you listening to me, dear?'

Akiko rambled on, waiting for Satoshi to suggest that they put Shigezō in a nursing home. But Satoshi, as if he had forgotten his promise, did not bring up the topic.

'Satoshi, I'd like you to take my place tonight and sleep downstairs,' said Akiko, now directing her anger at her son.

Satoshi was startled. Knitting his brows, he muttered: 'But Mum, I'm busy studying for my exams.'

'Oh? Then will you take my place when you've finished?'

'Do I have a choice?'

The college entrance examination, altogether different from what it had been before the war, now marked an important turning-point in a young man's life. Regaining her composure slightly, Akiko reminded herself not to upset her son unnecessarily at this crucial time. This left only her husband to appeal to.

'Please take my place tonight, dear. I'm not too steady on my feet after missing so much sleep. If this continues, it'll be the end of me. Try it for just one night. Then you'll know how agonizing it's been for me. Please take my place tonight, dear.'

'But I can't.'

'Why not?'

'Dad doesn't recognize me any more. Remember how he glared at me that night and called me a burglar?'

'Do you mean that I'll have to go on like this?'

Nobutoshi made no reply.

'This is the third time Grandpa has run away from home. The first time was the day your mother died. It was a good thing I ran into him on Itsukaichi Avenue! What a panic there would have been with Grandma dead and Grandpa lost. The second time was when Kyōko

130

was staying with us. And yesterday, I was able to go after Grandpa and Satoshi only because Satoshi had made sure he had thirty yen with him before he left. What if Grandpa should run away when there's no one at home? I don't know how we'd ever find him if he managed to get beyond Kitatama Ward.'

Nobutoshi still did not say anything. It was taking Satoshi such a long time to bring up the idea that Shigezō should be put into a nursing home that Akiko finally lost her temper.

'You probably think I should leave my job and stay at home. That's what you want, isn't it? But I don't just prepare tea at the office, you know. I have my own responsibilities. If I were to resign, my boss would be in a terrible fix. There are plenty of things at the office that only I know about. I simply can't leave and inconvenience everyone there.'

The wisest thing to do when a woman is having hysterics is to remain silent, thought Nobutoshi. The situation could easily get worse if he contradicted his wife, because she would then become completely distraught and would refuse to listen to reason. After letting her speak her piece, Nobutoshi said abruptly: 'I'll talk to a doctor.'

'The doctor who gave Grandpa a check-up said he was fine. He doesn't suffer from diarrhoea or even catch colds.'

'I was thinking of getting some tranquillizers.'

'You mean sleeping pills? I wonder if they'd work on him.'

'I'll ask the doctor.'

'But there's no surgery on Sundays.'

'I'll see one at the company clinic tomorrow.'

Shigezō, who had been as motionless as a clay figure until that moment, suddenly began to move his limbs in slow motion, getting unsteadily to his feet. Mesmerized, the Tachibanas watched him slowly stretch the upper part of his body and move his legs apart. Then he extended one of his elbows and bent forward, emitting a cry like that of some ominous bird.

Dumbfounded, his family watched him raise first one leg, then the other. Next, trembling, he raised and lowered his arms. It was not clear whether he was attacking or defending himself against an adversary. But his movements were very odd, as was the tone of his voice.

Satoshi turned to his mother and asked: 'Is Grandpa pretending he's some strange animal?'

'This is the first time I've seen him act like this,' Nobutoshi remarked, shaking his head. Was his father having hallucinations?

No longer able to look on in silence, Akiko grabbed the old man by his shoulders and cried: 'Grandpa, Grandpa! What's the matter?'

Shigezō fixed his eyes on his daughter-in-law.

'I'm doing callisthenics, Akiko.'

'Callisthenics?'

'Yes. A person has to get a little exercise.'

Nobutoshi, Akiko and Satoshi stared in amazement at the old man, who once again began to let out eerie cries and move his arms and legs in slow motion. To which period in his life had he reverted as he went through the exercises? Had he recalled from the depths of his memory that callisthenics were a good substitute for regular exercise? His movements were more bizarre than any rite performed by primitive man, and his family did not find them amusing.

'It's disgusting! How can a man that wretched want to go on living?'

The expression on Satoshi's face clearly indicated that he could not bear to watch Shigezō a moment longer. He rose and said to his parents: 'Dad, Mum. Please don't live this long!'

Then he ran up the stairs. His parents were too choked with emotion at these words even to look at each other. Meanwhile, Shigezō continued his callisthenics, uttering cries like those of an animal in its death throes.

13

When Nobutoshi described the situation at home, the doctor at the clinic immediately wrote out a prescription for the tranquillizers he had requested. Nobutoshi then asked if senility was an illness, to which the doctor replied: 'You must be referring to senile dementia.'

'I didn't know there was such a term. Is an old man who has hallucinations suffering from a kind of mental derangement?'

'What you've described just now seems to be a case of senile melancholia. As long as he doesn't get violent, you can't say he's ill. It's an illness of civilization very much like tooth decay.'

The doctor warned Nobutoshi to watch the dose he gave Shigezō, as the tranquillizer would tax his heart. He also advised him to try not using it for a couple of days if Shigezō began to show some improvement.

Nobutoshi returned home early that day and gave his father some of the drug just before going to bed. Shigezō swallowed the tranquillizer without protest. Nobutoshi, who was assisting his wife, was suddenly assailed by a foul odour, smelling like poison gas, which was coming from Shigezō's mouth. When he complained about it, Akiko said that she had been aware of it for some time.

'I think it comes from his dentures, because I haven't seen him clean them once. I can't bear the thought of touching them, so I've left them alone. Come to think of it, though, it's terribly unhygienic to leave them like that.'

Akiko gathered her courage, thrust her hand into her father-in-law's mouth and extracted the dentures. She was filled with a perverse but pleasurable sensation in doing so in her husband's presence.

Both Akiko and Nobutoshi screamed when a powerful stench, stronger than that of faeces, suddenly filled the room. It made them think of the putrefying odour of Dream Island, the gargantuan

133

garbage dump for the sprawling metropolis. Barely able to stop herself vomiting, Akiko threw the filthy dentures into the kitchen sink and turned on the water. As she vigorously scrubbed them clean with a brush, she recalled how nauseous she had felt some months earlier when she had come across the box of false teeth. Some of the food particles adhering to the dentures probably dated from that time.

The space under Shigezō's nose shrivelled to half its length, and his puckered lips resembled the opening of a money pouch. Furious, he flailed his arms and made strange noises, but without his teeth he could not pronounce his words clearly.

'Please rinse your mouth out, Grandpa.'

Akiko was completely horrified. Nobutoshi, who was equally appalled, was in such a dazed state that he was no help at all. Akiko grabbed Shigezō and made him rinse out his mouth with cold tea, reminding herself to get some of the special mouthwash she had seen in a television commercial. When Shigezō finished rinsing his mouth, Akiko had to struggle to get his dentures back into place, for Shigezō refused to remain still. Succeeding at last, she could make out what Shigezō was saying.

'You're so mean, Akiko! How could you pull my teeth out?'

'But Grandpa, you have to wash your dentures every day. They smell terrible! If you don't want me to wash them for you, you'll have to wash them yourself.'

'But they're not dentures. They're my teeth.'

'Then how was I able to take them out?'

'That's why I said they can't be removed.'

Like so many times before, Akiko felt confused; she never knew to what extent Shigezō comprehended what was going on around him. She shrugged and tucked him up in bed.

'He's suffering from what the medical profession calls senile dementia,' Nobutoshi explained.

'Senile dementia? Grandpa certainly has that!'

'The doctor said that it's the same kind of illness as tooth decay.'

'How is that?'

'According to the doctor, both senile dementia and tooth decay are diseases of civilization.'

'Tooth decay, too? I wonder why?'

'He said that there was no tooth decay before man began to cook his food. Peking Man probably had no cavities. I don't know about Egytian mummies, though.'

'But isn't that because man didn't live long enough for his teeth to decay? I think the usual lifespan then was about fifty years.'

'But don't you remember that Satoshi already had cavities when he was in kindergarten?'

'Yes, that's right! I didn't have a single cavity until I was at Girls' School. Satoshi must have inherited bad teeth from you.'

How quickly a woman changes the subject, thought Nobutoshi, feeling even more gloomy. In the meantime, Akiko mulled over their conversation. Suddenly, with a surprised look on her face, she asked: 'Is senility an illness of civilization?'

'Yes. It's also referred to as senile melancholia. But the doctor said it isn't exactly an illness.'

'Why is it considered civilized? Does it have something to do with the progress made by civilization and the average lifespan being longer?'

'I wonder.'

'Now that you mention it, there aren't any dotards in old Japanese legends. The old man makes his way up the mountain to gather firewood, and the old woman goes to the river-bank to do the laundry.'

'The old man and old woman were probably our age.'

'What an unpleasant thought! But you have a point there. We Japanese have always considered it disgraceful for a couple in their forties to have a child. Maybe that's why the folk tale has the baby popping out of a peach instead.'

Akiko laughed merrily as she presented her views on the peach-boy legend, but Nobutoshi still felt depressed. It had terrified him to hear the naked truth from his son's lips, and made him realize that he had to be fully prepared for old age.

Nobutoshi now picked out every article concerning the elderly in the weekly magazines he read while commuting to and from work. In an article on the remote jungles of New Guinea, his eyes were drawn to a passage describing how the Papuans would hang the aged from trees. 'Look at the fruit,' they'd shout, before cutting them down and slaughtering them. He also read about the Hottentots, who burned their disabled elderly alive. All these years he had merely skimmed through articles that reported how the elderly population of Japan was rapidly increasing, but now the words all but jumped at him off the page. What he found intolerable was the fact that in his mind he did not associate the word 'elderly' exclusively with his father. Twenty years had slipped by all too quickly since the end of World War II, and twenty years hence Nobutoshi himself would be counted among the elderly.

Nobutoshi tried hard to be philosophical about growing old, which was, after all, the fate of all living things. There is a time for green leaves to grow luxuriantly and for flowers to bloom. He had a son. And he himself would in all likelihood attain a comfortable position in society. After bearing fruit, a plant withers and decays, and so it was perfectly natural for a man to grow old. One might even look forward to leading a life of refined austerity in one's old age. The decaying process that preceded death was perfectly natural, and death was something one had to succumb to in time. But Nobutoshi could not bear the thought of ending his life like the last sickly leaf clinging to a branch of a bare tree or an over-ripe persimmon on a branch beyond one's reach, its unsightly form fully visible as it rotted away. He fervently hoped he would fall to the ground and die bravely when he grew old. Was his father like a sick leaf? Or an over-ripe persimmon? Nobutoshi could not find the right image. Was senility really an illness of civilization? Nobutoshi prayed that tooth decay would be the only illness with which he would be afflicted. Long after retiring for the night, he tossed and turned in bed. If he kept thinking such morbid thoughts, his mental health would surely suffer. Was not the mere fact that he couldn't leave the subject alone an indication that he, too, was suffering from senile melancholia? By now Nobutoshi was utterly disgusted with himself. Why hadn't he had some sleeping-pills prescribed for his own use?

Akiko had not had enough sleep during the last few days. Drained of energy, she fell into a deep, dreamless sleep, untroubled by any philosophical considerations. Hugging her pillow, she slept soundly and woke up the following morning feeling thoroughly rested. There was a light on in the room. She had left it on all night long, she remembered. Day had already dawned. When she glanced at her wristwatch, she was unable to make out the time. Creeping out of bed, she looked at the clock on the cupboard. It was six o'clock.

Akiko switched off the light and looked down at her father-in-law, who lay in bed blinking up at the ceiling.

'Good morning, Grandpa. Did you sleep well?' Akiko asked cheerfully.

'Yes.'

'You didn't get up at all last night.'

'No, I didn't.'

The medicine had worked! Akiko was so elated that she felt like cheering. Why hadn't she thought of tranquillizers sooner? Miracle of miracles, it had worked! She no longer had to be tormented night after night because of Shigezō's hallucinations. How marvellous medical science was! Diseases of civilization had lost their terror.

'All right, Grandpa, time to get up.'

136

'Akiko . . .'

'What is it?'

'My backside feels funny.'

'Oh?'

Shigezō had wet his bed. In a state of agitation, Akiko flipped over the covers, removed his underwear and got him into clean clothes. Then she folded away the bedding. In the meantime, Satoshi came downstairs and put two slices of bread into the toaster. After washing his face, he had his milk and toast and hurried out of the house.

Presently, Nobutoshi, his face swollen, came down the stairs.

'How was Dad last night?' he asked. Akiko replied morosely that he had slept through the night.

'That's great!' he exclaimed. But why wasn't Akiko bubbling over with joy? He had no time to ask, for he had to rush off to work.

Akiko was too shocked to tell Nobutoshi or Satoshi that Shigezō had wet his bed. Had the drug been so strong he could not get up to empty his bladder? Perhaps his incontinence was an indication that he had become even more senile. Grateful though she was that her sleep had been undisturbed, she knew that certain drugs produced harmful side-effects. She herself had at one time taken sleeping-pills, but she had either managed to go to the toilet or had waited until morning to empty her bladder. The thought that Shigezō's bed-wetting might be a sign of further deterioration, aggravated by the medicine, destroyed Akiko's joy in having had a full night's sleep.

Akiko prepared a box lunch for her father-in-law and accompanied him to the Matsunoki Centre. Then she made her way to the law office, arriving an hour late. Her colleagues were sympathetic when she explained why she was late.

Akiko filed away various documents, then sat down at the typewriter and began to bang away at the keys. As she typed out a very ordinary document that was to be presented in court, she rubbed her eyes with the back of her hand and brought her face up close to the handwritten copy, trying to make out the individual words. Again and again she blinked her eyes. Finally she looked at the page she had taken great pains to type and was appalled. Each column of characters had a white line running vertically through its centre. All she could see apart from the vertical lines were blurred outlines.

The two attorneys went out to attend a court session, leaving Akiko and the young secretary behind to look after the office. Akiko got up, took the morning paper from the desk of one of the lawyers and tried to read it. All she could make out were the headlines. The photograph of the Prime Minister was very clear, but when she tried to read the article accompanying it, she could only guess at what each character stood for.

'This is terrible! I can't read any more!' cried Akiko in dismay. 'Come to think of it, I couldn't see the time on my wristwatch this morning. What's wrong with my eyes?'

The girl looked at Akiko. 'Your eyes look all right to me. You're just tired, that's all.'

'But last night I slept more soundly than I have for months. I had no trouble typing yesterday. All these years I've been smug about having perfect vision in both eyes, and now I can't read. This is awful!' Akiko wailed, so upset that it seemed the world was growing dark before her eyes.

For a while the telephone rang constantly and Akiko was kept busy answering it, but all the while she was beside herself with anxiety because she believed she was going blind.

Later that afternoon, she realized she couldn't possibly work efficiently until she'd had her eyes checked. *If I knew the cause of the eye trouble, I might be able to calm down a bit,* she thought.

'I should see an ophthalmic surgeon, but I'm sure an optician can tell me what's wrong. I'll go and see one right away. Perhaps I've become long-sighted,' she said as she hurried out of the office.

But where was she to go? Having never been to an optician before, she was at a loss what to do. Then she remembered that every large department store had an optical department. Surely she could have her eyes tested there? Having decided which department store to go to, Akiko quickened her pace. Cold gusts of wind blew fiercely over the heads of the crowd pushing its way between the tall buildings. Akiko was dressed in a fur-lined overcoat she had bought three years earlier, and a pair of thick trousers.

Although the afternoon sun was shining, the wind was bitterly cold on her face. As she entered the department store, Akiko noted with surprise a sign suspended from the ceiling which announced in large letters, 'Spring Sale'. Why were women's magazines and department stores always two months ahead of the calendar? How could there be a spring sale when there wasn't a hint of spring outside? Akiko thought of Shigezō and reminded herself that the bleakness of winter would be with her family for a long time to come. With this dismal thought in mind, she went up to the information desk.

'Excuse me. Where can I find diapers and diaper covers for the elderly?'

'You'll find them in the Infants' Wear Department on your right as you go up those stairs,' replied a young beauty in a smart uniform and with a hat perched jauntily on her head.

Full of resentment, Akiko set off in the direction pointed out to her. She was almost certain that the girl had had cosmetic surgery done on her nose.

A sweet smell of milk seemed to issue from the Infants' Wear Department. Akiko looked around her. It was highly unlikely that she would find the nappies she was looking for in a place like this. The colourful assortment of infants' wear reminded Akiko of seaside rock. After wandering aimlessly about the department, she finally located the diaper covers for infants. Had the girl at the information desk heard only part of her enquiry? Or perhaps she had coolly and politely pretended not to hear. At the thought of this second possibility, Akiko lost her temper. Now she was positive that the girl had had a nose-job!

'Excuse me. Where can I find diapers for the elderly?'

'I'm sorry. This is the Infants' Wear Department.'

'I know that!' said Akiko sharply. 'That's why I'm asking you where I might find them. Doesn't this store sell diaper covers for old people? The girl at the information desk told me I'd find them up here.'

Akiko was in a defiant mood. Flustered, the sales clerk lapsed into silence, then disappeared into a back room. A moment later a young man, who seemed to be in charge of the department, emerged. He listened politely to Akiko's request, then replied, 'I believe you'll find them in the Medical Supplies Department over there.'

Why hadn't she realized that it was not only the elderly who had to wear diapers? I ought to have worded my enquiry more precisely, she thought as she headed for the pharmaceutical department where an assortment of vitamin pills were on display. Only one type of vinyl diaper cover for adults was available, but there were two kinds of diapers: disposable and cloth. Since they were far more expensive than she had imagined, she hesitated before deciding to purchase some disposable ones. Because there was a possibility of Shigezō soiling his clothes, she felt that she had to stock up. Akiko also purchased a bedpan. As she walked away carrying a large parcel in her arms, she wondered whether her father-in-law would wet his bed every night from now on. Perhaps he had already had an accident at the Centre and had made things difficult for the caretaker? Every morning, before taking him there, she would have to make sure that he had on a clean nappy. Was she breaking the regulations of the Centre by taking Shigezō there? They stated in black and white that only old people sound in mind and body were welcome there. Assailed by feelings of guilt, Akiko felt truly wretched.

Once outside, she stopped abruptly in the middle of the crossing, her eyes fixed on the green light. What in the world was she doing? It was a good thing she had made all her purchases, but hadn't she originally set out for the department store to have her eyes examined? How could she have forgotten? The light turned red, and angry drivers tooted their horns at her. Akiko remained motionless in the middle of the busy Ginza thoroughfare, her mind a total blank as she dodged the cars that sped by. Why had she bought the diapers instead of having her eyes checked?

She went back to the information desk and this time asked where the optical department was. The girl with the straight nose answered mechanically that it was located on the sixth floor and suggested that Akiko take the lift. The girl clearly did not recognize her as the customer who had asked about diapers. Feeling somewhat disappointed, Akiko went up to the sixth floor. The colourful paper-wrapped parcel containing the diapers and the bedpan rustled against her breast as she emerged from the lift. When Akiko asked for an eye test, a middle-aged optician took her into a small room. She seated herself in what looked like a dentist's chair and described the trouble she was having with her eyes. Being so small, her feet did not reach the footrest.

The last time Akiko had had an eye test was shortly after graduating from Girls' School before the war. On that occasion, first one eye and then the other had been covered and examined for short-sightedness. Medical science had made tremendous progress since then. The optician used two instruments resembling microscopes, then asked her to peer through what looked like a telescope. She was startled to see his eye at the other end. She was then asked to read the characters on an eye-chart on the opposite wall. Not a single character was split in half by a vertical line when Akiko read with just one eye. The room was darkened, and Akiko followed the movement of a beam of light through a special instrument. Next, the optician carefully examined her eyes while asking her which of two lights, each speckled with red and green dots, appeared darker.

'I've become long-sighted, haven't I?'

'Please be patient for a few minutes.'

Akiko refrained from asking any further question while the optician fitted her with steel-rimmed frames and carefully selected a pair of lenses which he snapped into place. Akiko's vision suddenly grew blurred.

'Everything's blurred now.'

'How about these?'

'I can see very clearly. That's *re*, isn't it?'

'Now your vision is better than normal.'

'Is that bad?'

'Yes, because your eyes will tire easily.'

For the next twenty minutes one pair of lenses after another was snapped into place.

'You don't seem to need lenses for either long- or short-sightedness,' he murmured.

Finally, he snapped two lenses into place, left the examination room and returned a minute later with a newspaper.

'Please read this for fifteen minutes.'

Akiko glanced at her watch to check the time, then proceeded to read the home affairs section of the previous day's newspaper. There were crime reports and one about a fire started by a madman. She read quickly through the two pages and was about to turn over when she noticed in one corner a two-line heading: 'Old Man Commits Suicide'. According to the article, a lonely old man on welfare, despairing about the future, had hanged himself. His body had been discovered by a social worker three days later. The seventy-eight-year-old man, a resident of Katsushika Ward, had been paralysed from the waist down. Akiko wondered if he had had to wear diapers. He could not have been senile if he hanged himself. No doubt he had been unable to endure the wretchedness of old age. Who was the more fortunate, Shigezō or the suicide? Shigezō did not know what it was like to be lonely and was totally unaware of how pathetic he was. Suicide would never enter his mind.

'How do your eyes feel?'

Akiko, who had been lost in thought, came back to reality. She glanced at her watch and saw that it was a quarter past the hour. Why had she been unable to read the time on her watch that morning?

'I had no trouble reading the paper.'

'Well then, I'll prescribe these lenses for you. What kind of frames would you like?'

The news that she needed glasses made Akiko feel that she had come to a turning-point in her life. Distracted, she selected her frames.

'Have I become long-sighted?'

'Oh no. You have what medical experts call exotropia.'

'Exotropia?'

'Yes. Your eyes have a tendency to diverge outwards, so I'm prescribing prism-powered lenses for you.'

'I wasn't aware of it.'

'It isn't that serious. Your work must require you to use your eyes a great deal. People have to use the muscles at the outer corners of their eyes whenever they read.'

'Do you mean that up to now I've been able to focus my vision using my own muscles and that I've suddenly lost the ability to do so?'

'I assure you that your eyes won't tire as easily from now on. The prism-powered lenses will help them focus on whatever you're reading.'

'Am I growing old?' asked Akiko in a loud voice.

The optician's tone became even more polite. She certainly was not growing old, he reassured her, for she had not become long-sighted. He told her that her glasses would be ready in a week. After paying in advance, Akiko felt utterly depressed. How terrible to have to wear glasses! She recalled a former classmate who was so short-sighted she could not distinguish one friend from another, but who had stubbornly refused to wear glasses until she was married. Some women, even after discovering that they needed spectacles, stoically went without them for as long as twenty years. Akiko felt as if an earthquake had struck without warning. Although the optician had emphatically stated that she was not long-sighted, there was no doubt in her mind that the reason she had to have prism-powered lenses was that she was growing old. She had to face the terrible truth.

Akiko had been able to sleep soundly the night before because Shigezō had not woken up in the middle of the night. How ironic it was that her fatigue should affect her after a good night's rest! One misfortune seemed to follow another. Although Shigezō was able to sleep undisturbed with the aid of tranquillizers, Akiko could no longer read without the aid of glasses. Reluctantly she accepted the fact that she was growing old. This was far more painful than the anguish of a vain woman who had to decide whether or not to wear glasses, and it made her recall how Satoshi had begged his parents not to live too long. When she stepped out of the lift on the first floor, she suddenly remembered that cod-liver oil worked wonders when one was suffering from over-tiredness; she therefore returned to the pharmaceutical department to buy some pills containing vitamins A and D. There she saw a middle-aged woman examining closely a diaper cover like the one she herself had purchased. If Akiko had not known what it was to be used for, she would never have noticed the woman. Akiko studied her for some time, her heart overflowing with compassion. The woman probably had an elderly relation to look after, perhaps her own father or her father-in-law. Fully aware of the

142

misery this stranger was going through, Akiko hurried away from the sales counter blinded by tears.

Akiko had some curry in a restaurant in a back street in the Ginza before returning to the office, where she found the two lawyers seated at their desks. She quickly explained why she had been away from the office and apologized for her absence. The lawyers, both of whom wore glasses, expressed their deep concern and plied her with questions.

'Is it what they call exophoria?'

'I believe it's called wall-eye in English.'

'Is eye trouble a sign of ageing?'

'I think it is. My eyes get so tired I've stopped reading books at night. I go to sleep as soon as I've had a nightcap. Maybe I should have *my* eyes examined.'

'I'm sure smog is harmful to the eyes.'

'Well, it can't do them any good.'

'Did you say that a person eventually loses the ability to bring his eyes together? I've heard of something called myasthenia.'

'Oh, I know what that is,' said the young secretary who had been listening in silence. 'A person with myasthenia can't raise his eyelids. My grandmother has that. Growing old is terribly sad, isn't it?'

Full of the vitality of youth, the girl laughed merrily. The three others in the room were rendered speechless by her insensitivity.

How tragic it is to grow old, thought Akiko. The young secretary's laughter sounded so cruel. She had probably never experienced a lapse in memory, and if she felt exhausted, all she needed was a good night's rest. She was too young even to imagine that her muscles would grow weak one day! When Akiko was young, she had not been considerate of the elderly, either. Twenty years earlier, she too had laughed merrily at life. Since she had been blessed with a cheerful disposition, people found it difficult to believe that she had been brought up by a single parent. But of late there was nothing amusing in her life. How appropriate it was to refer to middle age as the twilight years!

It had grown completely dark by the time Akiko arrived home. Her son, who had earlier accompanied his grandfather home from the Centre, was there to greet her.

'Grandpa's mind seems to be pretty clear today, Mum. I think it did him good to sleep well,' he said before disappearing upstairs.

'Welcome home, Akiko,' said Shigezō, his face expressionless.

Akiko returned his greeting, then, remembering what had occurred that morning, walked up to him and felt his crotch to see if

143

he had wet his pants. He was dry, probably having gone to the toilet by himself at the centre.

'Don't do that, Akiko!' cried Shigezō.

Akiko blushed. Had she been a younger woman, she would have burst out laughing.

14

One misfortune had followed another since the death of Akiko's mother-in-law. But when buds began to form on the branches of the sweet-smelling daphne in their garden, Satoshi took the nationwide trial college entrance examination sponsored annually by a publisher of educational books and got very good marks. Spring had suddenly come even to the Tachibana household. Now that they had some idea of his ability, Nobutoshi and Akiko breathed a sigh of relief. Satoshi still had over a year to study for the actual examination, so his family was delighted that he had done so well in the trial. If her son had done poorly Akiko would have been haunted by feelings of guilt, for she still made him collect his grandfather from the Centre on his way home from school. But he had done well. Akiko had been told that the best way to bring up children was to allow them to be independent, and she genuinely believed that Satoshi, though an only child, was trying hard to excel and make his own way in life because she worked full-time. It was sad that his grandmother was no longer with them, for she had taken Akiko's place at home and had lavished affection on her grandson when he was little. Akiko could just imagine how delighted she would have been at his success. As for Shigezō, he did not comprehend what had happened enough to take part in the rejoicing. In her excitement, Akiko had all but shouted in his ear that Satoshi had passed the examination with flying colours and that he would be enrolling in college the following year, but, much to her disappointment, he had hardly responded.

Ever since he had begun taking the tranquillizers, Shigezō no longer woke at night, and he seemed to be in complete control of his faculties during the day. Now, instead of getting up during the night to relieve himself, Shigezō wet his diaper every third night. One of Akiko's additional chores was to see that he had on a fresh nappy before she put him to bed every night. She had taken to washing his

145

dentures for him every day, so she gradually got used to this task too. Above all, Akiko was relieved that Shigezō slept soundly and no longer raved like a lunatic in the middle of the night. Worried that the tranquillizer might affect his heart, she put him to bed without giving him any on Saturday night. Though he fell asleep through force of habit, he behaved strangely on Sunday, showing severe symptoms of senile melancholia, such as cringing in a corner of the room and trying to crawl under the stairs. Akiko therefore gave him another dose of tranquillizer on Sunday night.

In front of the Senior Citizens' Centre was a mansion with cherry trees growing in its garden and Akiko took great pleasure in gazing at the blossom each time she accompanied Shigezō to the Centre. All too soon, however, the petals scattered like snowflakes in a snowstorm, and the entire neighbourhood was fragrant with the breezes of early summer as red leaves sprouted and eventually turned into a profusion of green. Despite its lush greenery, the district was notorious for its smog. Still refusing to accept the real reason for having to wear glasses, Akiko blamed her eye trouble on the smog. Although the true nature of photochemical smog was still not known, in Akiko's opinion, it was a demonic product of modern science and served as a symbol for a variety of illnesses.

Thanks to the tranquillizer, Shigezō's senile melancholia was not so severe, and because of her prism-powered lenses, Akiko's vision had been corrected. At first, she wore her glasses only when typing. With them on, she felt like the ballerina who wore red shoes, and once she took up a novel, she could not put it down until she had read it all. Though at first she had hated the very thought of glasses, she now wished that she had started wearing them sooner. All along she had blamed her headaches on her lack of sleep; now after wearing her glasses for a time, she was no longer distressed by nagging headaches and she became her cheerful self again.

In the past, the Tachibanas had gone off on a trip during the Golden Week.* After Satoshi had begun to study for his entrance examination three years ago, the trips had been discontinued. They had been looking forward to a trip to Hokkaido after Satoshi passed his examination, but while they had Shigezō to look after, no one in the family felt like discussing such an excursion. Giving the excuse that he needed a good rest, Nobutoshi spent the entire week at home. During the week, he came down with a bad cold.

'I'll prepare something that'll work wonders for your cold, dear.'

In the kitchen, Akiko scrubbed clean then grated some uncooked

*April 29 to May 5.

burdock which gave off a powerful smell. She mixed in some soya-bean paste and poured a little boiling water over the mixture, thus preparing what looked like soup for her husband.

'What in the world is this?'

'It's a cold remedy. Pretend you're under a magic spell and drink it.'

The soya-bean paste had helped to get rid of the strong smell. Shaking his head all the while, Nobutoshi sipped the brew, and from time to time threw a suspicious glance at his wife.

'I grated some burdock and was careful not to boil the soya-bean paste. It's good, isn't it?'

Nobutoshi was obviously impressed.

'I suppose it'll work.'

'Did you know about burdock? I read somewhere that chives, garlic and burdock aren't served in convents. They're probably regarded as aphrodisiacs.'

'You pick up the strangest things! Did you read that in some cheap magazine?'

'No. It's guaranteed to work.'

Since Akiko could not bring herself to say that she had been told about the remedy at the Centre, she avoided the truth. When she looked down at her fingertips, she saw that her nails had turned black from the burdock. What a frightening colour, she thought. She tried to wash the stain off with soap and water, then applied hand cream lavishly, wondering if dry skin was yet another sign of ageing. When she was young, all she had to do after soaking her hands in water was to wipe them dry and her fingers felt soft. Akiko suddenly wondered about the state of her father-in-law's fingernails and toenails. She had not cut them for him for the past six months.

Akiko felt that it would be good to do Shigezō's nails in her husband's presence, so she went to fetch the nail-clippers and sat down in front of her father-in-law.

'Let me trim your nails for you, Grandpa.'

Having rested during the week-long vacation, Akiko was able to speak gently to him. Shigezō silently held out his hands.

The romantic picture of a kind and gentle woman trimming her father-in-law's nails was completely dispelled the moment Akiko caught sight of Shigezō's fingernails.

'Come and look at this, dear.'

Almost all his nails were damaged, with cracks, resembling tiny bamboo whisks, running along their length. Akiko was surprised that they were not longer. His nails and fingers were hard and dry, and his chapped hands felt rough. Akiko tried in vain to trim the fingernails with the clippers; the only way she could cut them, she realized, was immediately after he had taken a bath. She went to fetch her night cream from the bathroom and rubbed some of it into Shigezō's fingertips. They reminded her of the wooden bucket she had used during the war. As kitchenware these days was made of plastic, there was nothing now that remotely resembled the old-fashioned wooden bucket with hoops fitted loosely around it. The bucket she remembered using had been badly stained and had had a cracked rim very much like her father-in-law's nails. Akiko wondered if signs of ageing appear first at farthest extremities of the body. While briskly massaging her night cream into Shigezō's fingertips, she noticed that her husband had disappeared upstairs, probably unable to stand the sight of the wretched old man a moment longer. Shigezō, however, was completely oblivious to what Akiko was doing. With his eyes half-closed, he looked as if his soul were wandering aimlessly between dream and reality.

Akiko dreamed that night, something she had not done for a long time. In her dream she was grating burdock; then, together with her husband, she sipped the cold remedy. What an unpleasant dream! Suddenly she woke up, a heavy weight pressing down on her body. Her first thought was that Nobutoshi had been aroused by the aphrodisiac, but, to her horror, it was her father-in-law.

'Akiko, Akiko,' cried Shigezō as he straddled her. Akiko twisted her body and slipped from under him.

'What is it, Grandpa? Is anything the matter? Whatever are you doing in the middle of the night!' she demanded, so exasperated she could not help shouting at her father-in-law.

'There's a burglar in the house. He's right in this room, Akiko. Let's get away from here!' urged Shigezō, trembling with fear.

'Nonsense. Why would a burglar take the trouble to break into a house like this? You must have been dreaming.'

'No, I wasn't. I saw him with my own eyes and splashed some water on him before I ran away.'

'Some water?'

At the mention of water, Akiko pushed Shigezō down on the bedding and felt his diaper. Just as she suspected, it was wet.

'If you wanted to go, Grandpa, why didn't you wake me up? Your diaper's soaking wet! That's why you're not allowed to drink any water before going to bed,' said Akiko while changing his diaper.

By now Akiko was wide awake. She had given Shigezō a tranquillizer at bedtime, but it no longer worked! He had begun taking it only a little over two months ago. Akiko was fully aware of the danger of gradually increasing a dose of sleeping-pills and she wondered if this was also the case with tranquillizers prescribed for the elderly. Though Akiko tried to reason with Shigezō, he stuck stubbornly to his story about the burglar. He grabbed Akiko violently by the arm and begged her to run away with him. Finding such madness unbearable, she told him off in a loud voice and made him get back into his bedding. But Shigezō refused to go back to sleep. Moments later he began to complain that he was hungry, so Akiko had to give him some bread to keep him quiet. Shigezō sat up in bed and munched away. Unable to bear this wretched sight any longer, Akiko went upstairs and roused her husband.

'Grandpa's awake, dear. It looks like the tranquillizer doesn't work any more. What should I do?'

'For God's sake, let me sleep!' Nobutoshi turned over in bed. Then, in desperation, he cried out, 'Kill him!'

'How can you say such a thing? Why, if I did that, I'd be called a hired assassin.' After working for a law firm all these years, the words slipped easily from Akiko's lips. She was furious at her husband for putting all the responsibilities on her shoulders.

'If you want to see him dead, you do the killing. You'll be guilty of patricide, but I'll keep my mouth shut. As for me, I absolutely refuse to take part in such a terrible crime. Do your own work!'

Whatever am I saying? thought Akiko, shocked at herself once she had recovered her senses.

'Please listen to me, dear. Do you think it'll be all right to double the dose? Ask the doctor at the clinic what a fatal dose would be. Grandpa's wet his diaper every night for the past few days. This time it was dripping wet. He complained about being hungry, and right now he's munching some bread. I'm afraid there won't be enough left for breakfast tomorrow morning.'

Akiko's voice gradually grew softer. Nobutoshi, breathing peacefully, pretended that he was being lulled to sleep by a lullaby. Resigned to her unhappy fate, Akiko went downstairs and found Shigezō fast asleep.

The next night Akiko was woken late at night by a loud noise. When she opened her eyes, she saw that her father-in-law had taken down the funerary urn containing the remains of his dead wife and had removed its cover. Seeing that he had a fistful of his wife's bones in each hand, Akiko screamed hysterically and knocked the bones out of his hands. She raced upstairs and cried: 'Wake up, dear! Something terrible has happened! Please get up.'

Nobutoshi, roused by his wife's shrill voice, was startled to see her holding the urn. 'What's happened?'

Akiko was trembling so violently that her teeth chattered. The eerie scene she had just witnessed was like something from a painting depicting hell. Akiko refused to go back downstairs.

'I tell you I can't take any more of this. Last night he climbed on top of me, and now this. He's become impossible again, now that the tranquillizer no longer works. Why didn't you ask at the clinic if it would be all right to increase the dosage?'

'I had one meeting after the other. I didn't even have time to see my dentist.'

'If that's your attitude, I don't care any more. I simply refuse to spend another night with your father. I feel so sorry for Grandma! It's cruel of him to torment her even when she's dead!'

'I wonder what possessed him to take down the urn?'

'Well, it looks as if he gnawed the bones.'

'Oh?' Nobutoshi blanched but said nothing more. Then he remarked casually: 'We'll just have to buy a burial plot for the family.'

To Akiko's disappointment, this was all her husband would say. But she realized that she could not leave things as they were. The night before, Shigezō had gone back to sleep after satisfying his hunger. At this moment, Akiko could not go downstairs and face her father-in-law again, so she asked her husband to give him a snack. Seeing the determined expression on his wife's face, Nobutoshi reluctantly made his way down the stairs to see what his father was doing. A few moments later, he shouted in a panic: 'Akiko. Come down! Father isn't here and the front door's open.'

Akiko ran down the stairs. Shigezō was nowhere in sight. She dashed out of the house and went round to the cottage, but the rain shutters were tightly closed and there was nothing to indicate that Shigezō had forced his way inside. Had he gone off in the direction of Ōme Avenue again? The same possibility had apparently occurred to Nobutoshi, for though he was wearing pyjamas, he slipped on a pair of sandals and ran out of the house.

'Satoshi!' Akiko shouted. 'Please get up, dear. Grandpa's run away again.' Running up the stairs, she roused her son, then changed out of her night clothes. No longer worried about whether Satoshi would get into college, she had no hesitation in waking him up in the middle of the night.

'All right, Mum. I'll follow the route he took last time. As soon as I find him I'll phone home, so wait for my call,' said Satoshi, confident that he would find his grandfather. Then he pedalled off on his bicycle.

Thirty minutes later Nobutoshi returned home out of breath and reported that he had searched the immediate area but had failed to find Shigezō. Akiko told him that Satoshi had gone out after Shigezō.

'Really?' replied Nobutoshi, impressed.

'I hope Satoshi finds Grandpa safe and sound. This is the first time he's run away with no one following him.'

'He's so old he can't possibly get very far.'

What an irresponsible thing to say, thought Akiko, her anger mounting. Shigezō moved sluggishly at home, but, once outdoors, he was capable of charging ahead like a wild boar. Had Nobutoshi fogotten his own sister's harrowing experience and Akiko's account of how she and Satoshi had stopped Shigezō on the outskirts of Nerima? Had all this gone in one ear and out the other?

'Besides, Satoshi's gone after him on his bicycle, hasn't he?'

Nobutoshi turned away, intending to go back upstairs, whereupon Akiko cried out in a shrill voice: 'You're not going back to bed, are you?'

'Of course I am. I have a busy day tomorrow.' Before Akiko could say another word, he made his way upstairs and went back to bed.

Akiko was seething with rage, but she exercised every ounce of self-control she possessed and remained immobile. As the wife of a company employee, she reminded herself, she must not pick a quarrel with her husband and cause him to spend a sleepless night. But how irresponsible and insensitive of him to go back to bed in these circumstances! Like father, like son, thought Akiko. Shigezō's blood obviously flowed through Nobutoshi's veins. She would probably be the first person Nobutoshi would forget when he grew old, and without a doubt he too would become senile. As she heaped imaginary abuse on her husband, Akiko began to feel uneasy. Since the weather was mild, she was not worried about Shigezō's catching a cold, even though he had run away wearing only his night clothes. But Satoshi hadn't phoned yet. Had he left without taking any change? Filled with anxiety, Akiko paced restlessly about the house. When at long last Satoshi called home, it was already growing light outside.

'Have you found Grandpa, Mum?'

'Not yet, dear. Where are you calling from?'

'Somewhere near Nerima Ward.'

'Oh dear!'

'Grandpa may be heading in the opposite direction. Don't you think you ought to call the police?'

'I'll do that. Come straight home, dear. And watch out for cars.'

'There are hardly any around. It really feels great out here! The air is so clean!'

151

'What are you talking about?' Akiko replaced the receiver, then immediately picked it up again and dialled 110. This was the first time in her life she had called the police, and she regretted that she had not woken her husband.

'Police Department,' said a voice at the other end of the line.

'Er . . . my father-in-law has run away from home, and we don't know where he is. Could you help us find him?'

'Yes, Ma'am. You say you're looking for an old man who has run away from home? At what time did he leave the house? How old is he? Could you describe him? What's his name? Tachibana Shigezō? Please give us your address and telephone number. How can we recognize your house ?'

The man who answered the phone spoke coolly and deliberately, repeating whatever Akiko said. Akiko was extremely nervous. She told him that although everyone in the family had helped to look for Shigezō, they had failed to find him. As for describing him, she confessed that she was too upset to think straight. Then, still terribly flustered, she mumbled that he was in his night clothes and had a diaper on. Immediately, she wished that she hadn't mentioned the diaper. By the time she replaced the receiver, Akiko was exhausted.

'Please wake up, dear. Satoshi has just rung to say that he couldn't find Grandpa. I phoned the police. It won't do for them to find you in bed when they arrive, so please get up.'

Rudely awakened for the second time that night, Nobutoshi dragged himself out of bed and made his way downstairs.

'If I have to go through this every night, it'll kill me for sure,' he muttered as he began to shave.

'Don't you think you ought to get into something decent, dear? The police are on their way. Are you going to thank them for their trouble in your pyjamas?'

'Why all the fuss? I don't have to get into a suit and tie to greet a policeman, do I?'

'How can you say that? The police are searching the city for Grandpa. You really shouldn't talk like that.'

'Who let him get out of the house in the first place?'

'Are you hinting that I'm to blame for all this? I wish you'd seen Grandpa gnawing on a bone! After all, he's *your* father, isn't he?'

'Will you stop saying that? What are you trying to insinuate?'

They were on the verge of a violent argument when a patrol car screeched to a halt in front of their house. Akiko ran out of the gate. There was Shigezō, his chest fully exposed, grappling with a policeman.

152

'Thank you for finding him, Officer. Oh, Grandpa! Where did you run off to?'

'Akiko, why did he arrest me? I didn't do anything wrong. I keep telling him that I'm no burglar, but he won't believe me. He's inhuman,' wailed Shigezō.

Moving very nimbly, the young officer turned Shigezō over to Akiko. He explained that the police at Shinjuku headquarters had noticed Shigezō acting suspiciously and were just about to take him into custody when Akiko called. In the meantime, Nobutoshi, who had hurriedly changed his clothes, made his appearance. 'I'm sorry we caused you such trouble,' he said, bowing low.

'Not at all. It's fortunate we found him unharmed.'

'Should we go to Headquarters to thank the officers personally?'

'No, there's no need for that. It's part of our job, after all. I'll be on my way now. Please take good care of him,' said the young officer, saluting smartly and returning to the patrol car. Satoshi, who had just returned home on his bicycle, gazed rapturously at the car as it sped away.

'Grandpa walked all the way to Shinjuku.'

'That's the route he took the time Aunt Kyōko ran after him. No wonder I couldn't find him!'

Akiko looked at Shigezō. He had nothing covering his loins, having lost his diaper and diaper cover somewhere along the way.

'I told the policeman my name over and over again, but he had it in his head that I was a burglar and arrested me. He was really nasty!'

'It's great that you could remember your name, Grandpa!'

'What was that? Akiko, Satoshi says such impudent things these days!'

Shigezō was still extremely agitated after his struggle with the policeman. As, surprisingly, his words made perfect sense, Akiko took the opportunity to try to find out what had been going through his mind. She asked him why he had left the house. Shigezō was puzzled by her questions, however, and did not respond.

Since he had had hardly any sleep, Akiko thought that it would be cruel to take Shigezō to the Centre that day, so she decided to stay at home and look after him.

'Akiko, I'm hungry. I kept telling the policeman I wanted a snack, but he wouldn't give me anything. He was so mean! I'm starved!'

Akiko began to prepare some noodles for him because there was no bread in the house. Satoshi said that he too would like some, so Akiko prepared three bowls. Just as they were all sitting down to eat, Nobutoshi came downstairs, dressed for the office. Akiko and Nobutoshi were still angry with each other, so Nobutoshi left the house without saying a word and Akiko did not wish him a pleasant day.

'Satoshi, didn't I beg you to talk to your father about putting Grandpa in a nursing home? Why haven't you? Grandpa is more than I can handle. You understand the situation, don't you?'

'But I've already talked to Dad about it.'

'When?'

'Ages ago, when the weather was still cold. One day when you were out, I suggested that we put Grandpa in an old people's home.'

'And what did your father say?'

'Actually, he didn't say anything.'

'So that's how he feels! It's obvious that he doesn't even want to contemplate it.'

'But, Mum. Even I'd think twice before sending you or Dad to a place like that.'

Although Satoshi had intended to sound sympathetic, his words pierced his mother's heart to the core. Would her son have to make a decision about what to do with her one day?

Akiko looked at her father-in-law and realized that she was not afraid of death. Whether she became senile like Shigezō or amorous like Mrs Kadotani, old age was a far more cruel fate than death. If Nobutoshi were to die, she would join him in death – even if they weren't on speaking terms at the present moment.

After Satoshi left for school, Akiko phoned the office to say that she would not be coming in that day. She gave an account of the previous night's events to the lawyer who answered the phone.

'Things must be pretty hectic for you!'

'Well, I feel trapped in a hopeless situation, because my husband's opposed to putting Grandpa in a nursing home.'

'You know, there are various kinds of nursing homes, and they're not at all like the old people's homes of long ago. But I'm afraid I'm in no position to recommend a home for your father-in-law.'

'I have to keep an eye on him every minute of the day. If the tranquillizer no longer works, it'll be next to impossible for me to get away from home. We had to call the police last night!'

'You really have got a problem on your hands, haven't you? Can't you get some form of day-care for him? Would you like me to ask a friend of mine who works at the Ministry of Public Welfare about it?'

'Would you, please? I'd really appreciate it.'

Akiko bowed as she replaced the receiver. She wondered how the Ministry of Public Welfare could be of any help in solving her problem.

Her boss called back in the afternoon and reported that he had been introduced to an official in the Department of Social Welfare for the Elderly, a division of the Ministry of Public Welfare. For further information, he had been advised that she should see a consultant at her local welfare office. Having given her the telephone number, he added that the consultant would probably introduce her to a doctor specializing in geriatrics.

Akiko thanked him for his trouble and placed the receiver back on the hook. Then she phoned the welfare office, and while reading over the notes she had jotted down earlier, asked to speak to the Consultant on Social Welfare for the Elderly.

'Yes, speaking,' replied a woman in a lilting voice. Akiko explained rather incoherently how she had learned that there was a consultant and mentioned that she was a resident of Umezato. She also described how her family had suddenly discovered that Shigezō had become senile. The woman chimed in appropriately from time to time, then asked point-blank: 'And what do you wish to do with him?'

'Well, as I was just saying, we don't know what to do. I'd appreciate any advice you might have to offer,' said Akiko, somewhat flustered.

'Yes, I understand the situation. I'll come and see you straight away. How will I recognize your house?'

Was the woman being businesslike or just pushy? Akiko could not decide, but she had certainly not expected the consultant to come round immediately. Feeling extremely nervous, she hurriedly tidied up the house and even managed to put the cottage in order. While getting Shigezō into a clean outfit, she kept telling herself that the idea of putting him in a home was not her own. It had first been proposed by her boss and was now being carried out by a civil servant. Akiko felt guilty about having gone this far without consulting her husband, but all she was doing, she tried to convince herself, was to ask an expert how to cope with the problem of looking after a senile old man. As proof of this, she had not even mentioned nursing homes. Akiko thought that she should emphasize the fact that she worked full-time. In all probability the consultant was married herself, and Akiko felt confident that what she had to say would fall on sympathetic ears.

The buzzer sounded. When Akiko opened the front door, she saw a woman of about her own age smiling broadly.

'Are you Mrs Tachibana?' she asked.

The woman was dressed casually. If she had had a shopping basket on her arm, she could have easily been mistaken for an ordinary housewife returning from the market. There was nothing about her to suggest a married woman with a responsible position outside the home. Akiko felt at once immensely relieved and exceedingly grateful that there were such people as professional social workers. This woman with such an impressive title radiated the same warmth and compassion as the young caretaker at the Centre.

Responding warmly to Akiko's friendly greeting, the woman entered the house, her eyes falling on Shigezō who was sitting in a corner of the room.

'Good afternoon, Grandpa,' the woman called out.

Shigezō focused his sleepy grey eyes on the visitor, but remained silent.

'We have a guest, Grandpa. Won't you say hello to her?'

'All right,' replied Shigezō, but he did not return the woman's greeting.

'This is what he's like,' said Akiko, making no attempt to conceal her lack of sympathy.

The woman sat silently on the *tatami*, studying Shigezō for a while. Then she asked for details regarding the family. What kind of jobs did Akiko and Nobutoshi have? What was their joint income? What did Shigezō do every day? Thinking that it would be in her best interests to be perfectly frank, Akiko described Shigezō's odd behaviour since the day his wife had died, his voracious appetite and his sudden fits of fear. In explaining the situation as fully as possible, Akiko repeated some of the information she had earlier provided over the phone.

'He's suffering from senile dementia, isn't he?'

The woman did not answer. Instead, she remarked, 'He's very old, isn't he?' with the same lack of emotion in her voice as the doctor.

'I was told at the Senior Citizens' Centre that they had men and women even older than Grandpa who had not gone senile. How did he come to be like this?'

'He isn't violent, is he?'

'No, but he yells at night about a burglar breaking into the house.'

'What about his bodily functions?'

'He's wet his bed from time to time ever since we started giving him tranquillizers.'

'Am I correct in assuming that he's able to go to the toilet by himself during the day?'

'Yes, but when I'm around I feel I have to help him. And there are times when he forgets to come out of the toilet.'

'If that's all, he's doing fine for a man his age. He lives in such a

156

pleasant environment! Besides being in excellent health and having no financial worries, he has his son, daughter-in-law and grandson living with him.'

Akiko felt rather bewildered. The woman was probably familiar with worse examples of senility, but the Tachibanas – Akiko in particular – were terribly distressed by Shigezō's wretched condition.

'You may be right,' she replied, 'but, as I've already mentioned, I work full-time. I've been suffering terribly from lack of sleep, since he gets up in the middle of the night. He's so senile I can't leave him at home on his own, and I worry constantly that something terrible will happen to him. I'm sure I'll find some peace of mind if he's admitted to an institution. That's what I wanted to talk to you about.'

'Are you referring to a nursing home?'

'Yes. I'd like to put Grandpa in a home, and I'll gladly pay the fee. I'm sure he won't feel unhappy in a place like that.'

'Such homes are available, of course, but don't you think he'd be much happier living at home? For your information, though, I'll leave you this pamphlet.'

The pamphlet, published by the Tokyo Bureau of Public Welfare, had the words 'A Guide to Homes for the Elderly' on its yellow cover. Glancing through the table of contents, Akiko noted that there were four kinds of homes: those for people with a low income, special nursing homes, low-cost homes and homes that required payment for services provided.

Akiko turned to the page describing special nursing homes, curious to learn more about them. The first paragraph stated that these homes were for people over sixty. According to paragraph 2, they were designed for old people who required assistance with their meals and in performing various bodily functions because of a serious physical or mental disability. Men and women who required medication or medical care, however, could not be accepted. Akiko wondered if this might be the right kind of home for Shigezō, since he obviously had a serious mental disability. But would he be disqualified because he had been taking tranquillizers?

Meanwhile the woman had walked up to Shigezō and was speaking to him intently. Sitting like a monkey with his arms around his knees, Shigezō looked up at her from time to time, his face devoid of expression.

Akiko continued reading the pamphlet. There were a total of twenty-one special nursing homes authorized by the Tokyo Bureau of Public Welfare, she learned. Fees charged were based on the amount of tax paid by the family; anyone with an income of over 156,000 yen had to pay the total cost of the services provided. Did that sum refer to the income of the old person? And what was the full charge for the special nursing?

The section on low-cost homes for the elderly stated that the monthly fees ranged from 25,000 to 26,000 yen. Senior citizens who qualified were: a) those without any relatives, and b) those who were unable to live at home due to family circumstances. Surely Shigezō belonged to the latter group? The monthly charge was low enough for Akiko to cover it out of her salary. It was very cheap when she thought that she would no longer be roused in the middle of the night to find Shigezō sitting on top of her.

When she began reading the qualifications for the fourth category Akiko was terribly disappointed. A person had to be over sixty and in good health; he also had to be able to take care of himself, get along with other patients and have one or two guarantors. Apart from paying approximately 20,000 yen per month, he was required to put down a deposit and pay a substantial lump sum. In all, there were only seven such institutions. To Akiko's surprise, three of them were exclusively for women. Was this because women outlived men? Akiko thought it sheer nonsense that a person meeting the above qualifications would need to go into a home.

'Akiko,' cried Shigezō.

Akiko looked up and saw Shigezō getting to his feet with the help of the social worker. He raised his arms and began to perform callisthenics in compliance with the woman's instructions. He had called out to Akiko because he suddenly felt uncomfortable.

'Akiko, who is this lady?'

'She's a visitor, Grandpa.'

'But she keeps saying the strangest things.'

At this the woman burst out laughing and walked back to where Akiko was standing. 'His mind is quite lucid, isn't it?'

'Yes, but only once in a while. He usually doesn't understand half of what we say to him.'

'Surely you could take care of him at home instead of committing him to an institution? My job is to go around day after day interviewing old people, and your father-in-law is truly one of the more fortunate ones. There are a great many who are worse off than he is.'

It cost Akiko a considerable effort to prevent herself crying out that it was she who suffered most. Instead, she pointed to the yellow pamphlet and quietly asked: 'What exactly is a special nursing home?'

'It's an institution that accommodates the bedridden elderly and those afflicted with a personality loss.'

'Bedridden elderly' was easy enough to understand, but Akiko had to enquire about the meaning of the term 'personality loss'. The woman threw a quick glance at Akiko and murmured: 'It refers to the aged who are incontinent, eat their own excrement or smear it all over themselves.'

Akiko was horrified. 'Are there people like that?'

'A great many, I'm afraid.'

'Do they actually eat their own excrement?'

'Yes. Not even psychiatrists who specialize in the elderly know very much about this perverse form of behaviour.'

Shigezō's senility was far less severe, but he did wet his bed and was once caught with his wife's bones in his fists. Akiko described these details to the social worker, her heart beating.

'What's more, he gets me up several times in the course of the night, so I can't perform my duties efficiently at the office the next day. I know that most people don't approve of women going out to work, but surely *you* sympathize with my plight.'

'I do indeed. But picture yourself in his place. Don't you think he'd be happiest spending his last years with his family? I appreciate that you work full-time, but someone in the family has to make sacrifices. After all, we'll both be old ourselves one day.'

Akiko could see that the discussion was not leading to the conclusion she was hoping for, so she bombarded the social worker with a barrage of businesslike enquiries.

'It says here that the low-cost homes are for old people who are unable to live at home due to family circumstances. Doesn't this apply to my father-in-law?'

'Well, yes, if you insist on sending him away. But the truth of the matter is that all these homes are full. The situation is so serious that even a person strongly recommended by us has to wait from between six months to a year before he's admitted.'

'You mean that he has to wait for one of the patients to die, don't you?'

'To be perfectly frank, yes.'

Adding up the numbers in a table, Akiko discovered that approximately 700 people could be accommodated in this category of home. The fourth category catered for less than 200 individuals. Akiko sighed. The job of the social worker with the impressive title was to serve the public. But with so few institutions, could there be any solution to the urgent problem of caring for the elderly? Remembering the woman's remark about someone in the family having to make sacrifices, Akiko asked bluntly: 'What happens when a person with no relatives becomes senile?'

'We give him top priority. But the problem is so serious that even he is put on a waiting list. Twice a week, a caseworker spends half a day helping the bedridden who live alone. They're deeply grateful for the care they receive, but it's far from adequate.'

How on earth did these lonely, bedridden old people manage to feed themselves and perform their bodily functions during the rest of the week? Akiko suddenly recalled the news article reporting an old man's suicide. Were even the special nursing homes, which could accommodate 1,800 old people, fully occupied? Were there over 2,000 elderly in Tokyo who were either bedridden or who had suffered a personality loss? Akiko shuddered at the thought.

'Well, I suppose it won't do me any good to discuss the possibility of putting Grandpa in a home any further. He may be quiet now, but he runs away the minute I take my eyes off him. I told you over the phone, didn't I, that he once ran away in the middle of the night? In the end I had to call the police.'

'Oh, so he's a runaway.'

'What do you mean?'

'No home will admit someone like that because they're terribly short-staffed.'

'Then what am I to do? Do I have to look after a senile old man whom even a nursing home would reject?'

As soon as Akiko had uttered these words, she felt deeply ashamed of her hysterical outburst. The social worker, however, was completely unperturbed.

'There's really no solution to this problem. It tears many families apart. The wife simply has to cope as courageously as she can.'

Akiko tried to remain calm, realizing that she would be wasting her energy if she vented her anger on the woman. Now that she knew no nursing home would admit Shigezō, she had to seek the advice of a specialist regarding medication and hospitals for the senile.

'The tranquillizers he's been taking for the past two months no longer work. Would it be all right to increase the dose?'

'You'll have to ask at the health clinic. Someone there will introduce you to a geriatrician.'

'Would he help a runaway like my father-in-law? Tell me, is this illness peculiar to the elderly?'

'It seems to be.'

'Senility is sometimes referred to as senile dementia, isn't it? And I was told that having hallucinations and screaming that a burglar's broken into the house are symptoms of senile melancholia. My father-in-law may be running away because he's seeing things, so couldn't he be considered ill?'

The social worker looked directly at Akiko and remained silent. After a long pause she very slowly opened her mouth as if she had made up her mind to provide Akiko with the cold facts. 'Mrs Tachibana,' she said, 'senile melancholia – and this also goes for senile dementia – is a mental illness. Thus, if you insist on sending him away, the only place that will take him is a mental hospital.'

Akiko nearly screamed. At last she understood why the doctor had been so evasive!

'Is it really considered a mental illness?'

'I'm afraid it is. If you put him into a mental hospital, they'll just give him tranquillizers and his life will be shortened as a result. That's why I advise you to take care of him at home. Even young mental patients, so long as they aren't violent, are usually kept at home. I'm telling you all this because your family seems to be so understanding. These days young people no longer have feelings of filial piety. The general trend among the young is to do whatever they can to live in separate households. This is the problem we are confronted with at present.'

While the social worker expressed her dismay at how post-war Japanese education had completely neglected to teach respect for the elderly, the bits and pieces of information Akiko had just picked up echoed in her ears. So senility was a mental illness! Senile dementia. Hallucinations. Personality loss.

All this time, Shigezō cowered in a corner of the room, staring vacantly into space. Akiko looked at her father-in-law, filled with a vague feeling of apprehension. Was he mentally ill? She was too tired to organize her thoughts. The social worker had come right away, but she had failed to offer any hopeful or constructive advice. What was now clear to Akiko was that the current welfare system for the elderly in Japan was appallingly backward and that official policy had so far failed to take account of the increase of old people in the population.

When the social worker had left, Akiko prepared lunch for herself and Shigezō. Although she desperately needed to get some sleep, she first had to check that the doors could not be opened from the inside. Every precaution had been taken to make it next to impossible for a burglar to break into the house, but now she had to make sure that Shigezō could not get out on his own.

Shigezō ate heartily as usual, noisily devouring whatever was placed in front of him. Watching him, Akiko lost her appetite altogether. Was he really a mental case? According to the social worker, even young mental patients were looked after at home. What Akiko feared more than anything was that she would have to look after her father-in-law around the clock. If that happened, it was only a matter of time before she became a mental case herself.

The sun was still high in the sky, but Akiko secured the rain shutters, spread out two sets of bedding and tucked Shigezō up in bed. His hunger satisfied for the time being, he began to doze off when Akiko stretched out next to him. Although her whole body felt lethargic from lack of sleep, a part of her brain remained very active. The phrases 'personality loss' and 'mental illness' echoed in her head. What would her daily routine be like from now on? A pall of gloom had descended on the entire house. Akiko felt that even with the shutters – and her eyes – wide open, the place would have seemed dismal.

She drifted off to sleep, only to be woken by Shigezō's cries. Dazed, she looked around the room, wondering where the horrible shrieks were coming from. When her eyes focused, she saw Shigezō pressed against the rain shutters, his arms stretched wide. 'What's the matter, Grandpa?' she asked.

'Oh, Akiko.'

'Would you like to go out?'

'Yes.'

'You didn't get any sleep at all last night, so why don't you go back to bed. I'll just die if I don't get some more sleep.'

'All right.'

Whatever the old man's intentions had been, he obediently went back to sleep when Akiko pushed him down on his bedding. This time Akiko remained wide awake. What on earth had he been doing with his arms pressed flat against the shutters as if he were a moth? He really must be mentally deranged, thought Akiko, drawing the most obvious conclusion.

A short while later, Shigezō slipped out of bed and began to crawl around the room, screaming incoherently. When he crawled over Akiko's bed, she realized that this was how he had got on top of her the other night.

'Grandpa!'

'Oh, Akiko. Is anything wrong?'

What a question to ask! Akiko could not put up with Shigezō's restlessness any longer, though she did not think that he had the strength to remain active like this for any length of time. She wondered if she should give him some of the tranquillizer. But just as she was about to prepare a dose for him, she recalled what the social worker had said about it taxing the old man's heart.

Akiko's common sense told her that the tranquillizer was certain to have harmful side-effects. Though it put Shigezō to sleep, it would

162

eventually cause a completely different kind of illness. The drugs developed in recent years were highly effective, producing immediate results, but their side-effects were truly frightening. Tranquillizers, while inducing sleep, weakened the heart. What effect would it have on Shigezō's heart if she gave him another dose at this hour, Akiko wondered. No sooner had she reached out for the medicine than she drew her hand back. Terribly agitated, she debated what to do. Perhaps they should both take some of the tranquillizer? But then this particular prescription had been made for the exclusive use of the elderly and might not work on her. What is more, if Shigezō slept soundly in the afternoon, he would probably be restless during the night and cause her to lose all sense of time.

As Akiko contemplated her dilemma, the minutes slipped by. Before long Shigezō began to complain about being hungry, so she got up to prepare a snack for him. When she opened the rain shutters, Shigezō, like a pet dog, went down into the garden and made straight for the cottage. Akiko quickly picked up some old newspaper and spread it out on the floor of the toilet before he got there. She then watched him from outside to see that he used the toilet paper properly. In slow motion, he went through all the steps as if performing a solemn ritual. When he finally emerged, Akiko went in and saw a fine specimen of excrement; she marvelled that it could have been produced by a man of nearly eighty-five. Had the Chinese herbal remedy at long last taken effect, she wondered, so that he no longer suffered bouts of diarrhoea? Then she remembered that Kyōko had repeatedly said that her father had drunk only herbs that promoted longevity.

Later, when she left the house with a shopping basket on her arm, she took Shigezō along with her, feeling that it was her responsibility to keep an eye on him all the time. Because of Shigezō's voracious appetite, there was not a single package of instant noodles left in the house. Akiko paused in front of the fish department at the market and noted that fresh fish was twice as expensive as the frozen variety. Looking over at Shigezō, she saw that his face registered an almost imperceptible look of interest. Although she thought the price exorbitant, she bought a fillet of fish marinated in soya-bean paste.

'Why, hello, Mrs Tachibana! How nice to see your father-in-law looking so well. My mother-in-law needs a lot of looking after these days,' said Mrs Kadotani as she stalked up to Akiko, chattering in her usual lively manner.

'What has happened to her?'

'Well, she can't walk any more.'

'Oh dear!'

Mrs Kadotani laughed, then recounted how her mother-in-law had fallen off the veranda and fractured one of the lumbar vertebrae in her spine. Since then, the lower half of her body had been completely paralysed. Akiko expressed her deepest sympathy for the old woman who, until recently, had been so hale and hearty. How she must be lamenting her fate!

'Not really. It's taught her a good lesson. Ever since I first came here as a bride she never once caught a cold and was constantly boasting that the only time she had ever stayed in bed was in childbirth. Shortly after my wedding, I came down with pyelitis and had to stay in bed for some time with a high temperature. How she tormented me then! I can't tell you how good it feels to get my own back now. She was always saying how she'd never be a burden to any of us, so it amuses me no end now that she's an invalid,' said Mrs Kadotani, sounding surprisingly cheerful.

'But you must be doing everything for her.'

'Yes, indeed. Grandma has to wear nappies, you know. She's terribly mortified whenever I change them for her. The tears stream down her face, and she keeps on saying that she wishes she were dead. Her favourite pastime was to call on the neighbours, so I suppose she feels lonely at home. She phones the Senior Citizens' Centre several times a day, but no one ever comes to visit her. I suppose she wasn't very popular with the other members.'

'Will she be back on her feet soon?'

'According to the doctor, she'll be bedridden for the rest of her life.'

'How awful!'

'She bursts into tears at the slightest provocation. Her own son and grandchildren avoid her like the plague because she's so unpleasant to be with. The whole situation is both pathetic and amusing.'

'I hope that nothing like that happens to either of us.'

'What a gloomy thought, Mrs Tachibana!'

'I feel so sad whenever I hear about the plight of the elderly, and I pray that I won't suffer a similar fate. I'm sure no one willingly grows old or becomes disabled.'

'I do believe you're an intellectual, Mrs Tachibana!'

'I suppose I am.'

'As for myself, I don't bother with such thoughts. I know I'll get terribly depressed if I do. I'm just an average person. I've been sick and sometimes I'm foolish, and I don't hesitate to squabble with my mother-in-law. Whenever I change her nappy, I give her bottom a little smack and tell her that this is what she gets for having tormented me so. Then I feel quite cheerful about the whole situation. As I have no idea how long she'll be with us, I can't very well brood about *my* old age.'

Mrs Kadotani's garrulity was no doubt a trait she had acquired from her mother-in-law. After saying her piece, she turned abruptly and walked away. Akiko stood open-mouthed as she watched the ample hips of the mother of four sway back and fourth. What a remarkable attitude, she thought. She had much to learn from her neighbour.

Nobutoshi returned home earlier than usual that night. 'Any dinner left for me?' he asked.

'The mackerel season is over, but I've bought you a fillet marinated in soya-bean paste. I'm sure you'll like it.'

'No thanks. I'll just have some *tsukudani*.'

While her husband hungrily slurped down his *chazuke*,* Akiko gave him a full account of the events of that afternoon. She concluded by telling him what the social worker had told her.

'Grandpa's a runaway, and so no nursing home will take him.'

'Oh?'

'A person has to be of sound mind and body to be accepted by those homes that charge exorbitant fees.'

'I see.'

'Senile dementia is actually a kind of mental illness. If it becomes necessary to send him away, he'll have to be placed in a mental institution.'

'Really?'

'No matter how old a mental patient is, if he isn't violent, they think he should be looked after at home. A man like Grandpa would probably be classified as feeble-minded.'

'Is that so?'

Nobutoshi showed no surprise as he listened to the information his wife had acquired that day. In the middle of her account, Akiko began to grow suspicious.

'You're behaving very strangely, dear. Did you know all this already?'

'Yes.'

Lately, Nobutoshi had learned more than he cared to admit about families who had an elderly person to look after. Men older than he, some of them colleagues at work, had provided him with a great deal of information about the problems involved. He had learned that the percentage of senior citizens had increased dramatically in Japan in recent years, and that very few measures had been taken to deal with

*Leftover rice over which hot tea has been poured.

165

the aged even in the advanced countries of the West. The more he investigated, the more he appreciated the gravity of each aspect of the problem – the psychological as well as the medical.

'If you knew all along, you should have said so,' said Akiko reproachfully.

'It wouldn't have done any good.'

Akiko remained silent.

As he ate his *chazuke*, Nobutoshi suddenly bit down on something hard. When he removed it from his mouth, he saw that it was a grain of rice covered with chaff. A rare sight indeed these days, thought Nobutoshi, suddenly transported to the distant past. His paternal grandmother, who had been alive and well when he was a young boy, had looked upon an unhulled grain of rice found in a bowl of rice as a lucky charm. Ecstatic whenever she found one, she would reverently place it on the Shinto altar as an offering. By the time World War II broke out, she had saved up one cupful. She thought it would be a good idea to sew one grain on each thousand-stitches belt,* so she had distributed the grains of rice among her neighbours who had relatives fighting in the war. According to her, a grain of rice had to pass through eighty-eight barriers before it got to the dining-table. The chaff was separated from the grain during the process of being dried, beaten, hulled and polished; it was then either burned or used as feed for domestic animals. A grain of rice which still had the chaff clinging to it – even after it had been pounded and polished, then cooked and served in a bowl – well deserved to serve as a charm for longevity. His grandmother had died by the time Nobutoshi went off to war, so he did not know if an unhulled grain had been sewn on his own thousand-stitches belt.

Nobutoshi gazed at the hard grain, which he had placed on the table, thinking that it could very well symbolize something altogether different. Was it not like his father? The old man had lived a long life. Despite the fact that he had suffered from ill health and had undergone numerous hardships, he had somehow managed to cling tenaciously to life without succumbing to diseases like cancer or diabetes. Still, the unhulled grain was inedible even after it had been cooked, and, like the beans that are scattered to see the old year out, it would never sprout even if it were planted.

'By the way, dear, Mrs Kadotani can't walk any more,' said Akiko, interrupting his thoughts.

Akiko reflected upon what the social worker had said about someone in the family having to make sacrifices. If any member of

*A red cotton belt sewn with a thousand stitches – supposedly by a thousand women – and worn by soldiers to protect them from danger.

166

the Tachibana family had to be sacrificed on Shigezō's account, it could only be herself. She also recalled the remarks made by Mrs Kadotani's daughter-in-law, who had stated that she did not allow herself to think about growing old.

In the meantime, Nobutoshi had put down his chopsticks and was maintaining a pensive silence. That very day, he had heard about an old man who lay in a hospital bed unable to see, hear or eat. He was given fluids through a plastic tube which had been inserted into one of his nostrils. Incredible though it seemed, the patient could be kept alive for twenty years, provided the pump to which he was hooked continued to operate. What did that man, probably even more senile than Shigezō, think about all day long? The man who was telling the story then described further details that were even more horrifying. The flesh against which the plastic tube constantly rubbed had begun to rot, and if the patient was not watched carefully, a fly could easily lay its eggs in the open wound. The thought of maggots writhing in the wound had made Nobutoshi feel sick with horror.

Several decades from now, would eighty per cent of the entire population of Japan be over sixty? If this were so, every able-bodied youth would be surrounded by four old people who could not support themselves, a terrible fate for any young man. According to statistics quoted by an acquaintance of Nobutoshi's, there had been a sudden decrease in the birth rate similar to that in France. At the same time, progress in medical science had greatly reduced the death rate of the elderly.

In more realistic terms, several decades from now, Satoshi, as a working member of society, would have to support two strangers besides his parents. He had also heard that by about the year 2000, there were likely to be more than 30 million people over sixty in Japan; the Japanese would be a nation of senior citizens. Although Nobutoshi prayed that he would be dead long before this happened, he did not have the courage to share his feelings with his wife. Still echoing in his ears was his son's fervent plea: 'Mum, Dad, please don't live this long!'

15

The doctor warned Nobutoshi that four times the normal dose of tranquillizer would be lethal. It was therefore with the utmost caution that Akiko increased the amount she gave Shigezō before he went to bed. For the first five days, the increased dosage sent him to sleep, but a week later, he was giving Akiko as much trouble as before. If Shigezō's life would be shortened in direct proportion to the increase in the medication, Akiko could not indiscriminately give him larger amounts. Night after night she agonized over her dilemma.

One morning, after Shigezō had had a good night's rest, Akiko accompanied him to the Senior Citizens' Centre. When she asked how things were at the Centre, the caretaker, who remembered her well, said:

'The women are as active here as they are at the other centres. Most of the senile members are men. The same is true at the nursing homes. I really don't know why this should be so. Some people say it's probably because men don't do anything at home. They're so used to working that they don't know what to do with themselves when they retire. Mr Tachibana is by no means the only example. Generally speaking, the women are high-spirited and the men quiet. Unless a man is playing *go* or *shōgi*, he'll just sit with his shoulders hunched and stare vacantly into space. That's how things are.'

For a while Akiko went to work regularly, happy that the woman at the Centre did not complain about Shigezō. But then, on several occasions, Satoshi could not find his grandfather when he went to fetch him at the Centre. Sometimes Shigezō would wander away and get lost; at other times, he would run away. Each time this happened, Satoshi had to call her at the office and notify the police. Akiko would then come rushing home from work, beside herself with worry and anger. In time, it became impossible for her to continue working regularly.

'You've lost a lot of weight, haven't you, Mrs Tachibana?' said the young secretary one day.

For days on end, Akiko found absolutely no relief from her lack of sleep and ceaseless worrying. She had not been overweight to begin with, and now she had lost so much weight that her shoulder bones and elbows protruded noticeably. Her eyelids were swollen and her eyes hurt. Occasionally she took a non-prescription tranquillizer. Her employers were very sympathetic and did not complain even though she often failed to turn up at work. In the meantime, the young secretary learned the office routine and became an expert about matters that Akiko had once considered her sole responsibility. Since she could even manage the Japanese-language typewriter, she would be able to fill the position admirably if Akiko were to leave her job altogether. The girl, who until recently had only run errands and served tea, had proved herself to be very reliable. Akiko felt utterly wretched. Studying Shigezō closely, she realized that soon she would have to take care of a man whose physical health had so deteriorated that he could not move about freely. By the time it became impossible for her to go to the office at all, her employers would probably be able to get along without her. She supposed that this was what was called natural selection. And yet, right there at home was a senile old man who had somehow escaped the weeding process.

One Saturday, while stocking up on frozen foods in the basement of the department store, Akiko wondered how long this routine would continue. Half a year had already slipped by since that snowy day.

When Akiko emerged from the subway station, she saw that it was raining. The rainy season had begun. Her arms were so laden with parcels that she could not have opened her umbrella even if she had thought to bring it. Tying a scarf around her head, she started walking, heedless of the rain. It was a good thing I wore an all-weather coat today, she thought, as she marched forward in the dismal rain. When her vision grew cloudy, she realized that she still had her glasses on. Propping up her parcels against a telephone pole, she removed her glasses. Something so convenient can be such a nuisance at times!

While Akiko waited for her washing-machine to reach the end of the wash cycle, she stored away the frozen foods. She put the damp, freshly-laundered underwear into the dryer before going to fetch her father-in-law from the Centre. Akiko could not very well present an expensive gift to the caretaker, who was a civil servant, but she wanted very much to express her gratitude to her for having been so understanding; she therefore took with her a copy of a recent best-seller as a token of her appreciation. Thanking her, the woman remarked that Akiko was an ideal daughter-in-law. Flattered, Akiko bowed low and left the Centre with Shigezō.

'You were good today, weren't you?' said Akiko, praising Shigezō for not running away.

'Akiko,' said Shigezō, suddenly stopping. 'I hate that place. There are only old people there.'

'But you know I can't leave you at home by yourself, Grandpa. Can't you make new friends?'

'All I see are old men, Akiko. I hate it there.'

Who does he think he is – a young man? Akiko thought in disgust. She had brought two umbrellas from home, but Shigezō had dropped his and was getting soaked in the rain. Looking back, she spotted the abandoned umbrella on the road some way back; it was still open and was rocking back and forth in the wind. Akiko hurried to retrieve it. Then, closing her own umbrella, she held on to Shigezō tightly under the ancient black umbrella and marched forward.

'Akiko, I really hate the Centre. All I see there are old people. There isn't a single young person in the group,' said Shigezō. He repeated the same complaint over and over again. Akiko was taken completely by surprise, for this was the first time that he had complained about the Centre.

'There's one young person. And she takes good care of you, doesn't she, Grandpa?'

'Well, yes.'

Shigezō suddenly quickened his pace. 'Grandpa, Grandpa,' cried Akiko, tapping him on the shoulder.

Shigezō turned round and gave her a hard look. 'Well, if it isn't Akiko. What is it?'

There was no continuity in Shigezō's concept of time. In his mind, the time he left the Centre and the present belonged to entirely different time zones. He had probably begun walking faster because he had suddenly thought of something urgent; when Akiko tapped him on the shoulder, he completely forgot what he had been doing a moment earlier.

They were nearly home when Shigezō stopped again. A small truck tooted its horn as it overtook them. Since the major roads had been turned into one-way streets in recent years, traffic had increased noticeably in the narrow streets and become a danger to pedestrians.

'Grandpa, is anything the matter?'

Akiko looked up to follow Shigezō's gaze and beyond the fence on the other side of the road saw a tall tree with a luxuriant mantle of leaves. Nestling in the lush greenery was a magnolia, its blossom dazzlingly white.

Because of the rain, Akiko had had her eyes fixed on the muddy road as she walked along, holding her umbrella aloft, while Shigezō had refused to get under the umbrella. He had been the first to notice the magnolia. Akiko was deeply moved by the exquisite blossom, the large petals wet with rain and glowing white high above the narrow road. She stood in silence for some time, her eyes fixed on the blossom. Shigezō had stopped too, apparently overwhelmed by its beauty. Akiko marvelled that he was still able to distinguish between beauty and ugliness. Was this why he had complained about the Centre? Couldn't it be said that as long as he could appreciate the magnolia he was still very much alive?

Akiko usually gave Shigezō a bath once a week. She hesitated to bathe him this particular Saturday because it was the wettest time of the year, but realized that if she did not do so, he would accumulate two weeks of grime. As soon as dinner was over, she made Shigezō, who was feeling sleepy, remove his clothes and soak in the tub. In the nude, Shigezō was clearly in excellent physical condition, having changed very little since he was examined by the doctor. He had, however, lost a little weight and now had deeper wrinkles. His hip bones seemed to protrude more noticeably than before. Akiko had got used to bathing her father-in-law by now; she energetically scrubbed his body, bringing the soap to a rich lather as if she were washing a dog or a horse. She still felt squeamish about washing the lower half of his body, however, and tried her best to get him to wash himself. She handed him a bar of soap, but he only played with it, and when she directed his hands down to his crotch, he started playing with his testicles. Since it was mainly to clean his anus and genitals that Akiko gave Shigezō a bath, she finally lost patience and washed his crotch for him. She found this task exceedingly unpleasant, and therefore left it to the very last. After washing the lower part of his body and splashing the suds off with warm water, she breathed a sigh of relief.

The telephone rang.

Akiko knew that Satoshi was attending a seminar and would be returning home late. Perhaps it was Nobutoshi, calling to tell her that he would also be late?

'Grandpa, please get back in the bath for a few minutes. I'm going to answer the phone. You can manage that, can't you?' asked Akiko, assisting the old man so that he would not slip and hurt himself. Then she ran to answer the telephone. Saturdays were always so hectic!

'Hello, Akiko. How are things with you?' It was Mitsuko, her sister-in-law. It had been some time since Akiko had heard from her.

'Terrible. I feel as gloomy as the weather outside and I'm just barely managing to keep going. What is it?'

'Bad news, I'm afraid. Things are just as gloomy here.'

'Is someone ill?'

'You guessed correctly. It's Shizuko. Her condition is very grave.'

'What? Shizuko? Do you mean our old friend?'

'Yes. She's dying of cancer and has less than a week to live. Her husband phoned me and asked us to come to the hospital to say goodbye to her. What should we do?'

'Isn't this rather sudden? The cancer must have spread very rapidly. What kind is it?'

'It isn't all that sudden. Shizuko had an operation a year ago, remember? She told me then that it was only a benign tumour, but in fact it was already too late by then. The operation was just a formality. Her husband was the only one who was told that she had a year to live.'

'Oh dear. Why did she wait so long to have something done about it?'

'Remember how Shizuko refused to wear glasses to correct her vision?'

'Oh yes. She was stubborn about the oddest things. But I can't believe she's dying. How old is her child? Is there no hope at all? And does she know that she's dying?'

Once Akiko grasped the fact that an old friend was dying, she was profoundly saddened and wanted to know every detail of her condition. If she were going to visit her in the hospital, she had to decide when and where to meet Mitsuko. But how could a woman of her own age be dying of cancer?

'Don't you know that women over forty are prone to cancer? We ought to have regular check-ups. Mrs Yamada mentioned that she's examined once a year at the Cancer Centre. Shizuko wouldn't be dying if she had been more careful.'

Akiko had heard about the high risk of cancer among middle-aged women. Nevertheless, it was shocking to learn that someone very close to her was dying from the dreaded disease. As the next day was Sunday, Akiko decided that she would ask her husband to look after the house while she and Mitsuko went to visit Shizuko in hospital. Long after replacing the receiver, she was still in a state of shock. She pictured in her mind the lovely magnolia she had seen earlier, and it somehow reminded her of Shizuko as she had known her during

172

their school days. She had been a fair-skinned, rather plump girl who had an air of tranquillity about her. How could someone as healthy as that fall ill?

Akiko heaved a deep sigh. The phrase 'the uncertainty of life' came into her mind. Although she had recently become aware that she herself was ageing, she firmly believed that a person of her age was still young. After all, a member of her family had lived forty-five years beyond the age of forty without having suffered from cancer.

She returned to the bathroom, opened the door, and stood transfixed. Her father-in-law, his face turned upward, was lying in the bath, the water up to his forehead.

'Grandpa! Grandpa!'

Akiko plunged one foot into the water and lifted Shigezō up into her arms. He retched and vomited a huge volume of water, then went on coughing up water onto the wooden slats on the floor. Akiko was in a panic. Shigezō's body was bigger and heavier than she had imagined. His long limbs, now grown limp, sprawled lifelessly on the slats; not a muscle twitched. Suddenly convinced that her father-in-law was dying, Akiko felt her body grow cold.

'Grandpa! Grandpa!' she cried hysterically, shaking the old man with all her might. Shigezō opened his eyes, his lower eyelids quivering.

'Grandpa!'

He was still alive! Akiko gave him artificial respiration, as she had learned during the war. She turned Shigezō over on his back, straddled the lower half of his body, and rhythmically pressed her palms against his chest. Shigezō was still gasping for breath. Akiko desperately tried to organize her jumbled thoughts as she continued the artificial respiration. Gradually she regained her composure.

She placed her ear against Shigezō's chest and listened for his heartbeat; the pounding sounded like a cataract. She quickly phoned the doctor to report the accident and was even prepared to call for an ambulance if he happened to be out. Fortunately, the doctor had just returned from a house-call. He and his nurse set out at once for the Tachibana residence. In the meantime, Akiko dried Shigezō from head to toe, dressed him in his night clothes and laid him down on his bedding. Feeling for his pulse, Akiko whispered urgently in his ear: 'The doctor will be here any minute now, Grandpa. Just hang on. He'll be here soon.'

When the doctor arrived, he pressed the stethoscope against Shigezō's chest and asked: 'Did he have a stroke in the bath?'

'I don't know. I thought at first that he might have dozed off, but his eyes were wide open. He was completely still. My sister-in-law had phoned to tell me that a friend of ours was dying of cancer. I was so shocked by the news that I kept prodding her for details and by the time I got back to the bathroom, he was up to his forehead in water. I was terrified! I managed to get him out of the tub, and he began to vomit up water.'

'He nearly drowned.'

'Will you be able to save him? Oh, Doctor, you must save him!' cried Akiko. As she was describing the details of the accident, the legal term 'accidental homicide' had suddenly appeared from her memory; she felt absolutely wretched.

The doctor worked quickly and efficiently. He instructed the nurse to prepare an injection, then checked Shigezō's pupils and moved the stethoscope around on his chest. After the injection, he said very calmly; 'He'll be all right. It's a good thing his heart is strong.'

'But he hasn't said a word. Grandpa! Grandpa!'

'Mrs Tachibana, you can't expect a man who's had a brush with death to start chattering away.'

The doctor's easy banter helped Akiko to regain her composure. While the nurse held up the hem of Shigezō's night clothes, the doctor gave him two more injections in his sagging buttocks. Then he checked his blood pressure. While the doctor was listening to his patient's pulse, Shigezō opened his eyes for an instant.

'Grandpa!'

'He'll be all right,' said the doctor, answering on his patient's behalf. 'I'm impressed that you knew about artificial respiration.'

'I learned it at school during the war. I even learned how to tie a tourniquet, but this is the first time I've had a chance to use these techniques in real life. And I was almost hysterical at the time! I really thought he was going to die when I saw water pouring out of his mouth. Then his eyes flickered. That's why I tried to resuscitate him.'

'You did an excellent job, especially as he had just swallowed all that water. There's nothing to worry about now.'

'But Grandpa can get around on his own and go to the toilet without assistance, so he shouldn't have had any trouble standing up in the bath. The water wasn't very deep. How could this have happened? Is it because he's suffering from senile dementia?'

'Oh no. Because of his age, he was probably just a little absent-minded. You must have heard of people on beaches and in swimming-pools drowning in water shallow enough to stand in, haven't you? Didn't you say yourself that he could have fallen asleep?'

174

'Well, that was my first impression. But his eyes were wide open. There's no doubt about that. He seemed to be in a sort of trance under the water. If he had just touched the bottom with his hands or feet when he began to go under, he wouldn't have been completely submerged. Actually, all he had to do to keep his head above water was to put his hands on the edge of the bath.'

How *could* Shigezō have nearly drowned? Akiko asked herself again and again, trying to allay her sense of guilt.

'Akiko!' cried Shigezō when at last he opened his eyes.

'Oh, Grandpa. It's me. Do you recognize me?'

'Akiko, who are these people? That woman's dressed like a nurse. Who is she?'

'The doctor and his nurse are here. I'm so glad you're all right, Grandpa!'

'Is he a doctor? I hate doctors. I don't mind nurses, but I don't like doctors at all.'

'Well then, I'll have to excuse myself,' said the doctor with a laugh.

Akiko heaved a sigh of relief. Nevertheless, she was appalled to hear her father-in-law speak so rudely to the doctor.

'My father-in-law has been taking tranquillizers at bedtime because he keeps seeing things at night and shouting that someone's broken in.'

The doctor thought for a moment, then announced that he would give Shigezō a sedative injection. Shigezō protested vehemently when he caught a glimpse of the needle.

'I don't want an injection, Akiko. That's why I hate doctors. Keep him away from me!'

Shigezō resisted valiantly, but his movements were so slow that the doctor and the nurse had no trouble pinning him down. After giving Shigezō the injection, the doctor smiled at Akiko and repeated that she had nothing to worry about. Seeing with her own eyes how energetic Shigezō was, Akiko was finally convinced. She bowed, then accompanied the doctor and the nurse to the door. How terrified she had been when she had lifted Shigezō's limp body from the tub! Now, however, she was in complete control of her emotions.

Listening to Shigezō's easy breathing, Akiko remembered what Mitsuko had said to her over the telephone. What was the world coming to? An old classmate was on the verge of death, and an eighty-five-year-old man had nearly drowned in shallow bath water. Happy memories of her friend Shizuko came flooding back, but strangely enough, the scene of Shigezō submerged in the water kept recurring in her mind's eye. The news that her friend was dying had shocked her, but seeing Shigezō so close to death had apparently affected her even more profoundly. Although Mitsuko had reminded her that they were of an age when cancer was a real risk, Akiko was not frightened in the least. As far as she was concerned, death was not that frightening. Her friend, the mother of a young child, was dying, and still Akiko could not sort out her feelings. On the other hand, Shigezō's near-drowning had shocked her profoundly. Was this because she was not directly responsible for Shizuko's condition? What would she have done if Shigezō had drowned in the bath? Even if the police had not treated it as 'accidental homicide', feelings of guilt and remorse would have haunted her for the rest of her life.

Akiko realized that her father-in-law's brush with death had completely altered the way she felt. When she visited the hospital, the terrifying reality of losing an old friend would no doubt come home to her. But at the moment, considering the circumstances, she could not feel guilty about her present lack of grief.

As soon as Nobutoshi and Satoshi returned home, she gave them a full report of everything that had happened, hoping that it would help to calm herself down. She was still in a highly agitated state. Akiko felt immensely relieved when neither her husband nor her son rebuked her for having been off her guard.

'I just can't believe it! Not in our bathtub,' said Nobutoshi.

Despite the lateness of the hour, Nobutoshi decided to take a bath himself now that the effects of his evening's drinking had worn off. As he went in and out of the bathroom, he kept on expressing his disbelief.

'The water doesn't even come up to my waist!' he shouted. Then when he emerged:

'I tried getting into different positions, but it's impossible to drown in that bath.'

'Well, there he was in the water, staring up at the ceiling. He didn't even put up a struggle!'

'How did he get like that in the first place?'

'My first impression was that he had dozed off, but his eyes were wide open.'

'You must have reached him just as he went under.'

'Perhaps. But he sicked up a lot of water as I lifted him out, and then went limp. I really thought he was dead. I was so frightened! Chills run down my spine when I think of it.'

After Nobutoshi and Satoshi had gone to bed, Akiko lay down and closed her eyes. In her mind's eye, the image of Shizuko was juxtaposed with that of Shigezō submerged underwater. Now that she had calmed down and was sure that Shigezō's life had been saved, the terrible truth that she was about to lose a close friend began to

176

weigh on her heavily. Had Shizuko lost a lot of weight? Akiko could not imagine what her friend, once so plump, would look like as she lay dying in a hospital bed.

Both she and Mitsuko were at risk from cancer. Was it an illness associated with ageing? No, Akiko remembered, there was that frightening type that afflicted children.

She had almost forgotten that she had arranged to meet Mitsuko the next day to go to the hospital with her. Shigezō's accident had upset her so much that she was afraid she would be unable to get any sleep that night, but because she had used up her last drop of energy she soon fell into a deep slumber. Outside, it was still raining. Akiko did not even dream of her friend.

In the middle of the night, she suddenly woke up. Glancing over at Shigezō, she saw that he was sleeping on his back. Something was wrong with him; he was breathing with great difficulty. Akiko felt his forehead and was startled at how hot it was. She leaped out of bed, took out the thermometer and put it under his arm, remembering that his normal temperature was 96.1. Was she imagining things? No, he did seem to be having difficulty breathing. Akiko checked the thermometer. It registered 102.

She raced up the stairs, shook Nobutoshi awake and told him that his father had a high fever. Then rushed downstairs again and phoned the doctor. She felt the old man's pulse. It was racing.

'Do you think he'll be all right, dear?' she asked Nobutoshi.

'Calm down, honey. He may have simply caught a cold.'

'Because he nearly drowned in the bathtub? But the doctor assured me that he'd be all right.'

The doctor arrived with a cross look on his face after coming through the rain. This time he was alone; if he had expected his nurse to accompany him on house-calls in the middle of the night, she would probably leave her job. Akiko suddenly remembered what Shigezō had said about hating doctors. Strange that she should think of something amusing at a time like this!

The doctor placed his stethoscope against Shigezō's chest.

'He has acute pneumonia.'

'Is it because of what happened earlier?'

'No. He's very old. The bad weather we've been having lately may have had a debilitating effect.'

'What about penicillin? Won't that help?' Nobutoshi asked quietly.

The doctor's glasses glinted. After a moment's pause, he said solemnly: 'If his fever doesn't go down, I'm afraid he'll last for only three more days.'

Akiko and Nobutoshi looked at each other in silence, the doctor's words echoing in their ears.

The doctor gave Shigezō three injections: two in the arm and a big one in his shrivelled buttocks. Shigezō did not twitch a muscle.

Nobutoshi found that his father's death would be far easier to accept than he had imagined. Shigezō was so decrepit that he had nearly drowned in the bathtub. No, it was not at all surprising that his father should be dying. However, Nobutoshi was disturbed by his calm reaction to this piece of news.

In the meantime, Akiko vividly recalled the white magnolia she had seen that afternoon in the rain. It was still raining, and it looked as if the rain would continue all night. Shigezō had stopped to gaze up at the magnolia. Perhaps he had been drawn to its beauty because he instinctively sensed the approach of death.

But Akiko had no time to dwell on such thoughts. She searched the house for two ice-bags which she had not used for years: one for Shigezō's pillow and the other for his forehead to help bring down the fever. Although she had not received specific instructions from the doctor, she could not let someone with a high fever rely solely on drugs. The ice-bag she placed on Shigezō's pillow did not give her any trouble, but the one she had filled with water and ice cubes for his forehead had sprung a tiny leak the size of a pinprick. Akiko went to great pains to repair the leak.

Nobutoshi returned home with the drugs prescribed by the doctor.

'It's raining cats and dogs out there. It's worse than usual for the rainy season. I bet there'll be landslides up in the mountains and whole villages will be swept away.'

Akiko suddenly thought of her husband's younger sister.

'You must inform Kyōko, dear.'

'I suppose so.'

Despite the lateness of the hour, Nobutoshi dialled his sister's number and briefly explained the situation. Then he replaced the receiver.

'She wasn't a bit surprised. When I told her that Father's condition was serious, she asked me when he was expected to die. That's disgusting!'

How typical of Kyōko, thought Akiko, but she did not dare to put her feelings into words.

The doctor had left instructions about the drugs. If Shigezō was unable to take them every two hours, they need not force him. But Nobutoshi and Akiko propped Shigezō up so that even though he had his eyes closed he somehow managed to swallow the dose, which

178

they had dissolved in sugar water. For some time after they had tucked Shigezō up in bed again, Nobutoshi watched his wife fussing with the ice-bags on his father's forehead and pillow. Then he went resolutely up the stairs as if he had made up his mind to get some sleep.

Akiko desperately needed to sleep, too, but she had to stay awake. According to the doctor, Shigezō had only three more days to live. As he was seriously ill, it was her duty to nurse him and, if necessary, to stay home from work, while her husband reported to his office. Akiko had not thought of asking Nobutoshi when his sister would be arriving, nor had he said anything about it before disappearing upstairs. Fortunately, it was Saturday. Surely he would not play golf tomorrow!

The ice cubes in the bag on Shigezō's forehead soon melted, and the water quickly turned lukewarm. Worried that the supply of ice in the freezer compartment would not be sufficient, Akiko made more ice cubes. The doctor had told them that, if the fever did not abate, Shigezō would die. Akiko knew that the cause of the fever was internal and that the ice-bags applied externally could not bring it down, but she could not remain idle while her father-in-law lay dying. Only three more days of suffering on her part and then she would be free of all her troubles. Akiko's emotions were in turmoil as these thoughts passed through her mind.

'Has something happened?'

Akiko turned and saw her son standing by the door to the toilet.

'Grandpa has a high fever. We had to call the doctor. He diagnosed acute pneumonia and said that Grandpa has only three more days to live.'

Satoshi disappeared into the toilet. From where she was in the kitchen, Akiko heard a powerful jet of water, and memories of how she used to get up in the middle of the night to help Shigezō out into the garden came flooding back to her. How different that sound had been!

Satoshi came out of the toilet and slowly walked over to where his grandfather was lying. Without a word, he sat down cross-legged near the old man's pillow.

'The ice cubes melt so quickly! The doctor gave him an injection to help bring down the fever, but it worked for only about fifteen minutes.'

Akiko added more ice and carefully placed the ice bag back on her father-in-law's forehead. Shigezō remained motionless, his eyes closed. He was still having great difficulty breathing, but he was fast asleep.

179

'Is Grandpa really dying, Mum?' Satoshi asked the question that Akiko would probably have asked herself if she had been bold enough to probe into the depths of her heart. Ever since she was a child, she had believed that death was the most momentous event in one's life. Yet in certain cases it was surely much more difficult to go on living. Satoshi went back upstairs without waiting for a reply.

Exhausted from putting ice cubes into the ice-bags at regular intervals, Akiko resolved to get some sleep. Before she could go back to bed, however, she still had to check Shigezō's diaper. With the help of her dryer, she had been able to get the freshly-laundered diapers dry even during the present rainy spell. She took up a folded diaper and, turning back the bottom of Shigezō's quilt, pushed up his nightclothes to remove the diaper cover. Just as she had expected, his diaper was soaking wet. Unlike a baby's nappy, however, it gave off a foul odour. With a practised hand, Akiko slipped a fresh diaper into place, and gently lifting his penis which had probably been limp for the past twenty years, fixed it in place with the cover. She gave Shigezō a little spank, then froze, appalled by her own action. Was she not behaving with disrespect towards a dying man?

After Akiko had disposed of the wet diaper, she went back to bed. But as soon as she closed her eyes a vivid image of her father-in-law drowning in the bathtub appeared in her mind. Though she tried her utmost to drive out the distressing memory, she kept remembering his limp body sprawled out on the wooden slats. Akiko had thought that he was dead, and had been petrified with fear. What had upset her most of all was the thought that her negligence had caused his death. How relieved she had been when the doctor had assured her that Shigezō would be all right! But he had probably caught pneumonia as a result of the incident, so was she not to blame for his critical condition after all? The thought was more than she could bear. What if Kyōko probed into the cause of her father's illness and discovered that it was Akiko's fault? The thought that even her husband might become suspicious of her made Akiko fear that she was losing her mind. This was certainly not the time to think about how unpleasant it was to look after a senile old man. Had she struggled in vain during the past six months? She wondered why she felt so distressed.

When she opened her eyes, Akiko saw that the ice-bags had again grown limp. The bag with a leak finally broke while she was adding more cubes. Unperturbed, she proceeded to wring a towel in a basin of iced water and placed it on Shigezō's forehead. When she checked his temperature, it was 103.

Akiko got no sleep that night. Before long, day began to dawn. Both Nobutoshi and Satoshi slept late on Sunday mornings. When

180

the rain finally stopped, Akiko rushed out to the pharmacy to buy a new ice-bag. She also bought a feeding-cup in case Shigezō, who must have been terribly thirsty from the fever, could not manage a glass. As the local market was closed, she walked all the way to Kōenji and bought several oranges at the department store, which was already bustling with activity minutes after it had opened.

Not long after Akiko returned home, Shigezō opened his eyes. 'You recognize me, don't you, Grandpa? Of course you do. See these oranges? I'll squeeze some for you.'

Shigezō closed his eyes a moment later, but at least he was still alive. Akiko's spirits rose. She cut an orange in half and squeezed out the juice. Then she poured it into the feeding-cup and helped Shigezō to drink it a sip at a time. His eyes were still closed, but he pursed his mouth as if he were savouring the delicious flavour. How very much alive he is, thought Akiko as she watched his deeply lined neck quivering as he swallowed.

Even though she had had a sleepless night, Akiko decided to prepare a special Sunday brunch for her family, who usually had only tea and toast in the morning. She prepared a traditional Japanese breakfast, including rice and miso soup. At about eleven, Nobutoshi and Satoshi came downstairs. Their eyes glowed with delight when they saw the salted salmon, seaweed, and soup, to which Akiko had added eggs.

'How's Grandpa?' asked Satoshi, stuffing his mouth full of hot rice.

'He still has a high fever. That ice-bag finally broke, so I had to go out and buy a new one.'

'Nursing Grandpa must be pretty hard work for you, Mum.'

'I didn't sleep a wink last night. When you've finished eating, dear, please take my place.'

'I'll take your place, honey,' said Nobutoshi, looking up from the newspaper. 'You'd better go and get some sleep.'

Akiko asked Satoshi to clear away the breakfast dishes and gave her husband detailed instructions about Shigezō's medication and the ice-bags. Then, her legs unsteady, she made her way up the stairs. Too tired to take out her own bedding from the closet, she crawled into her husband's without bothering to change into her nightgown. The musky odour made her realize that it was a long time since she had slept with her husband. At last she fell into a deep sleep.

Some time later Akiko was awakened by Satoshi. 'There's a phone call from Auntie,' he announced.

'You could have asked your father to talk to her. Why do I have to answer the phone?'

'But she said that you were going to meet her today.'

Akiko had assumed it was Kyōko. Of course, Mitsuko was also Satoshi's aunt, she realized.

'I'm terribly sorry, Mitsuko.'

'Has anything happened? I waited for half an hour. This isn't like you at all.'

'Grandpa developed acute pneumonia last night and has a high fever. The doctor said that he has only three more days to live. I was up all night and just had a bit of sleep while Nobutoshi and Satoshi looked after him. Please forgive me.'

'I can imagine how difficult it must be for you. You can't possibly leave the house, can you?'

'I'm afraid not. I should have got in touch with you sooner. I really am sorry.'

'Please don't apologize. I'll go by myself to the hospital; I've already told Shizuko that I'd come and see her today. I've bought her a little present.'

'Please tell her that I'll visit her when things settle down.'

Bowing again and again, Akiko replaced the receiver. Because of the excitement of the previous night, she had forgotten completely about going to the hospital. After Shigezō's near-drowning, she had not had a moment to herself to think about her friend. Now, on a sudden impulse, she had said that she would visit Shizuko after things had settled down. She was shocked to realize that by this she meant that she would visit the hospital after Shigezō's death. Shigezō had only three more days to live; Shizuko, on the other hand, had at least a week.

Akiko began climbing the stairs, intending to get a little more sleep. She stopped halfway and asked: 'When will Kyōko be arriving, dear?'

'Haven't you read the paper? All trains on the Tōhoku Line have been suspended because of the damage caused by the rains. She probably won't get here today.'

Nobutoshi filled the ice-bag carefully with cubes, but then dropped it on Shigezō's forehead. Aghast, Akiko said: 'Remember, dear, Father has a high fever. You practically threw the ice at him! Don't you realize that the bag will hurt him if there's nothing but ice in it? You should add a little water. And have you checked his nappy?'

'No, not yet.'

Men are so helpless, thought Akiko, clicking her tongue in irritation. She came back downstairs and angrily flung aside the bottom of the quilt. A terrible smell filled the room. Nobutoshi and

Satoshi recoiled, then leaned over to have a look. What they saw filled them with revulsion. Akiko ordered her son to bring her a damp towel, then asked Nobutoshi to hand her a fresh diaper. Furious, she began to clean up the blackish excrement. She had got used to Shigezō wetting his diaper, but this was the first time she had had to change a soiled one. It must have required a great amount of energy to force out all that excrement, she thought. How puzzling that a man, fast asleep and with a high fever, could manage such a feat. She had a difficult time getting Shigezō clean. His penis and testicles were smeared with excrement. Finally she had to fetch a bucket of soapy water. She was extremely agitated performing this unpleasant task while Nobutoshi and Satoshi stood stiffly by, mistakenly assuming that Akiko was accustomed to performing this ritual. After flushing the filthy water down the toilet, she made her way upstairs again, determined to get a little more sleep. If Shigezō really had only three more days to live, she would be kept busy all the next day. She probably wouldn't get much sleep that night either, and Nobutoshi would be leaving for work early the next morning. She told herself that it was her duty to keep Shigezō alive at least until his daughter arrived.

Kyōko finally came the following evening. She was wearing a short-sleeved two-piece suit under her raincoat, and was carrying a white vinyl suitcase. Akiko was astonished that her sister-in-law was not exhausted after travelling such a distance. She simply took one look at Akiko's face and launched into a monologue.

'As Mother died when it was snowing, Father must be thinking that the least he can do is to die when it's raining. We really did have a lot of snow this winter, didn't we? The last time I was in Tokyo, the snow had already melted, but we had quite a bit of snow earlier this year. Every time it snowed, I thought of Mother. It didn't surprise me at all to hear that Father was dying. After all, what's the use of living if you don't know what's going on around you any more? All his brothers and sisters are dead, and I imagine most of his friends are, too. How can he go on living when he doesn't even recognize his own son and daughter? I'm sorry his fever hasn't come down. I bet he wants desperately to be relieved from his suffering.'

How can Kyōko say such things when her father is so close to death? thought Akiko.

She told her sister-in-law about the times Shigezō had run away from home and how upset the family had been each time.

'Really?' Even though Kyōko had once had to chase after her father herself, she was so unmoved by Akiko's account that Akiko might as well have been talking about a complete stranger.

183

'A runaway? Oh dear! Do you mean that even the Ministry of Welfare has given up on such people? Where I come from, there'd be such a fuss if the police got involved. But then in a small town someone would stop a runaway right away. In Tokyo it's like running through a jungle. Come to think of it, though, there are quite a number of 'runaways' out in the provinces. The father of a distant relation of my husband is one! Not too long ago he walked all the way to a nearby town! Luckily, our town barber happened to see him there behaving strangely and brought him home.'

Kyōko laughed merrily. All this time Shigezō slept soundly. Despite his voracious appetite in the past, he did not ask for food. Akiko felt sorry for him and tried to get him to take some fresh orange or apple juice. When she pressed the feeding-cup to his lips, Shigezō would purse his mouth and somehow manage to swallow half the contents.

'How can a man who's supposed to die tomorrow drink at all?' asked Kyōko.

Akiko wanted to tell Kyōko how Shigezō had stood in the rain, gazing in rapture at the magnolia, but she resisted the impulse. On Tuesday evening there was still no sign of Shigezō's fever abating. The doctor made a formal house-call once a day, visiting briefly every morning to see how his patient was doing. On each occasion, he gave Shigezō an injection. No one, not even Kyōko, had the courage to ask him how much longer Shigezō would live.

Kyōko decided to sleep in the cottage. All night long she and Akiko took it in turns to look after Shigezō. By Wednesday Kyōko had run out of topics of conversation, so she asked: 'By the way, Akiko, what are you planning to do with the cottage? Though the property is small, it's all that Father and Mother left behind.'

'But we're the ones who built the cottage for them, and it's registered in Nobutoshi's name.'

'They have surface rights to the place if they've lived there for ten years,' argued Kyōko.

Akiko experienced a moment of extreme discomfort. It was so unseemly to fight over an inheritance! She suddenly felt very cold, before realizing that Kyōko hadn't brought up the subject out of any selfish motive. Talking about the cottage was probably her way of dealing with the painful thought that her parents had left nothing of value behind.

'When I think about it, Father led such a wretched life! All he ever did from the time he was young was to complain. Nothing ever pleased him, he was always grumbling. His only concern was that delicate stomach of his. I still feel sorry for poor Mother, having to put up with him. At the marriage interview with my husband, the only thing Father wanted to know was whether he had a strong stomach! You should have seen my husband's face! He told Father that the only time he had had a stomach-ache was when he once ate too much as a child. Father seemed to be satisfied with that. Of course, my husband has his faults, but he's easier to live with than Father. Father made himself unhappy. He was so bad-tempered and spiteful that he didn't have a single friend! What did he live for all his life? He never showed any interest in a hobby.'

Akiko felt pity for Shigezō, having a daughter like Kyōko, who went on and on in this vein even though she knew that he did not have long to live. Nevertheless, she could not help agreeing with her. Shigezō hadn't had any particular interests and he had been extremely difficult to get on with. He hadn't made friends with his neighbours, or gone to the theatre or worked on bonsai. Cooped up in a tiny cottage with his wife, he had not had enough stimulation to avoid becoming senile. Mrs Kadotani had insulted Shigezō by saying that senility was a state of mind, but there was a great deal of truth in what she said. Akiko resolved to keep both her mind and body active. She would cultivate various interests to keep her busy in her old age. Growing old should not be someone else's problem.

Four days after Shigezō first developed a high fever, Akiko came downstairs after her nap and found Kyōko watching television. Startled to see a change in Shigezō, Akiko dashed over to him. His body seemed to be turned slightly to the right. 'Grandpa!' she cried. She felt faint when she discovered that his body was cold to the touch. Trembling, she took his pulse. It was steady. She slipped a thermometer into his armpit. Kyōko turned around for a second, then went back to the television.

Shigezō's temperature had come down to 97.7, which was only slightly higher than his normal temperature. Even to Akiko's untrained eyes he seemed to be out of danger.

'His temperature's dropped, Kyōko.'

'Then we'll have to get the doctor to come over right away.'

'Yes, I'll call him.'

Akiko felt vastly relieved, thinking that Shigezō had passed the crisis. Kyōko, on the other hand, believed that her father was about to breathe his last. When Akiko phoned the doctor's office, she was told that he was out making house-calls and would probably be calling at their place first. No sooner had she replaced the receiver than the doctor arrived at the house with his bag. Practically flinging herself at him, Akiko reported that the fever had abated. The doctor

185

listened carefully to Shigezō's chest with his stethoscope, then looked up in relief.

'It's a miracle that he's pulled through. His heartbeat is quite steady. He has a remarkably strong heart. He'll be all right now, so you needn't worry any more. This is good news!'

Akiko thanked the doctor and, bowing, saw him out. For a while both Akiko and Kyōko remained speechless. Then Akiko phoned her husband.

'What did he say?' asked Kyōko.

'All he said was "Oh, really?"'

'There's nothing much a person can say at a time like this. But I brought my funeral outfit with me, and my mother-in-law even gave me an obituary gift. This is such a disappointment!'

Akiko felt immensely relieved. During the past few days, as Shigezō clung to life, she had stopped feeling so guilty. It was a good thing that she had made him drink the fruit juice! Though the quantity had been small, it had no doubt helped him to keep up his strength. She also congratulated herself for not having increased the dose of the tranquillizer even though she had been so distressed by his screams in the middle of the night. Hadn't the doctor said that Shigezō's heartbeat was steady and his heart strong? This was not only because he had a strong constitution, but also because Akiko had been careful in doling out the medicine. If she had given him large doses, his heart would have given way long before he caught pneumonia. Akiko felt giddy with relief. Suddenly feeling very hungry, she was overcome by an irresistible urge to go on a binge. She picked up her wallet and shopping basket and set off to the market. Once there, she wanted to buy everything in sight.

For dinner that night Akiko served a great variety of dishes – stewed fish, pork cutlet and barbecued chicken. She ate as heartily as her son, but Kyōko was still so disappointed that she only had some *chazuke* and fish. Nobutoshi was out, probably in a bar somewhere; celebrating his father's miraculous recovery. The three at home had very little to say to each other.

'Has Grandpa really recovered?' Satoshi asked. Getting no reply, and finding it extremely difficult to talk to his aunt, he excused himself and disappeared upstairs.

'Hello,' whispered a voice.

Startled, Akiko looked over at Shigezō and saw that his eyes were open.

'Grandpa, you're awake! Isn't it wonderful that your fever's gone? Can I get you anything? How about some juice? I know, I'll prepare some rice gruel for you.'

186

A faint smile seemed to play on Shigezō's face as he looked up at Akiko. As he was wearing his dentures, the lower half of his face was without expression, but charming wrinkles formed at the corners of his eyes.

When Akiko went into the kitchen, Shigezō cried out again. 'Hello!'

'Have you wet your diaper, Grandpa?'

Shigezō smiled. Akiko checked his diaper and saw that it was wet. Watching her sister-in-law expertly change her father's diaper, Kyōko laughed merrily.

'This is ridiculous! What does he mean by "hello"? I'm not coming at all next time, even if you tell me he's dead.'

Akiko said nothing, but in her heart she made a strong resolution. All these months she had hated every minute she had had to spend looking after her father-in-law. But, starting today, she vowed to prolong his life for as long as she possibly could, knowing in her heart that she was the only one in the family who was able to do so. The rain had stopped earlier in the day, but now it began to drizzle again. That night Akiko listened intently to the sound of the rain.

16

After four days of high fever, Shigezō did not make an immediate recovery. His movements were now even slower than before and he looked unwell. He had lost a considerable amount of weight and he became even more taciturn. As he now walked about very little, Akiko no longer had to worry about him wandering off. He no longer complained about being hungry, although he continued to eat whatever he was given. The most noticeable change was that his hair had turned completely grey.

Akiko heard from Mitsuko that Shizuko's condition had suddenly deteriorated and that she had died the day after Shigezō's temperature returned to normal. Akiko expressed her deep regret that she had not visited her friend in hospital.

'It's a good thing you didn't go,' remarked Mitsuko. 'Shizuko had grown terribly thin. You couldn't possibly imagine what she looked like at the end. She was a mere shadow of her former self. She didn't know that she was dying and kept on saying how lucky she was that she didn't have cancer. I got so upset at one point that I changed the subject and told her what you were going through. By the way, how have things been with you since your father-in-law nearly drowned?'

'By a miracle he survived. The doctor said his heart is stronger than that of most men his age. His temperature's back to normal and he's been eating rice gruel since yesterday.'

'Really?' said Mitsuko after a pause. 'Do you mean to tell me that our friend died but your father-in-law survived? You were lucky! I'm sure you'd have felt guilty if he had died. But from now on you'll be kept busy looking after him.'

'I know, but lately things have quietened down a little.'

'The future's not going to be easy. We've both reached the age

188

where we have to watch for signs of cancer, and even if we don't get it, we can't fight old age.'

'That's very true, Mitsuko. I often wonder what people will do about the elderly in the future. I feel it's my duty to take good care of Grandpa.'

Akiko had not told a soul how she had resolved to do her best to prolong her father-in-law's life for as long as possible. And now she had good reason for wanting to keep him alive.

She knew full well that Shigezō, who by some miracle had recovered from his recent illness, had gone far beyond the limits of old age. Lately, he often smiled with his eyes without opening his mouth or uttering a sound. In all these years, Akiko had never seen such a benign expression on Shigezō's face. He had always looked displeased and had grumbled about one thing or another. Neither Kyōko nor Akiko could recall ever seeing him happy and content. Since his recovery from acute pneumonia, however, he always had an angelic smile on his face. He smiled when Akiko guessed his wishes correctly and when she served him his meals. He smiled whenever he beckoned to her. Sitting by himself, from time to time he would break into a smile for no apparent reason.

'Satoshi would smile like that right after he was born. I used to wonder whether he was dreaming, as it was before his eyes were able to focus on objects. The doctor called it a mindless smile. I remember thinking that babies were really like little angels. Grandpa's just like that, don't you think?' asked Akiko. 'I wonder if this is what it's like for a man to become a god.'

Nobutoshi and Satoshi seemed to agree with her.

'Who was it who said man endlessly transcends man or something to that effect?'

'I think it was Pascal.'

'I didn't know you were familiar with the quotation, Satoshi.'

'I know that one. But do you think it describes a man like Grandpa?'

'Probably not. But then again, perhaps it does.'

'Well, Grandpa has certainly transcended the ordinary man.'

In some ways, Shigezō was indeed more god than man now; his life was spontaneous and pure. He no longer went into the toilet, a place of defilement, nor did he chose a time or place to relieve himself. Akiko had to make sure that he was wearing his diaper at all times. As the rainy season drew to a close, Mrs Kadotani, who was at her wit's end trying to get her mother-in-law's diapers dry, finally gave up and asked to use Akiko's dryer. Whenever she came with her damp laundry, she sat down and chatted with Akiko.

'Things have been difficult for me, but the washing-machine has been a real lifesaver. I can't imagine how I'd feel if I had to wash these diapers by hand.'

'I give my father-in-law his meals at set times, then put on a disposable nappy just before he's likely to have a bowel movement. It's so much easier for me afterwards. I've finally devised a system that works.'

'It's a little easier for me, as my mother-in-law can still talk. She is able to tell me when she needs to use the bedpan. Of course, it's a different matter when I'm not at home.'

'I'm sure it's not so much bother to clean up after a woman. It's very messy in the case of a man.'

'I suppose it is, with all those additional parts to wipe clean,' said Mrs Kadotani, laughing merrily.

Akiko had taken leave of absence from her job. Now that she had time on her hands during the day, she was pleased to see her neighbours when they dropped in. Talking to other women who had old relatives to look after, she learned that she was not alone in her suffering and took great comfort in this knowledge.

One day Mrs Kihara came to visit.

'You're lucky he's not a chain-smoker. Before my father-in-law died, he used to light one cigarette after another. He often forgot where he put them. The house was always full of smoke. It became so dangerous that I couldn't take my eyes off him for a minute. Even now my husband says it's a miracle the house didn't burn down, considering he once set a waste-paper basket on fire! The minute my father-in-law got up in the morning, he lit a cigarette, and he smoked non-stop all day long. He would often forget the cigarette he'd been smoking a minute earlier and light another. He smoked between eighty and a hundred cigarettes every day.'

'No! As I remember, he was healthy to the very end.'

'He was. He'd go out to buy his own cigarettes. When I asked him to cut down on smoking for the sake of his health, he refused, saying that to someone his age life was no longer precious.'

'What was he like towards the end?'

'He became senile. Everyone says that he died an easy death. He was in perfect health until the very end. I would leave a large bowl of water near his bed because he refused to stop smoking, and in the morning it would be full of cigarette butts. He must have died satisfied. I was so glad I didn't take his cigarettes away.'

Mrs Kihara paused for a moment, then laughed. She had not come to talk about her father-in-law, but rather to ask Akiko if she would consider renting out the detached cottage. A distant male relative of hers had got married while still attending college and was looking for a place to live. She wondered whether the Tachibanas would consider renting the cottage to the young couple for a period of two years; her family would act as guarantors.

Even as Akiko replied that she would have to consult her husband before giving a definite answer, she began to make certain stipulations.

'If they're willing to look after Grandpa during the day, they can stay in the cottage rent-free. My boss has asked me to work three days a week. Grandpa's quiet and easy to look after now, but I don't want to leave him at home unattended. I get bored at home as there's so little for me to do. But I suppose a young couple wouldn't agree to look after an old man.'

'I wouldn't be so sure of that. Remember that we'll be old ourselves one day.'

Akiko was taken aback by the sharp tone of Mrs Kihara's voice. Her neighbour was obviously very proud of the way she had taken care of her senile father-in-law.

'I don't think it's a good idea to let them have the cottage rent-free. Why don't you set the rent at something like 20,000 yen and then say that you'll pay them 10,000 or 10,500 yen to keep an eye on your father-in-law. That way would be best for everyone.'

'I just hope they'll agree to those terms!'

'The summer vacation will be starting soon, so I'm sure they'll be delighted. Please speak to your husband about them. For my part, I'll explain to the young couple that they're being considered as potential tenants provided they agree to look after your father-in-law.'

Not long after Mrs Kihara's departure, Mrs Kadotani dropped by. She had recently visited a nursing home and complained that her mother-in-law would probably never be accepted into a home because there was an able-bodied woman to look after her. Although the facilities at the home were nice and clean, she felt very sorry for the six old people who had to share each room, their beds lined up in a row. In her opinion, it hardly mattered that the facilities were outstanding.

'Whenever I change her diapers, my mother-in-law says that she wishes she were dead. She must feel she's a terrible burden. I really hated her when she used to torment me, but now I think that one day I may be like her. Now that I've actually been to a nursing home, my views on ageing have changed. Fate may be kinder to me if I take good care of my mother-in-law. I don't suppose what I'm saying makes much sense to you.'

'On the contrary, I know exactly how you feel. I sometimes wonder if I'm having a religious experience, because at times I feel as if I were serving a god.'

'That's because your father-in-law has become so senile. My mother-in-law has a long way to go before she reaches that stage.'

Akiko always took Shigezō with her when she went shopping. Before his pneumonia, he had had the mentality of a five- or six-year-old child. Now, he seemed to think and behave like a child of three. Whenever he found himself in front of a pet shop, he refused to move. Crouching in front of the cages, he never seemed to tire of gazing at the birds moving about inside them. On sunny days Akiko would quietly watch the birds with him. His eyes would also light up when he found himself in the fish department of the local market.

'What shall we have for dinner today, Grandpa? Would you like this fish or do you prefer a fillet? How about some smoked fish?'

Shigezō's choice semed to be the smoked fish, for he was beaming happily. As it was expensive, Akiko bought only one portion for him and chose a cheaper kind for the family. Smiling was now his only means of expressing his wishes. She wondered whether her mother-in-law had ever known that he was capable of smiling so sweetly.

When Akiko told Nobutoshi about Mrs Kihara's request, he was far from keen.

'Did you say that they're married college students?'

Akiko was still worried that Satoshi might fail his college entrance examination, which he planned to take the next spring. Nobutoshi, on the other hand, was more concerned that the young couple might be student activists who had participated in the recent disturbances; he was afraid that they would disturb the neighbours.

'Mrs Kihara said that her family would act as their guarantors. If you're so distrustful, would you like me to draw up an agreement? I'm an expert at it, so it wouldn't be any trouble.'

'But if they're part of the New Left, a written document won't mean anything to them.'

'What makes you think they might be activists? Let me ask Mrs Kihara about it.'

'Even if they aren't, don't you think it's outrageous for a young couple to get married while they're still at college?'

Satoshi suddenly burst out laughing. 'You're so old-fashioned, Dad!'

Both Nobutoshi and Akiko were taken back. They suddenly had to face the fact that next year Satoshi would be a college student himself and that he could conceivably even get married.

192

The generation gap was much in the news these days. Adults had always complained about the younger generation, but recently the newspapers and magazines had vied with each other to be the first to report the student disturbances. Accompanying these articles were photographs of the most violent scenes. Not surprisingly, parents of young adults spent their days in a state of constant anxiety. They knew that if they were excessively strict, their children would rebel – perhaps even run away from home; on the other hand, if they spoilt them they might find themselves with juvenile delinquents on their hands. Parents were therefore caught up in a terrible dilemma. One reason for Akiko and Nobutoshi's apprehension was that since the beginning of the year Satoshi had begun to let his hair grow. He tried his best to convince his parents that long hair was now the fashion, but they were not convinced. They were afraid that if they ordered him to cut it, he would let it grow even longer in defiance. It occurred to them that possibly he let his hair grow simply because he did not want to spend his allowance on a haircut, but neither Nobutoshi nor Akiko had the courage to ask him about it. When they found themselves alone together, they often quarrelled about whose responsibility it was. It was after one such quarrel that they quite unexpectedly agreed to rent the cottage to the college students. They felt that it might get them used to the changes that lay in store and prepare them to face Satoshi's immediate future.

'I agreed to pay them 10,000 yen to look after Grandfather on Mondays, Wednesdays and Fridays. Mrs Kihara visited Grandpa, and afterwards she said that he wouldn't be difficult to take care of. You know, dear, she had quite a hard time with her father-in-law before he died.'

'Taking care of the elderly seems to be a problem in every household.'

'It does, doesn't it? I've been thinking seriously about how to keep myself from ageing too quickly. They say that a person should have a hobby. I think I'll practice calligraphy at home on Tuesdays and Thursdays. I loved my lessons as a child. Maybe I'll take a correspondence course.'

'Oh?'

The songbird in the cage hanging from the eaves began to sing. Shigezō, who obviously had no trouble with his hearing, looked up and smiled. Akiko had bought the bird at a pet shop as a present for Shigezō on his eighty-fifth birthday. One of her responsibilities was to see that the bird always had a fresh supply of food and water. Not only was Shigezō unable to look after the bird, but there was even the danger that, like a little boy, he would kill it by fondling it too roughly. The cage was therefore hung up high where he could not reach it. Shigezō, who no longer watched television, never tired of gazing at the bird.

The day the young couple were scheduled to move in, Akiko got up early and gave the cottage a thorough cleaning. Without a moment's hesitation, she hurled the box of false teeth into the dustbin. The young couple finally arived, bringing with them two sets of bedding, several scarf-wrapped bundles and a small suitcase.

'I'm Yamagishi.'

'And I'm Emi.'

The two young people introduced themselves informally, merely nodding to Akiko. She helped them move their things into the cottage, then took them into the tiny kitchen to show them where the main gas switch was located. To her surprise, the only kitchen utensils they had brought with them were a pot, a frying pan, two bowls and chopsticks.

'When did you get married?'

'Yamagishi, can you remember?'

'Wasn't it some time last summer?'

'You're probably right. I can't believe it's almost a year ago. How time flies!'

'And we really haven't accomplished a thing.'

'True.'

Akiko began to suspect that they were not legally married, as Emi called her husband by his last name. She was also left in the dark about a number of other things. There was a youthful plumpness about Emi. She was fair and petite and, all in all, quite a beauty. As if she had read Akiko's mind, she giggled nervously and explained that when she first began to live with Yamagishi in his boarding-house, their friends had come to visit them in an endless stream. They had had a great time, she confessed, but they had been unable to get down to any serious studying.

'When will you two be graduating?'

'I graduated this year, but Yamagishi didn't. He was a little too active during the student disturbances. Since then he's had second thoughts and is now serious about getting his degree. He's always been fond of academic work, but for a time he was completely disenchanted with the whole educational system. I'd very much like him to get his degree, so we agreed to move to a place where he could get some work done.'

'I see.'

Akiko's heart felt heavy. They were young and attractive, but they had been student activists. And Mrs Kihara had assured her

194

there was nothing for her to worry about! Although her neighbour hadn't actually lied, she had not been very candid about the young couple, either. The only thing that comforted Akiko was the hope that they really did enjoy studying and had moved to a quiet place where they would not be bothered by their friends.

Noticing that Shigezō was peering into the cottage from beyond the veranda, Akiko went over to him and introduced him to the young couple.

'Hello, Grandpa,' said Emi in a loud voice, looking down at him. Akiko was surprised when Shigezō looked up at Emi and smiled.

'So this is the ten-thousand-yen Grandpa,' exclaimed Yamagishi, throwing a glance at Akiko.

The young couple were in an enviable position, as their tuition and living expenses were paid for by their parents, who lived in the provinces. They had met and fallen in love during a student strike, but only told their parents about their relationship after they had begun living together. Their parents had taken the news quite calmly. After all, it was not nearly as shocking as the report that their children were locked up in a police cell. Akiko picked up all this information in the weeks that followed. Learning that the young couple had once spent a night in jail, she grew pale and went immediately to confront Mrs Kihara.

'Oh? They don't strike me as being radicals. But then, Mrs Tachibana, that's the way students are these days. A few of them may become professional revolutionaries, but most take part in protests only while they're at college. There are other things I've seen on the news that I find far more disturbing. Take inflation. It's appalling that no one does anything to stop it,' exclaimed Mrs Kihara, venting her anger on Akiko.

Akiko felt instinctively that she should not tell Nobutoshi what she had learned about the tenants, afraid that he would say 'I told you so.' She couldn't keep it completely to herself, however, and told Satoshi about the activities of the young couple.

'Wow! Aren't they something?'

Akiko immediately wished she hadn't told him. For a while she was terribly worried that he would visit the cottage and come under their influence, but during the summer vacation he diligently attended summer school in Yoyogi. When he got home from school, he would take a nap, and then get up in the middle of the night to begin his studies. He didn't have a moment in which to chat with the Yamagishis.

Akiko found it hard to believe that Shigezō and Emi were getting along so well. After recovering from his recent illness, Shigezō could

195

not even recall Akiko's name. When he wanted something he said 'Hello.' He was no longer afraid of strangers. He had become very much attached to Emi, and so far there had been no trouble during the three days each week that Akiko was away at work. When Emi went shopping with Shigezō in tow, she took the opportunity to go for a stroll, sometimes as far as Seibi Mountain. So long as Akiko remembered to hang the bird-cage from the eaves of the cottage before leaving for work, Shigezō would sit all day long on the veranda gazing dreamily at the bird. Now and then he would doze off. Occasionally he would flash a smile at Emi.

Akiko often worried that her father-in-law would disturb Yamagishi, who appeared to be busy at his studies. Much to her surprise, she learned that Emi had been accepted into graduate school. She noted that the young couple always seemed to be reading. It was an ideal match between a promising student and a talented young woman, both of whom were willing to sacrifice everything for the sake of their studies. Their meals were very simple: bread and noodles, with some ham and eggs for protein. Although they received a monthly allowance from home, it was not enough to cover all their expenses. They had therefore reduced their food budget to the barest minimum. Akiko could not help but notice their plain fare. Their indifference to what they ate reminded her of the situation in Japan immediately after the war. As the monthly rent of 20,000 yen was a great deal of money in the eyes of the young couple, they could not afford to do without the 10,000 yen they earned by taking care of Shigezō.

Before leaving for work, Akiko always made sure that Shigezō had on a double layer of disposable diapers. Returning home from work one day, about two months after Emi had started looking after Shigezō, she was surprised to find him dry. When she went over to the cottage to thank Emi, the girl said: 'I don't mind changing his diapers. It's a smelly job, but if I make sure he doesn't sit down after having his lunch, it's really no trouble at all. He seems to have a bowel movement every day at about the same time.'

'Yes. He has no problems with his digestion.'

'He's really no different from us. After all, we eat the same food, don't we?' said Emi, laughing.

Akiko was genuinely grateful for the young couple's help. On her days off, she would often prepare enough stewed fish or chicken and rice to share with the Yamagishis. They never failed to express their deep appreciation when she delivered the food to the cottage.

When the young couple called Shigezō, he always went over to the cottage immediately.

'Grandpa, come and join us,' cried Emi one morning. Shigezō smiled to indicate that this was precisely what he wanted to do.

'Grandpa seems to be so happy!' said Akiko as she handed him over.

'Yes,' replied Emi. 'He's never discontented, and he looks happily at the bird all day long. Such an elegant life! He's like a wise old sage. Isn't he in some ways the ideal man?'

'He's got a crush on Emi,' said Yamagishi.

'Oh?'

'He doesn't say hello or smile at me. I'm beginning to think that a man can't live without a woman, whatever his age. Being a man, it makes me feel both happy and sad.'

Akiko then told the couple how Shigezō had quickly forgotten his son but had recognized her until fairly recently. Very much amused, the Yamagishis listened attentively.

'It isn't all that bad to forget everything,' said Yamagishi. 'Emi keeps calling Grandpa the ideal man. Early man had no need for toilet paper. You know, Aunt, it was in the sixteenth century, during the reign of Toyotomi Hideyoshi, that the Japanese began to build privies as a part of the house and discovered that human excrement made excellent fertilizer. These developments accompanied the growth of cities. Grandpa must have regressed to an earlier stage and become like the men who lived in Japan before the sixteenth century.'

Akiko was so startled when Yamagishi addressed her as 'Aunt' that she found herself lost for words. Shigezō obviously meant more to the couple than mere money; they were studying and analysing him. Nevertheless, Akiko could see that they were too young to think about growing old. The same was true of Satoshi. Although he had begged his parents not to live as long as Shigezō, he could not possibly imagine that one day he too would be an old man. Young people were too self-centered. The Yamagishis were happy, so they assumed that everyone else was. Spending one's time gazing at birds was an elegant pastime only if one was able to lead a life of leisure.

Apart from his usual 'hello', Shigezō hardly said a word. The Yamagishis often imitated him, calling out 'Hello' to each other. The young couple found that looking after Shigezō was no trouble at all; rather, Shigezō brought a welcome change into their dull lives. Akiko considered herself very fortunate. As for Shigezō, he preferred Emi to anyone else and seemed to be delighted whenever she spoke to him.

Now that she went to work only three days a week, Akiko's take-home pay was smaller. On the other hand, she was warmly welcomed at the office and no longer felt depressed about the possibility of losing her job. The other four days she stayed at home and had all the time in the world to savour the little pleasures in life. A special festival day was observed on the thirteenth and twenty-third day of each month at the Myōhō-ji Temple in the adjoining district of Horinouchi. On those days Akiko would take Shigezō by the hand and set out for the temple. While he sat watching people trying to catch goldfish, Akiko often went to the potted-plant stalls to buy some young seedlings. Not having done any gardening for the last ten years, she took great pleasure in planting morning glories, sunflowers and salvia in their tiny garden. Although she had planted the sunflower a little late in the season, it grew taller every day, like a developing child. By the time a bud appeared, the plant had grown to the height of Akiko's shoulders. Once, when she was sticking the handle of a duster into the ground as a support for the sunflower, Akiko realized that it stood on the exact spot where Shigezō had relieved himself night after night. Remembering with amusement Yamagishi's scatological observations, she wondered if Toyotomi Hideyoshi had in any way resembled Shigezō in his last years.

When the morning glories began to bloom, Akiko was filled with a sense of happiness every morning when she opened the doors.

'Look, Grandpa! They're in bloom. I've counted seven today. Can you see that blue one over there?'

Akiko gave the bird some water and birdseed, and suspended the cage from the eaves. The bird chirped happily as if it too appreciated the flowers. Shigezō smiled contentedly. These days he woke up every morning in a cheerful mood.

By mid-afternoon, the heat was so intense that the morning glories wilted. The air conditioning was left on all day at the law office, which helped Akiko to get through the day, but at home the heat was unbearable. Even though she sprinkled the garden with water, the heat crept into every room of the house, like steam rising from the ground. Shigezō sometimes sprawled out on the *tatami* and took a nap. Occasionally he crawled about and woke Akiko in the middle of the night, so she gave him a tranquillizer every other night. He was badly affected by the intense heat, and though he still ate the same amount, he lost a considerable amount of weight. Neither Nobutoshi nor Akiko said anything to each other, but both of them realized that his days were numbered.

One day Akiko saw Shigezō go down into the garden and bend down in front of a clump of fiery red salvia. Akiko was afraid that the direct sunlight might be too strong for him. She watched him closely, curious to see what he would do next. Shigezō suddenly reached out

198

his wrinkled right hand and pulled a salvia out of the ground. He pulled out several more, until finally Akiko felt that she had to stop him.

'Don't do that, Grandpa. Flowers are to look at, not to touch.'

Shigezō turned around at the sound of Akiko's voice. With a solemn expression on his face, he got up and made straight for the cottage. Akiko had asked the young couple to look after her father-in-law three days a week, while she herself took care of him during the remaining four. Shigezō paid no attention to that arrangement. Whenever he wanted to see Emi, he simply went over to the cottage. Afraid that he would disturb the young couple while they were working, Akiko was always running after him.

Shigezō had walked off wearing an odd pair of garden clogs. Akiko also grabbed two clogs of different heights and hobbled after him. When she caught up with him, she looked into the cottage and for a moment her heart stood still. Had she got a glimpse of something she ought not have seen, she wondered in a panic.

The doors were wide open, and the young couple, scantily dressed, were in each other's arms. Shigezō called out his usual greeting as he walked up to the lovers without hesitation. The two bodies came apart, and Emi, dressed in the skimpiest of bikinis, rose to her feet.

'Oh, hello there. What is it, Grandpa? Flowers for me? How lovely, thank you. Look, dear. Grandpa's brought me some flowers.'

'Aren't you lucky! This terrible heat must have gone to his head.'

The young man was wearing a pair of swimming trunks: he looked fairer than Akiko had imagined and rather puny. Emi, on the other hand, had a stunning figure. She got a glass of water from the kitchen to put the flowers in.

'Don't you think these flowers are pretty, dear?' she asked, turning to her husband.

'Hello,' said Yamagishi, mimicking Shigezō.

'What is it, dear?'

'Let's cool off again.'

'OK.'

The heat was so intense that, from time to time, the young couple slipped into their bathing suits and sought relief by sprinkling each other with water. Then they lounged comfortably against the pillars and continued with their reading. Sometimes their legs would intertwine or Yamagishi would pillow his head on Emi's lap.

When presently Shigezō returned to the main house, Akiko did not have the heart to rebuke him. Later she told her husband about the salvia.

'Did he really give her flowers? How romantic! I wonder if Dad ever did anything like that when he was young.'

'I wouldn't know. We could be seeing a side of his personality we've never witnessed before.'

'I never expected him to be this happy in his last years. What's the girl's name? Emi? She must look fantastic in a bathing suit. She's a real beauty, isn't she? I wish I'd seen her!'

'And to have given her some flowers too. But then Yamagishi would probably have thrown you out of the cottage!'

'I'd better watch my step. He looks like a tough guy.'

'Actually, he's much more puny than I thought, and he's a real bookworm. We'll have to be careful Satoshi doesn't turn out like that.'

'You know, honey, I've changed my mind a bit.'

'About what, dear?'

'The Yamagishis. They may be young, but according to what you've said about them, they've really gone out of their way to be kind to Dad.'

'Yes, they have. Emi even changes his diapers without my asking her to. It isn't really out of the kindness of her heart, though. She told me it's because she can't stand the smell. Those two don't know how to be tactful!'

Both Akiko and Nobutoshi had noticed that Shigezō was steadily growing weaker. He found having a bath very tiring, so they washed the bottom half of his body every other day using a pail of water. They also reduced the amount of tranquillizer they gave him at night, as he was able to go to sleep after a smaller dose. Akiko looked after her father-in-law with even greater care than before.

One day Satoshi came home with a musical baby's rattle he had bought at a toyshop. He and Akiko watched Shigezō closely to see what he would do with it. The old man picked it up tentatively and shook it. Appearing surprised by the sound it made, he stared at it with a puzzled expression on his face. He shook the rattle again and again, then, calling to Akiko, shook it for her.

'What a lovely sound!' she remarked, while Shigezō beamed with delight.

Satoshi had been the first to notice that Shigezō had begun to behave like a little child and had bought the toy with his own spending money. His parents were moved by his thoughtfulness. Shigezō smiled peacefully, content with the bird, the flowers and the rattle.

200

But the tranquillity was short-lived. One day towards the end of the hot summer which had left everyone feeling enervated, Shigezō locked himself in the toilet of the cottage. Yamagishi happened to be out that day and, as it was Tuesday, Emi had gone out shopping without taking Shigezō along. Akiko called Shigezō back to the house several times, but every time he headed straight back to the cottage at the first opportunity. Finally, she let him have his way, feeling sure that the couple would not mind.

An hour or so later, Emi appeared at the kitchen door. 'Mrs Tachibana, something terrible has happened! Grandpa's locked himself in the toilet.'

Shigezō had locked the door from the inside and would not open it or make any response.

'Grandpa! Grandpa!' cried Akiko in a panic.

The women's first thought was that he had fallen into the privy, but they realized he was safe when they heard a loud thumping noise and Shigezō's heavy breathing. What on earth was he doing in there? And why was he making so much noise?

Emi and Akiko called frantically to Shigezō, but he refused to come out.

A wooden latch slipped into place from inside kept the toilet door firmly closed. It would have been an easy matter to break the door down, but it would cause much inconvenience afterwards. Akiko decided to force the latch open with a fork. In the meantime, Emi went outside and announced that she would try to get in through the window.

By the time Akiko got back from her kitchen with a fork, Emi was trying to squeeze in through the tiny window, which she had slid open. The toilet had two windows: the one on top had a lattice nailed down over it; the lower one, though it opened easily enough, was narrow. Emi could not even get her head through it.

'The cottage is more solid than it looks. A burglar couldn't possibly get in through here.'

Akiko squatted down and tried to look inside. What was he doing in there? Akiko sighed. When she took a deep breath, she nearly choked on the foul stench.

Gathering her wits, Akiko finally succeeded in prying open the door. Shigezō was on the floor, hugging the porcelain urinal and kicking the floor in frustration. He had managed to pull the urinal from the wooden panel, but apparently it must have been too heavy for him to carry. Why he had taken it down was a mystery.

'Grandpa!' cried Akiko, tapping Shigezō on the shoulder.

Shigezō looked up first at Akiko and then at Emi; then he smiled, even though he was panting for breath. Akiko took the urinal in her arms, while Emi dragged Shigezō out of the toilet.

The stench of the urinal, which had not been cleaned regularly, made Akiko feel dizzy. The smell clung to Shigezō, who had been hugging the filthy thing for nearly an hour.

Akiko led him back to the main house and got him out of his clothes. Then she too changed into a clean outfit. To her annoyance, her hands smelled, no matter how hard she scrubbed them.

'Whatever were you doing in there, Grandpa?' asked Akiko again and again in exasperation. But Shigezō, drained of energy from having grappled wih the urinal, was in no state to reply. After getting Shigezō to drink a little weak tea, Akiko spread out the bedding and put him to bed. The old man, exhausted, dozed off almost immediately.

Still worried about the toilet, Akiko went back to the cottage.

'How did Grandpa manage to remove the urinal from the wall? All the screws have come out. The wooden panel and the wall are ruined. He must have pulled at it with all his might. Goodness, he's awfully strong,' said Emi, her astonishment undiminished.

The two women carried the dirty urinal outside. Akiko sprinkled a little cleanser on it, then scrubbed it vigorously. While doing so, she recalled that when the old couple had lived in the cottage, the urinal had never been as dirty as this, nor had it smelled so badly. There was no reason in those days why she should clean the urinal for them, but lately she had been concerned about the slovenly ways of Emi and her husband. By nature very fastidious, Akiko was always cleaning things and tidying up the house; though she worked full-time, her house was immaculate. She and Emi were poles apart. She had never seen Emi give the cottage a thorough cleaning. Goaded by her anger and resentment, Akiko scoured away at the urinal until it looked brand new. After wiping it dry with a cloth, she took it up in her arms, and only then realized how heavy it was. Now she knew why Shigezō had been unable to get to his feet.

Emi, embarrassed by how filthy the toilet was, got down on all fours and wiped the floor with a damp rag.

'I wonder what Grandpa intended to do with it,' Emi remarked when Akiko came back with the clean urinal.

'I haven't the faintest idea. He's obviously exhausted, though. He went to sleep straight away.'

'I can believe that!'

Akiko and Emi had some difficulty putting the urinal back up because the holes in the wooden panel and the wall were now too

202

large. They had to shift it a little to the right of its original position. Just as they finished, Yamagishi returned home.

'What's happened?' he asked, looking first at Emi, then at Akiko, with a puzzled expression on his face.

'Mr Hello tore down the "morning glory".'

'What's that?'

'Another name for the urinal.'

'What did he do that for?'

'It's a mystery.'

Laughing gaily, Emi gave her husband an account of the day's events. Akiko recalled all too vividly the stench that had clung to the urinal. Feeling embarrassed for the young couple with their slovenly ways, she set off back to the main house in the middle of Emi's soliloquy.

That night, Satoshi and Nobutoshi were astonished when Akiko told them what had happened. However, she kept the story of how she had scrubbed the filthy urinal to herself.

Shigezō did not get up the next morning. His temperature was normal, but his entire body was limp from exhaustion. Though Akiko was supposed to have gone to work that day, she stayed at home and asked the doctor to come round.

The doctor, accompanied by his nurse, arrived in the afternoon. After spending some time in listening to Shigezō's chest, he said: 'He's grown noticeably weaker, probably because of the heat.'

The doctor appeared somewhat embarrassed when Akiko recounted how Shigezō had wrenched the urinal from the wall; he was unable to explain his patient's strange behaviour. He gave Shigezō a vitamin shot and a heart stimulant, explaining that there was no need to give him any drugs as he was not ill. 'Take good care of him,' he said as he left.

Shigezō got up from bed four days later, looking a little thinner. All he could say was 'hello', for he had forgotten the rest of his vocabulary. He smiled as he watched the bird singing in its cage and smiled when he shook the musical rattle. He was truly the embodiment of innocence.

The young couple were worried about Shigezō and came to visit him. They were greatly relieved to see him looking better.

'Under the old feudal system, farmers were neither spared nor killed. Modern medicine has accomplished the same for old people.'

'But Mr Hello still dreams. He spends each day in a trance. Don't you think that's better than having your body break down? My grandmother suffers from rheumatism, and her face is more deeply lined than Grandpa's. He doesn't seem to suffer any pain or illness.'

With these remarks, the Yamagishis returned to their cottage.

Akiko was impressed by their observations. How true it was that in this day and age the old did not die easily! And Shigezō did indeed spend his days in a dreamy trance, a pleasure given perhaps only to those who have lived a long life. Probably, in Shigezō's eyes, the bird in the cage was the Kalavinka of Paradise, and Emi a heavenly angel.

Life became peaceful once again. The lingering heat of summer finally passed and at the Fujieda Law Office the potted cockscomb which Akiko had bought at the Myōhō-ji Temple bazaar was at its most colourful. Akiko took potted plants to the office because they lasted longer than cut flowers, and she usually left each one there for about ten days. But as there was little sunshine in the office, the red cockscomb quickly began to fade, and Akiko thought of replacing it with another. No major problems had arisen at the office as a result of her working only three days a week. The young secretary had learned how to manage the office efficiently. The two lawyers were worried, however, when they learned that the girl had a serious suitor. They were broad-minded and would not interfere in her love-life, but it was a different matter when their secretary began to think seriously about marriage. If she decided to resign, they would have to look for another girl right away, for Akiko was still unable to work for them on a full-time basis. Matters would be different if Akiko were to report at the office every day as before; then there would be no need for concern. The two lawyers had felt uneasy from the start about having a young girl whose future was so uncertain.

Strangely enough, Akiko looked upon this new development as a challenge. So this was the difference between being needed and not being needed! These days Akiko worked so diligently she could do two days' work in one. Even if the girl got married and left her job, Akiko was positive that she could manage without help. Just the thought made her feel rejuvenated. It suddenly occurred to her that perhaps it was because the elderly were not needed that their situation was so pathetic.

On the day that the first signs of winter were in the air, and Akiko was wearing her coat to the office for the first time, the secretary approached her for advice on a personal matter. She confessed that she and her fiancé were discussing marriage. Then she brought up a matter that was even more serious.

'I'm terribly worried about my grandmother. She's nearly ninety-seven . . . I haven't told my fiancé about her yet. After all, I have to help support her until she dies. If one of us six grandchildren shirks his duty, the others will too, and Grandmother will be in a terrible fix. My share of the burden is pretty light because so many of us are involved, so even if I don't tell my fiancé about it, I think I can continue to make my contribution from my own spending money. My fiancé is old-fashioned and keeps urging me to give up my job. I'd very much like to be a full-time housewife and let him support me, but he's an only child and lives at home with his parents. Much as I'd like to set up a separate household, it would be difficult on his salary alone, so I want to continue working on a part-time basis. I'd like to propose that you work on Monday, Wednesday and Friday, and I'll come on Tuesday, Thursday and Saturday. Would you please speak to Mr Fujieda about this? I really would appreciate it because it's difficult for me to bring it up.' She paused for a moment. 'No one knows how much longer my grandmother will live. I haven't told my fiancé about her in case he changes his mind about marrying me. I'm also scared that his parents might object to his marrying a girl with this sort of family responsibility. I know it isn't right to wish that she'd die soon, but our whole family would feel relieved if she did. After all, she herself doesn't know whether she's dead or alive. She can't even open her eyes, and no one knows whether she can hear anything. She's been bedridden for years. We never dreamed she'd live this long. We had to hire a special nurse to look after her at the hospital. That's why it all costs so much. But we'd feel terrible if she died while being moved to a cheaper place. Five years have passed since we thought she was dying. Five years! We all joke about getting rid of her, but of course we wouldn't dare kill her.'

Although she sympathized with the girl, her cheerful outlook caused Akiko great pain. Only the young were able to go through an ordeal like this and remain unaffected. She herself could never joke about Shigezō.

Akiko was lost in thought. The world seemed to be teeming with old men and women. And what about the girl's proposal that they work on alternate days? Akiko felt certain that her employers would have no objection; however, she too found it difficult to broach the subject, for they were both responsible for an elderly member of the family. If either she or Nobutoshi died before Shigezō, what would Satoshi do? One part of her mind told her that her fears were absurd, but as she now knew personally a young woman who was financially supporting a grandparent, she could not help thinking that the same fate might be in store for her son.

When she got home Akiko went straight to the cottage. Shigezō was dozing next to Emi who was engrossed in a book. Although the doors and windows were closed, it was very chilly in the cottage. Akiko made a mental note to dress Shigezō in an extra layer of clothing the next day.

205

'Thank you for looking after him. Grandpa, let's go home.'

Shigezō followed Akiko obediently, glancing back at Emi and smiling innocently. Emi, however, who was lying on her stomach, continued reading and did not even bother to return Akiko's greeting. Yamagishi was nowhere to be seen. Akiko wondered why Emi was so sullen, but she did not have the time to analyse the young couple each time they behaved strangely. She took Shigezō by the hand and returned to the main house.

These days Shigezō was no trouble to look after. He did not smoke, he did not complain about being hungry, and he no longer ran away from home. His vocabulary was limited to the word 'hello'. Shigezō himself was not conscious of the fact that he was incontinent. It was infinitely easier to look after him now that he was content to shake his rattle and gaze at the bird. Many old people were unable to walk, but Shigezō could still get about on his own. Compared to the young secretary's grandmother, who had been lying in a hospital bed for twenty years, Shigezō was no problem.

But Akiko's happy mood was shattered one day at dawn. Akiko, who still slept downstairs with Shigezō, was suddenly roused from her sleep by a strange odour. For some reason, the smell seemed to penetrate her ears rather than her nose, and she was unable for a moment to comprehend fully what was happening. She sat up in bed and looked around. It was then that she saw Shigezō on all fours, moving about in the corner of the room. Certain that the foul smell came from that direction, Akiko got up and went over to him.

'What on earth are you doing, Grandpa?' she asked. As she stood petrified with horror, she saw Shigezō slowly rubbing his right hand back and forth over the *tatami* mat. The *tatami* was smeared with a thick substance that looked like gold paint. Pinching her nostrils with her left hand, Akiko hurriedly opened the rain shutters to let out the foul air. Then she grabbed Shigezō from behind and dragged him into the bathroom. He struggled, his filthy hands flailing the air. Once she had got him there, she did not know what to do with him. There was no hot water, but the bath still contained a little warm water from the previous night. Akiko scooped some of it out with a basin and poured it over Shigezō's hands. The horrible smell filled the tiny bathroom. Shigezō's night kimono was smeared with a mud-like substance at the knees. Akiko did not know whether he had deliberately removed his diaper or whether it had come off while he slept. Why had he had a bowel movement in the middle of the night, when he usually had one at about one in the afternoon? She took off all Shigezō's clothes and, in a fit of anger, washed his body with lukewarm water. There was no time to worry about him catching a cold.

Shigezo's bedding was a pathetic sight, for his diaper had apparently slipped off in his sleep. He had probably begun to smear his faeces on the mats when he noticed it had come off. After getting Shigezō into a clean robe, Akiko threw the soiled sheets and bedding out into the garden.

'Please get up, dear,' said Akiko, rousing Nobutoshi. Together they removed the three soiled mats and carried them out into the garden.

'What a mess! Why did he do this?' asked Nobutoshi in bewilderment.

Though Akiko had left the water running in the bathroom, the smell pervaded the room. She heated some water. Dissolving a little detergent in a bucket of hot water, she went down into the garden and began to scrub the mats. Nobutoshi watched her helplessly as she worked like one possessed, trying her best to drive the memory of what she had seen from her mind. Both Nobutoshi and Akiko fully realized the gravity of the situation. At the extreme end of the ageing process was what the experts referred to as personality loss. In severe cases, the elderly person ate his own excrement or smeared it on his body. Some of them then formed their excrement into round pellets and threw them about like children playing with mud; others smeared it on the wall. The Tachibanas had heard all about this advanced stage of senile dementia. Akiko poured water on the mats until all three were soaking. She also washed the sheets out in the garden, then emptied the bucket. The filthy water swirled at the foot of the cockscomb, which had begun to wither.

Akiko could do nothing to get rid of the smell in the room that day. Because she had not had enough sleep the night before, she had no appetite; what's more, she had a throbbing headache. Taking Shigezō by the hand, she set out for the pharmacy to buy an air-freshener and some aspirin.

'Grandpa, why did you do this?' she asked when they got back. 'I can't stand this awful smell. Every time I think about what you did, it fills me with horror. I hope you didn't eat any of it.'

Akiko nagged endlessly, desperately hoping to find some way out of what she regarded as an intolerable situation. When she raised her voice in anger, Shigezō, realizing that she was talking to him, looked at her and smiled. His innocent, angelic smile was so disarming that it dispelled her rage.

It was a sunny day, so Akiko left the mats out to dry. Her mood, however, remained gloomy. She shuddered at that thought of what the future might bring. Was last night's incident going to recur night after night?

Since he had become senile, Shigezō had had no trouble with his stomach, and his bowel movements had been regular. Last night's incident had occurred near dawn. Akiko was curious to know what kind of bowel movement Shigezō had had the previous day. Perhaps there had been a sudden change in his digestive system. She decided to ask Emi about it.

'Grandpa, let's go and see Emi,' said Akiko, afraid to let him out of her sight for a moment. She assisted him down into the garden and pointed to the mats.

'Do you remember what you did last night?' she asked in a harsh voice. Shigezō gazed dreamily at the mats without a shadow of a smile.

Akiko called out a greeting when she got to the cottage. Yamagishi, his hair dishevelled, wearing a ski jacket, opened the door.

'Emi isn't at home,' he said, looking extremely cross. He was carrying his thesis in his hand and was clearly not pleased to have visitors.

'Oh? I just wanted to ask her how Grandpa was yesterday. When will she be back?'

'I don't think she will be back.'

Sorry about having disturbed him at his studies, Akiko quickly returned home. But what kind of greeting was that? The least he could have done was to ask if there was anything wrong with Shigezō.

It was Saturday, but Akiko was in no mood for housework, so she took Shigezō by the hand and set out for the market. There she ran into Mrs Kihara and on her way home met Mrs Kadotani. She did not feel like chatting, and simply could not bring herself to describe what had happened. Although she badly wanted to know whether something similar had happened to Mrs Kihara's father-in-law, she did not have the courage to ask. And if she were to mention the incident to Mrs Kadotani, she would be bound to find it amusing and immediately tell her mother-in-law all about it. Akiko had to be very careful what she said to a woman like that.

Akiko took her groceries home, then suddenly thought that she ought to consult the doctor. She and the old man set out for the clinic. They waited for some time in a room full of patients. When Shigezō's name was called at last, he completely failed to respond, even though his eyes were wide open. Akiko tapped him on the shoulder and led him by the hand into the examination room.

208

The doctor listened patiently to Akiko's account of the previous night, but did not seem at all surprised by what he heard.

'Is that so? He does appear to be run down,' he said in a subdued voice.

After examining Shigezō with his stethoscope, and checking his blood pressure, the doctor told Akiko that he would prescribe some medicine for Shigezō's stomach, which appeared to have got weaker. There probably isn't any medicine for personality loss, thought Akiko bitterly. Nevertheless, she placed her trust in the doctor. Instead of using the term 'senile dementia', he had said that Shigezō seemed to be 'run down'; what a tactful way of describing the old man's wretched condition! At the extreme end of senility, human life simply ran down.

Akiko walked home hand in hand with Shigezō. She was no longer angry or irritable. Even if Shigezō repeated his behaviour of the previous night, Akiko was determined to do her best for him. Tomorrow was Sunday and Nobutoshi would be at home to help her. If he was the kind of man who went off to play golf in such a situation, she would not hesitate to divorce him.

That night Akiko gave Shigezō some medicine for his stomach and some tranquillizer. She had intended to keep an all-night vigil, but with the approach of dawn, she dozed off. Suddenly she woke up with a start and groped to feel Shigezō's diaper. When she saw that her father-in-law, half-asleep and holding his breath, was having a bowel movement, she sprang out of bed and slipped a bedpan into place, congratulating herself for getting up just in time. The stomach medicine had apparently helped, for the bowel movement was perfectly normal. Unperturbed, Shigezō continued his peaceful slumber.

Having nothing further to worry about, Akiko slept soundly and woke up on Sunday morning feeling thoroughly refreshed. When Nobutoshi and Satoshi came downstairs and looked anxiously around the room, she was able to tell them that all had gone well.

'Mum's become an expert, hasn't she?' said Satoshi in admiration.

Akiko herself felt confident that from now on she would be able to cope with any eventuality.

That afternoon, Shigezō tottered off in the general direction of the cottage. Meanwhile, Akiko told her husband what the doctor had said about his father.

'Oh? So Dad's run down, is he?'

'I suppose that's one way to describe his condition.'

'In spite of that, he still seems to be attracted to young women. Dad must have gone over to see Emi.'

'We're lucky she doesn't mind.'

'Ten thousand yen isn't much for all the care they give him.'

'I agree. That's why I occasionally let them have a share of what I cook. Yamagishi really appreciates it. He says it reminds him of home. The Yamagishis eat the simplest meals – noodles, rice, bread and milk. Emi's the kind of girl you'd expect to find attending graduate school. She wouldn't waste her time doing household chores.'

'You seem to admire her!'

'I can't get over the fact that she doesn't clean the cottage or do the laundry. She told me that she and her husband wash their underwear at the public bath. Apparently, compared to the life they led behind student barricades, their present life is infinitely more hygienic. I couldn't just ignore their situation, so I offered to do their laundry in the washing-machine. Emi immediately brought over a huge pile of dirty shirts she had planned to take back to her parents' home.'

'How can you call that a marriage?'

'Young people seem to do things differently these days!'

Akiko felt that she must not let Emi spend too much time with Shigezō as the ten thousand yen she paid the couple was for looking after him only three days a week. When she had finished her cooking, she placed some piping-hot muffins on a plate and took them over to the cottage.

Yamagishi, dressed in the same clothes as the day before, stuck his head out when she knocked.

'Hello', said Akiko. 'Sorry for leaving Grandpa in your care for so long. Grandpa, it's time for your afternoon snack. We'd better be getting home.'

'Mr Hello isn't here,' said Yamagishi.

'Oh? I thought he had been with Emi all this time,' said Akiko, feeling the blood drain from her body. 'Where is Emi?' she asked, her voice rising.

'She walked out on me the night before last. We've decided to live apart.'

Akiko ran home in a panic. 'Something terrible has happened, dear! Grandpa's disappeared. He hasn't been at the cottage at all today. And Emi's been away for the past two days. What shall we do?'

Nobutoshi grew pale. In a loud voice, Akiko asked Satoshi to come downstairs. The three of them rushed out of the house, each heading in a different direction, but could see no sign of the old man. Although Shigezō had slowed down lately, they realized it would be a mistake to assume that he could not have gone very far. They phoned the police, then searched frantically in and around the house, even looking under the floor of the cottage. They also went to look for him at the two Senior Citizens' Centres, in case he had decided to go there. Not surprisingly, both the Umezato Centre and the Matsunoki Centre were deserted as such facilities were rarely made available to members on Sundays. Three hours had passed and there was still no sign of Shigezō.

'What can we do?' wailed Akiko. 'It's all my fault. I wrongly assumed that he'd gone to visit Emi. How could I have been so careless? It's already dark, and we still haven't heard from the police. What'll we do if he's been hit by a car?'

'We'll worry about that later.'

'How can you remain so calm, dear?'

'Well, I've been preparing myself for some time. I wouldn't be surprised if he suddenly died.'

'Do you think Grandpa's going to die?' asked Akiko without thinking. The world seemed to grow dark when she realized that her husband had also sensed Shigezō's death approaching.

She made her way to the Matsunoki Police Box and, bowing to the policeman, explained which routes Shigezō had taken in his past wanderings. Although the young officers were very courteous, they did not seem to know much about the problems of the elderly. They could not understand why an old man should periodically run away from home and rush along Ōme Avenue like a streak of lightning. Akiko's frantic explanations and urgent entreaties left them bewildered.

'We've contacted our patrols all over the city. We'll find him. Just be patient.'

'Yes, sir. Thank you very much.'

Hours later, Shigezō was still missing. Akiko began to fear that he had been killed in a car accident and begged the police to check recent traffic deaths. She was gently rebuked.

'We'll inform you as soon as we find anyone fitting your description.'

It was very late when the Nerima Police Station reported that Shigezō was being held at a police box in Kasuga-chō.

'Whereabouts is that?'

'Beyond Toshimaen.'

This time Shigezō had headed in an entirely different direction. Previously, he had walked along Ōme Avenue, heading either east or west; this time he had taken a route leading north. It was not surprising that the police had taken so long to find him. However had he managed to get that far? The very thought of the distance from Nerima Ward to Suginami made Akiko feel faint. Considering how weak Shigezō was, it was incredible that he had managed to cover it.

Nobutoshi set off in a taxi to fetch Shigezō and presently returned home with his father in his arms. Shigezō, too weak to struggle with his son, whom he had not recognized, appeared to be utterly exhausted. Nevertheless, when he saw Akiko, he beamed happily. The moment his head hit the pillow, he fell asleep.

'The doctor doesn't usually make house-calls on Sundays, but he may make an exception in this case. I'll ring and ask him.'

'I hope he will. When the police found Dad, he was having a hard time breathing. They didn't know his address. They told me to hang an identity disc round his neck if he was in the habit of wandering off like that. We never thought of that.'

'An ID tag? That's a good idea! He hadn't run away since his bout of pneumonia, so I suppose I became a little careless.'

Akiko phoned the clinic after she had taken Shigezō's temperature and checked his pulse. When the doctor told her to make sure that Shigezō got plenty of rest, Akiko calmed down considerably. She had trust in the doctor and it was a great comfort to speak to him over the phone and to know that he lived near by. Shigezō slept soundly that night, without the help of a tranquillizer. He was still in a deep slumber the next morning, and Akiko stayed home from work to watch over him. Afraid to move from his side for long, she was under a tremendous strain. When she set the birdcage down near him, Shigezō shifted his eyes to look at it but did not smile.

The doctor called in the afternoon and mumbled that, in view of the seriousness of his condition, it might be better to have Shigezō admitted to hospital. Akiko immediately phoned Nobutoshi's office. They both agreed to leave everything in the hands of the doctor. The doctor said that he would make the arrangements with the hospital. Before he left, he instructed Akiko to get Shigezō's things ready so that he could leave the house the following morning. Was Shigezō dying? Akiko remembered what the secretary had said about her grandmother. It was quite possible that Shigezō would die only after a long period in the hospital. She thought about Shigezō's physical deterioration and felt guilty about sending him away from home so that she might be free to lead her own life.

That evening Nobutoshi returned straight home from the office, and the Tachibana family had dinner together for the first time in months. It was a particularly lively occasion, with Satoshi telling his parents what had happened at school that day. Shigezō slept through the entire meal. Akiko hesitated to wake him so that she could feed him the chive porridge she had prepared. While clearing away the dishes, Akiko wondered what else, besides his night kimono, diapers and bedpan, she should get ready to take to the hospital. Nobutoshi was reading the evening paper and Satoshi was watching television. Suddenly Satoshi looked across at his grandfather and cried: 'Mum, something's wrong with Grandpa!'

Shigezō's eyes were closed, but his expression suddenly changed and his face grew visibly longer. A gurgling sound, which was definitely not a snore, rose from his throat. Frantically, Akiko felt for his pulse and found none.

While Akiko phoned the doctor, Nobutoshi gazed blankly at his father whose face had grown deathly pale. Nobutoshi wondered if he too had blanched. Memories of the war years when he had seen men dying all around him came flooding back. This experience, however, was entirely new.

Soon after, the doctor arrived. He seemed to be in no great hurry. Raising one of Shigezō's eyelids, he examined the pupil with his miniature torch and quietly pronounced him dead.

Nobutoshi and Satoshi stared at the dead man in blank amazement. Having witnessed the death of the old man at the Matsunoki Centre, Akiko immediately folded Shigezō's hands. Her calmness frightened her. Shigezō had always worn a pair of trousers and a cardigan around the house, but he also had a complete set of formal kimono. The first thought that came into her mind was the question of whether she should dress him in the kimono for the funeral or leave it as a keepsake. I must consult Kyōko about this, she thought. Remembering how practical Kyōko was, she decided not to dress him in his kimono.

Before going out to inform the neighbours of Shigezō's death, Akiko bathed the corpse. She poured some boiling water into the alcohol that had been left over from the time she had made plum wine and wrung out three towels. One of these she handed to Nobutoshi, the other she used to wipe Shigezō's body while undressing him. Satoshi took up the third towel but did not know what to do with it; Nobutoshi also stood by helplessly. Akiko handed her son the towel she had used to wipe Shigezō's neck, chest and armpits; then she took the clean towel he was holding and proceeded to wipe Shigezō's back. No matter how hard she rubbed, Shigezō's skin would not redden. Satoshi rinsed out the used towel. All three were keenly aware of the fact that only those very closely related to the deceased were there to bid him farewell.

Though Nobutoshi and Akiko were supposed to wipe Shigezō's body together, Nobutoshi was of no help at all, so Akiko asked him to give his father a shave. Nobutoshi nodded, stood up and asked: 'Would it be all right to use an electric shaver?'

213

Akiko did not think it would be appropriate, so she went to get the safety razor she used for shaving under her arms during the summer months, and handed it to her husband. She slipped a half-used bar of soap into a small bowl. 'Pour the water in first, then add a little hot water. You saw how I filled the container, didn't you?'

Akiko's emotions were under complete control as, addressing no one in particular, she explained how to perform the ancient ritual of purification.

While Nobutoshi gave Shigezō a shave, Akiko was left with the task of wiping the rest of his body. She removed the diaper, which was wet, and carefully wiped him clean. His penis, wrinkled and limp, appeared unchanged from when he was alive. Oblivious of Satoshi's presence, Akiko absently wiped Shigezō's crotch. This was the last time she would have to perform this task. Instead of being relieved at the thought, she felt only a profound sadness. She used a chopstick to insert some cotton into Shigezō's anus, then put on a new diaper and diaper cover.

'He doesn't need them any more, does he?' asked Nobutoshi.

'No, but it's better this way,' replied Akiko.

Their words sounded strangely ordinary. For whose benefit was the clean diaper – Shigezō's or Akiko's?

When Akiko's mother-in-law had died, her death had been unexpected. It had been Akiko's first experience of a funeral. She had run blindly around the house, not knowing what to do, helped by Mitsuko and the neighbours. This time, much to her amazement, she herself attended to every single detail. By the time Mitsuko and her husband, the Kiharas and Mrs Kadotani arrived for the wake, Akiko had taken delivery of the sushi which she planned to serve for dinner.

On the occasion of her mother-in-law's death, the cottage had been used for both the wake and funeral. As the cottage was now rented out to the Yamagishis, all the mourners assembled in the large room downstairs. It did not take Akiko long to move the necessary items into the room. She arranged the white and yellow chrysanthemums Mitsuko had brought.

Akiko had been so flustered last time that she could not remember what words of condolence had been said and how she had responded. Now she remained perfectly calm. She offered her apologies to all the mourners for having brought them out at night. She even pressed her hands to the floor in greeting her brother and Mitsuko and apologized to them for the great distance they had had to travel. How strange that she should be so cool and collected! She remembered Satoshi's remark that she had become an expert in such matters. What Akiko failed to notice was that the mourners were anxiously

214

studying her every move. Mitsuko in particular observed her closely, her heart full of pity.

Akiko was desperately worried that someone would notice the three *tatami* mats. She had scrubbed them so thoroughly they were stained a darker yellow than the other mats in the room. She had sprayed the room with an air-freshener and once even with some perfume, but she was still convinced that they gave off a peculiar smell. What would she do if someone noticed and complained? What excuse could she possibly give the mourners? She had no desire to tell anyone about the appalling incident. If only she had kept it a secret from Nobutoshi and Satoshi! She promised herself she would never mention it again.

When the priest finished chanting the sutras, Akiko had the temple contribution ready. While pressing her hands together in prayer, she remembered the priest's bedridden father and asked him how he was.

'I'm sure he'll be around for many more years. Whenever I officiate at a funeral, I must confess that I envy the bereaved family. I sometimes think I'll die of cancer or some other terrible disease before my father dies of old age. It's quite possible, you know,' said the young priest, looking surprisingly cheerful as he drove off in his car.

Akiko's brother and his wife and the Tachibanas' neighbours all returned home late that night, leaving Nobutoshi, Akiko and Satoshi alone in the house with the dead man. Akiko had learned at the time of her mother-in-law's death that the incense near the bed of the deceased person must not be allowed to go out. She therefore lit two joss-sticks at a time, planting them firmly in the ashes of the censer.

'Kyōko keeps on asking whether Dad's really dead. She says she won't come unless he is. What an idiot that woman is!'

'That's because of the false alarm we had. Remember how she complained at the time about having wasted her train fare?'

'Emi hasn't turned up yet, has she?'

'Did you tell her husband?'

'Yes, but all he said was "Is that so? How sad!" Young people these days don't know how to behave.'

'Emi's been gone since Friday night. Yamagishi told me that they're getting a divorce.'

'Really? Just like that? On what grounds?'

'I didn't have time to ask. But Grandpa must be terribly disappointed that Emi wasn't at his wake. I'll try to get in touch with her tomorrow.'

Nobutoshi yawned. Akiko realized that no one had shed a tear over Shigezō's death. Nobutoshi said that he wanted to lie down for a while and went upstairs.

215

Satoshi sat silent in the corner of the room, his arms around his knees. Being tall and lanky, he looked so much like Shigezō! Nobutoshi, who was of medium build, probably took after one of his grandfathers.

Suddenly remembering that she had forgotten to cover the birdcage for the night, Akiko got to her feet. As she did so, Satoshi said: 'I wish Grandpa had lived a little longer.'

Akiko's mind went completely blank. At a loss for words, she quickly threw the black cotton scarf over the birdcage. The sound of her son's footsteps echoed behind her as he ran up the stairs. Holding the cage in her arms, Akiko sat down. The bird flapped its wings against her breast and let out a mournful cry. Tears welled up in Akiko's eyes and rolled down her cheeks. It was not until some time later that she realized she was crying. She hugged the birdcage to her breast and sat there for what seemed an eternity.

DISCOVER JAPAN, VOLS. 1 AND 2
Words, Customs, and Concepts

The Japan Culture Institute

Essays and photographs illuminate 200 ideas and customs of Japan.

THE UNFETTERED MIND
Writings of the Zen Master to the Sword Master

Takuan Sōhō / Translated by William Scott Wilson

Philosophy as useful to today's corporate warriors as it was to seventeenth century samurai.

THE JAPANESE THROUGH AMERICAN EYES

Sheila K. Johnson

"Cogent...as skeptical of James Clavell's *Shogun* as it is of William Ouchi's *Theory Z.*"—*Publisher's Weekly*

Available only in Japan.

BEYOND NATIONAL BORDERS
Reflections on Japan and the World

Kenichi Ohmae

"[Ohmae is Japan's] only management guru."—*Financial Times*

Available only in Japan.

THE COMPACT CULTURE
The Japanese Tradition of "Smaller is Better"

O-Young Lee / Translated by Robert N. Huey

A long history of skillfully reducing things and concepts to their essentials reveals the essence of the Japanese character and, in part, accounts for Japan's business success.

THE HIDDEN ORDER
Tokyo through the Twentieth Century

Yoshinobu Ashihara

"Mr. Ashihara shows how, without anybody planning it, Japanese architecture has come to express the vitality of Japanese life."
—*Daniel J. Boorstin*

NEIGHBORHOOD TOKYO

Theodore C. Bestor

A glimpse into the everyday lives, commerce, and relationships of some two thousand neighborhood residents living in the heart of Tokyo.

THE BOOK OF TEA

Kazuko Okakura
Foreword and Afterword by Soshitsu Sen XV

A new presentation of the seminal text on the meaning and practice of tea—illustrated with eight historic photographs.

GEISHA, GANGSTER, NEIGHBOR, NUN
Scenes from Japanese Lives

Donald Richie

A collection of highly personal portraits of Japanese men and women—some famous, some obscure—from Mishima and Kawabata to a sushi apprentice and a bar madame.

WOMANSWORD
What Japanese Words Say About Women

Kittredge Cherry

From "cockroach husband" to "daughter-in-a-box"—a mix of provocative and entertaining Japanese words that collectively tell the story of Japanese women.

THE THIRD CENTURY
America's Resurgence in the Asian Era

Joel Kotkin and Yoriko Kishimoto

"Truly powerful public ideas."—*Boston Globe*
Available only in Japan.

THE ANATOMY OF DEPENDENCE
The Key Analysis of Japanese Behavior

Takeo Doi / Translated by John Bester

"Offers profound insights."—*Ezra Vogel*